RETRIBUTION

EVIL FOR EVIL IN
ETHICS, LAW, AND LITERATURE

RETRIBUTION

*EVIL FOR EVIL IN
ETHICS, LAW, AND LITERATURE*

MARVIN HENBERG

TEMPLE UNIVERSITY PRESS

PHILADELPHIA

Temple University Press
Philadelphia 19122
Copyright © 1990 by Temple University.
ALL RIGHTS RESERVED
Published 1990
Printed in the United States of America

The paper used in this publication meets the minimum
requirements of American National Standard for Information
Sciences—Permanence of Paper for Printed Library Materials,
ANSI Z39.48–1984 ∞

Library of Congress Cataloging-in-Publication Data

Henberg, Marvin.
  Retribution : evil for evil in ethics, law, and
literature / Marvin Henberg.
       p.   cm.
  Includes bibliographical references (p.   ).
  ISBN 0-87722-724-1 (alk. paper)
  1. Suffering.   2. Consolation.   3. Punishment.   I. Title.
B105.S79H46   1990
128—dc20   89-20585
                                                    CIP

FOR AGNES HENBERG

Acknowledgments

Research for this book was supported by a year's fellowship from the National Endowment for the Humanities and a grant from the Earhart Foundation of Ann Arbor, Michigan. The author is grateful for the generous support of both these organizations.

Most of the book was written during a 1987–88 sabbatical leave granted by the University of Idaho and spent at the Institute of Criminal Justice, University of Southampton, England. The author would like to thank members of the Faculty of Law at Southampton, especially Denis Galligan and Andrew Rutherford, for providing a hospitable and stimulating atmosphere.

Contents

RETRIBUTION

EVIL FOR EVIL IN
ETHICS, LAW, AND LITERATURE

Introduction

Suffering is a raw fact of human existence that begs to be transformed into something other than itself. Suffering alone—unmodified, unanalyzed, drawn into no larger pattern—proves as intolerable to the mind as to the body of one who undergoes it. If given the choice, human beings would doubtless avoid suffering altogether, but the choice is never ours. Even those of us blessed with goods of life ranging from comfortable shelter and abundant food to ample physical security cannot banish suffering from our lives. It occupies whatever space is open, with exaggerated injuries swelling in the minds even of those, objectively, with scant reason for complaint.

Broadly speaking, retributive thought is the effort to contend with the inevitability of human suffering. Raw, unintelligible suffering is denied; there *must*, the retributivist cries, be a reason for it. Perhaps the suffering is merited, or perhaps it will be compensated for in a manner yet to unfold. In its quest for explanation, retributive thought shares in the primary rationalist assumption of Western philosophy that the universe is fundamentally intelligible. We do not simply suffer, we suffer for a reason—or for a whole complex of reasons. A larger explanatory pattern awaits discovery. If only we knew more, we would understand our wounds and heartaches, achieving a kind of solace in their stead.

When linked to the quest for solace, the search to explain suffering invites a metaphysical turn. Long before the Stoics cultivated indifference to pain and pleasure by self-consciously imitating an indifferent universe, men and women looked to nature for clues to their plight. Finding precedent in the alteration of the seasons, they trusted that a period of suffering would yield to a period of good fortune in the manner that winter yields to summer. A combination of luck, fortitude, and perseverance might return the cycle to fruition, putting an end to suffering, however temporarily. It is only a small imaginative leap from perceiving the mere fact of alternating cycles to conceiving of an expanse of suffering as "paying for" a previous expanse of good fortune.

At this high level of generality, retributive thought produces what we may call *metaphysical solace*—the comfort implicit in perceiving a larger order and assimilating ourselves to it. In offering abstract consolation, retributive thought may lack many familiar trappings. In place of evil for evil we may have good for evil, or evil for good. There may be no concept of merit, demerit, fault, praise, blame, or desert. There is only suffering as a raw currency, its payments exacted by the whim of nature or capricious gods. Despite scant discernible moral content, such views may nonetheless provide solace in the face of such natural evils as tempests, earthquakes, drought, and pestilence. Why agitate ourselves at what lies beyond human control?

Enter deliberate evil committed by one human being against another and the perceived alteration of good and evil no longer produces solace. When we suffer at the hands of others, we are racked by feelings of resentment and indignation; a new and different response clamors for recognition. We become actively engaged, responding to deliberate evil by doing evil in return. Yet even in this more familiar guise of demanding *like for like,* suffering still serves as the currency of retribution. We insist on "paying back" a fitting evil for evil done to us. Even when we are incapable of "settling the score," a transformed metaphysical solace may await our pleasure. Perhaps some larger agent—a moralized deity or an inherently retributive cosmos—will do for us what we are unable to do for ourselves. We are comforted while waiting patiently for the evildoer to be punished later in this life, through his descendants, or in an afterlife.

Metaphysical solace, in its way, appeals mainly to the timid and the powerless. If history is any guide, those capable of returning evil for evil done to them seek an altogether different kind of solace. Let us call it *vindictive solace,* the comfort derived when evildoers suffer appropriately for their offenses. Thus the time-honored ideal of Rhadamanthus, judge in Hades: "Should a man suffer what he did, right justice would be done." [1] In one stroke, these words seem to capture the essence of moral response to deliberate wrong. No aim could be simpler, no objective less subject to dispute. The words satisfy, for evil returns, in a sense, to itself. Suffering lodges where it originates; if the doer suffers what he does, the victim's body is little more than a temporary abode for anguish as it rounds toward home.

The vindictive solace produced at the prospect of an evildoer's suffering what he does is as complex as it is morally controversial. Critics of retributivism associate this aim with the satisfaction of an animal thirst for vengeance—a passion that they insist morally sensitive agents must disavow. To allay one's sense of grievance by relishing the suffering of another is, we are told, devoid of charity and elemental compassion—we ought to do better.

Perhaps so, but can we? Take the following example. In the spring of 1989 near Matamoros, Mexico, agents of the U.S. and Mexican governments discovered shallow graves containing the corpses of thirteen victims of an alleged satanic cult. The dead were mutilated as part of a ritual presumed to guard against the arrest of cult members, who earned their living by smuggling drugs. On apprehension, one of those accused of the murders was taken to the burial site and compelled to exhume the decomposing bodies. He reportedly suffered severe nausea, but was only belatedly and grudgingly given a mask to staunch the odor.[2]

Reactions to this ad hoc punishment will vary, and I shall not judge here whether we should cheer or condemn the authorities responsible. Persuasive or not, however, the case in favor of compelling an accused murderer to dig up his decaying victims speaks volumes about the kind of solace people feel at the prospect of a doer suffering what he does. Why should anyone else—an innocent person—have to suffer the revulsion of digging up fetid corpses when the chore can be imposed on a person responsible for their slaying?

Not only does suffering end up where it belongs in the ideal of Rhadamanthus, but hope lingers that the doer will learn from his experience. The ideal is Janus faced: One pair of eyes gazes backward toward the original evil, the other pair forward to a time when the doer may refrain from committing a similar offense. Its backward-looking face wears a fierce expression, serving in the putative moral justification of punishment, whereas its forward-looking face is benign, perhaps smiling, serving as putative grounds for conscience and self-control. Here the use of retributive thought is admonitory, its proffered solace intimate and internal. A person who refrains from doing evil attains the repose of a clear conscience. What is more, the person may reinforce the solidity of this repose by forgiving evils done to her or him. This third kind of solace we shall name the *solace of self-control*.

At first blush it seems paradoxical to consider refraining from and forgiving evil as constituents of retributive solace. Quite commonly, in fact, forgiveness is conceived of as the antithesis of retribution—namely, as the return of good rather than of evil for evil done. The important point, however, is that forgiveness is a derivative act—at home conceptually only in a larger panorama where retribution is the normal response to deliberate evil.[3] The solace of self-control, based on an inner sense of keeping to the moral high road, is parasitic on retributive thought in the following way. One may keep to the moral high road in part because of retributive warning and admonition: Disease, blight, poverty, or hellfire (people variously may think) await those who depart from the straits of conscientious self-control. Forgiveness of and restraint from evil have rarely, if ever, been practiced as universal moral doctrines. Instead they find themselves embedded within a larger retributivism that proffers reward to those who refrain from and forgive evil while threatening punishment to those who are either unforgiving or who persist in evil despite repeated opportunities to reform.

Where forgiveness fails or is deemed inappropriate, legal and institutional punishment may rise to replace it. Whatever its putative rationale, legal punishment involves the deliberate infliction of evil on human beings. Despite the wishfulness of certain quests for metaphysical solace, the cosmos fails to be retributively self-regulating. Someone or other—a human being—is required to serve as the agent of the evil inflicted on criminals. Thus arises a fourth and final kind of solace, which we may call the *solace of duty*. In one respect it is the converse of vindictive solace, for, rather than assuaging resentment or indignation, it is directed at the sympathy a conscientious person feels at witnessing or hearing of the suffering of others. Resentment and indignation are natural retributive emotions, but they are complemented by compassion. The solace of duty allows one who is an agent of deliberate evil to think of the imposition of suffering as a moral imperative. Without such exculpatory solace, how may we ask particular individuals—police, judges, and jailers—to devote their lives to the institutional requiting of evil with its like?

Understanding retributive thought as the quest for solace in the face of suffering goes a long way toward explaining its protean nature. Retribution is no single doctrine or unified set of doctrines, but a sprawling variety of doctrines, many of them at odds with one another.[4] Its proper scrutiny requires a combination study in moral psychology and in the history of ideas before we may presume to shoulder the philosopher's burden of justifying legal punishment. On a long view, what is perhaps most astonishing about retributive canons of justice is their ability to persist in the face of multiple criticisms that, on an analytical plane, seem devastating. How, for instance, can retribution be morally satisfactory when we consider that responding to evil with evil adds to the sum of suffering in the universe? Should we not, following a utilitarian doctrine, be primarily concerned with alleviating future suffering? What compassionate person would choose to add to the sum of suffering when it lay in his or her power to do otherwise?

The trouble is that suffering itself precludes us from being or remaining disinterested. We are keen to alleviate our own suffering as well as the suffering of those whom we love. Archimedean points of moral theory, such as the notion of an abstract sum of suffering, are persuasive only to detached observers in ideal worlds created by rational reconstructions of human nature. At times we must and should detach ourselves, but we must not allow our impartial prescriptive judgments to parade as descriptions of moral life as practiced by the great diversity of human beings in the great diversity of cultures to which they belong. Moral theory often paints "the problem of punishment" as a logical confrontation between consequentialist and nonconsequentialist modes of thought. Accordingly, the retributivist (a nonconsequentialist in moral theory) looks only to the past, whereas the consequentialist (a nonretributivist in moral theory) looks only to future consequences in the justification of moral action.[5] This mode of analysis does violence to the history of retributive thought, neglecting among other things the retributivism inherent in theories of conscience and self-control. Sometimes retributivism is taught, not with the aim of punishing others, but with a view toward self-punishment—toward producing the sort of conscientious human beings who, via inward sanctions of guilt and shame, enforce morality for themselves. In this guise, retributive thought is tied less to a literature of legal punishment than to a literature of moral education, replete with warnings and admonitions. To call this literature nonretributive simply because it is essentially forward looking is to insist on logical niceties at the expense of plain fact.

Accepting or rejecting retributivism could never hinge on a point as simple as an all-or-nothing decision about which—past deeds or future consequences—should dominate in moral theory.[6] Grounded in the retributive emotions of resentment and indignation and closely allied with the emotions of sympathy and compassion, retributive thought comes packaged in various (to use the image of W. V. Quine and J. S. Ullian) webs of belief.[7] These webs derive their rigor from the fabric of our biological nature, their characteristic shape from the cultures we inhabit, and their particular mode of suspension from an interweaving of allied metaphysical and practical ideas. Each web has its own aesthetic, its own pattern of suffering and solace. Some are spun with narrow interstices for entrapping offenders both large and small; others have wide gaps, permitting the small offender to escape. Some hang in remote corners, capturing few prey and needing only occasional maintenance; others are set in busy corridors, snaring many victims and demanding continual repair.

A variety of factors—pattern, size, texture, adhesion, location, tensile strength, and the like—coalesce in the shaping of retributive webs. A web's suspension is as much a function of the tension among its strands as of their interconnection. Inevitably, then, beliefs seemingly at odds with retributive thought—beliefs about forgiveness, mercy, and clemency—are woven into the overall design. We cannot fully understand a retributive web unless we understand both its limits and the ways in which its strands pull against each other. Take, for instance, the four kinds of retributive solace—metaphysical, vindictive, the solace of self-control, and the solace of duty—outlined above. From a perception of the tensions among them, we must not expect them always to be commensurable. Sometimes the pursuit of one will impede or preclude pursuit of another, as when the quest for vindictive solace (assuaging a desire for revenge) hampers one's ability to attain the solace of self-control (the repose of one who refrains from evil).

Short of embracing or rejecting retributivism outright, the role of moral thought is to determine which retributive web best suits our mature and culturally sensitive judgment. That some retributive beliefs will be woven into the fabric of our lives is inevitable—or at least such is the tragic thesis I hope to portray in convincing detail. The thesis is tragic because abstract moral theory taunts us with the enticing aim of banishing deliberate suffering from the cosmos. Thought experiments can create worlds in which evil is never requited with evil; worlds, even, in which the fundamental biological imperative of predation is banished.[8] But alas, these worlds are ideals of subtraction that omit whole chunks of robust human experience. We can, in practice, no more rid ourselves of retributivism than we can escape suffering or cease searching for solace in the face of it.

This book's approach to retributive thought as an incessant, uneasy, and fallible quest for solace in the face of suffering falls into three main divisions. Part I—"Justifying the Ways"—explores the moral psychology of retributivism from a naturalistic perspective. Turning on its head the allusion to Milton's grand ambition to "justify the ways of God to men,"[9] this section of the book argues that the demand for retribution is inspired by and carried out by us, *Homo sapiens,* as part and parcel of our evolutionary heritage. We cannot shift the burden onto anyone or anything else. Allied claims, metaphysical or otherwise, about the retributive nature of God or of the cosmos are derivative, a projection of our own natures writ large.

In Chapter One, "The Scope of Retributive Thought," I demonstrate the degree to which a restrictive focus on punishment distorts the vitality of the retributive point of view. To understand retributivism is to understand that it is a view about returning evil for evil, with punishment standing as only a single option among a range of possible retributive responses to wrong. To avoid prejudging important moral issues, I introduce the concept of *hard treatment* to cover all varieties of deliberately imposed suffering.[10] Retributivism as the cry for imposition of hard treatment pervades a vast number of cultural practices in addition to the practice of legal punishment. Once we see the phenomenon in all its breadth, we likewise appreciate its persistence and imperviousness to rational critique. As a product of evolution, the retributive impulse is nonrational. All manner of "higher" criticisms and appeals to more "enlightened" standards are, in a sense, beside the point. The ideal of the doer suffering what he does remains irresistible because it finds a deep resonance in our emotive and cognitive natures. The chapter ends by dividing the retributive impulse into two basic components. The first, or reactive, component is a product of evolution that *Homo sapiens* shares with other social mammals. Where flight is precluded, most individuals of a social species will meet hostility with hostility, aggression with aggression. It is at this point that the second, or epistemic, component of retribution comes into play. For a species with relatively high intelligence, the problem arises of setting limits on its hostile responses. Thus human beings are disposed to measure according to a principle of like for like. As much as we receive, we return: no more and no less. Unlike the reactive component of retribution, which belongs to evolution alone, the epistemic component is a product of culture elaborating on a biological tendency.

Chapter Two, "Retaliatory Genes," takes up the reactive component of the retributive impulse. Building on the work of Edward Westermarck and J. L. Mackie, I argue that the retributive emotions of resentment and indignation serve as the foundation for a prereflective morality of hostile response to perceived threat. Recent work by Robert Axelrod and William D. Hamilton suggests that such a response, genetically coded, is a robust mechanism for defeating rivals in a variegated environment of individuals employing alternative prereflective responses to threat. Intraspecifically among social mammals with short memories and limited capacities for harming each other, the mechanism remains relatively crude. Flight or submission by the individual defeated in an agonistic encounter constitutes a "forgetting" of the grounds of conflict, giving rise to a prereflective analog of forgiveness. There is no need for further limitation of aggression.

For creatures with long memories and the technological capability to harm each other over distances, however, it is imperative to establish a limit to the reactive retributive impulse. Chapter Three, "Justice and Causality," argues that the epistemic component of retribution—limiting a hostile response according to a like for like formula—also has a naturalistic basis. This thesis is substantiated by exploring parallels between the like for like of retribution and analogous principles of sympathetic magic and primitive causal reasoning. Even so, biology is far from moral destiny. The more interesting story lies, not in our genes, but in our various cultural means of selecting among retributive practices. It is here that the essay in moral psychology yields to a study in the history of ideas.

Part II—"The Spell of *Like for Like*"—gives grounds for circumspection about analytical approaches to retribution. Like for like is protean, applicable to an astonishing variety of human concerns, but this great strength is also a great weakness, for the formula is as vague as it is adaptable. Like for like requires interpretation before it can serve to set moral limits. The formula, it turns out, is far from the essence of retributive thought, far from a timeless analytical grid to lay over a culture's retributive practices in assessing their morality. Instead, like for like is the gossamer from which different cultures and different individuals spin an impressive array of retributive webs. Each such web, designed to trap a characteristic prey, is as unique as the thinker who spins it. To grasp retributive thought in all its scope and complexity, we must examine more than its gossamer. We must investigate the ways in which like for like is interpreted—fashioned into a web with a particular size, pattern, and mode of suspension. The full story of a retributive web is the story of the beliefs and values that give it shape.

Part II presents a study of eight such retributive webs. In one sense the selection of cultural niches is arbitrary: Any number of other niches in any number of other historical eras would have served equally well. In another sense, however, the selection is far from arbitrary, for I have chosen retributive webs that illustrate the contradictory ways in which like for like may plausibly be interpreted. I have also selected webs that illuminate not only the idea of retribution as a moral basis for legal punishment but also the neglected concept of retribution as a basis for conscience and self-control. The historical portion of the book undermines the prospect that some univocal thing called "the retributive theory of punishment" is subject to ultimate proof or disproof.[11] Neither cultures nor individuals speak in a yes-or-no, thumbs-up or thumbs-down fashion when it comes to retributive institutions. Instead, certain retributive webs are culturally sanctioned, while others are disapproved. The process is in some measure nonrational, and reform—when it occurs—is achieved by appeal to values other than that of retribution itself.

Developing a sympathetic appreciation of the diverse and contentious values shaping various retributive webs constitutes the main project of this book. The emphasis is warranted in part by the overall project of propounding, in Part III, a fresh means of assessing the morality of legal punishment. Equally, the emphasis is warranted by the intrinsic fascination of the subjects chosen for scrutiny. Readers with little interest or background in moral theory will be happy to find that the studies in Part II stand on their own.

Chapter Four, "*Lex Talionis*," explores the like for like formula in its familiar biblical setting, as well as in the less familiar settings of ancient Near Eastern law. The chapter focuses on links between exact retaliation and the allied metaphor of compensation, or repayment. It also explores the role of retaliation in the blood feud, an issue that carries over into Chapter Five, "Suffering unto Truth." This chapter examines the story of Orestes in light of the ancient Greek doctrine of pollution. Far from being a mere superstition, as many are wont to think, the pollution doctrine is part of an effective, future-oriented retributive system for deterring and punishing homicide.[12] As both avenger and polluted one, however, Orestes points up a weakness of the system when confronting familial homicide. Thus Aeschylus' optimistic use of Orestes' trial to celebrate the state's harnessing of retributive passions is juxtaposed against Euripides' bleaker view that such passions can never be subdued and put to productive use.

"Order in the Soul" (Chapter Six) considers Plato's penal theory. Generally considered a proponent of a nonretributive, curative theory of punishment, Plato nonetheless persists in thinking a measure of pain essential in treating offenders. He also recommends various retributive eschatologies as part of proper moral instruction. Putting these elements together, Chapter Six argues that Plato retains a retributive core in his penology. (His theory, in fact, turns out to be a precursor of the permissive retributivism endorsed in Part III.) Though Plato insists that evil must meet with evil, he denies that the degree of deliberately imposed suffering should bear equivalence to some feature of the offense. Instead, the degree of pain applied in punishment is, for Plato, a function of what is necessary to restore harmony in the offender's soul.

Whereas Plato's retributive eschatology is speculative and undogmatic, the

Qur³an presents a very different and highly dogmatic view of the afterlife. Chapter Seven, "Self-Surrender," traces the social implications of the Prophet Muhammad's reiterated warnings of hell in forging a Muslim consciousness and so giving rise to persistent retaliatory objectives in Islamic law. Similar themes are pursued in Chapter Eight, "Eternal Torment," where the doctrines of hell and purgatory in the thought of Saint Thomas Aquinas are considered in depth. Hell surpasses all other creations of retributive thought, and in discussing its torments both Aquinas and his poetic disciple, Dante, opt for a mirror image of God's plenitude in endowing the goodness of creation. The damned in the Aquinian hell meet with both an endless variety of pains and an inflexible insistence on no surcease of pain—each justified by the mesmerizing logic of like for like. Among the torments Aquinas adduces for the damned in hell is the "worm of conscience"—a worm exercising a purely punitive function.

The moralizing world of the revenge tragedy in Renaissance England is the setting for Chapter Nine, "Theatre of Judgment." The genre presupposes in its audience mixed attitudes of horror and satisfaction as intricate patterns of revenge are enacted according to various ideals of poetic justice. These ideals spill from the stage in an extended metaphor of the world as *The Theatre of God's Judgements* [13]—a metaphor, ironically enough, used by critics to condemn the stage. God's hand was thought nowhere to be more certain than in the miraculous detection of murder and in the striking down of atheists. A presumed lack of conscience made atheists abhorrent to the age, but at the opposite end of the spectrum stand figures whose consciences are, if anything, too acute. The chapter concludes with a look at theatrical figures inflated with the notion of valuing honor more than life, and so seeking satisfaction through dueling.

The theme of honor provides a link between dueling and one of the mainstays of Chapter Ten, "Punishment and Duty." This chapter interprets Immanuel Kant's retributive theory of punishment in the *Rechtslehre* in light of his comments on honor and conscience in the *Tugendlehre*. In neglecting the *Tugendlehre* it is easy to misconstrue Kant's theory. While it remains true that he views legal punishment as a moral duty, this obligation is as much a duty to oneself as to others. In making this point, we discover in Kant the idea of conscience as a purely juridical faculty, pronouncing sentence without the emotive sanctions of guilt and shame.

If we put Aquinas's punitive conscience together with Kant's juridical conscience, we derive "The Retributive Unconscious," as seen in Chapter Eleven's exploration of Fyodor Dostoevsky's *Crime and Punishment*. The novel's protagonist, Raskolnikov, commits a hideous murder under the illusion that he is immune from the torments of guilt and shame. These forces, however, set to work in his unconscious, so that Raskolnikov can no more escape self-punishment than he can refrain from murdering in a doomed effort to render his prior suffering intelligible. Dostoevsky develops this portrait of the fully retributive conscience via brilliant parallels between the protagonist and other characters of the novel, most especially the angelic Sonia and the devilish Svidrigaylov.

Consideration of Dostoevsky concludes Part II, the implications of which for classical retributive moral theory are largely skeptical. Despite its biological foundation and elaborate buttressing by cultural norms, the retributive ideal of like for like cannot stand. It seems so right because it speaks to an impulse deep within our natures, but, once interpreted (as it must be to be institutionalized), the principle is vitiated by its own plasticity. Among other things, Part II shows the degree to which, plausibly within each of its various retributive webs, the like for like formula accommodates a vast but inconsistent panoply of hard treatments meted out to offenders.

Retributive hard treatment, we feel, must "fit" the offense, must reflect moral equivalence. But what aspect of the offense do we select? A review of answers from Part II, each plausible in its own setting, suggests the enormity of the problem. Perhaps the "fit" should be with the economic value of the loss, a penal restitution common in ancient Near Eastern law. Perhaps the degree of suffering originally inflicted is our criterion, as suggested by the *lex talionis*. Or perhaps the social station of the victim is our measure, in keeping with the honor-bound precepts of the blood feud. Perhaps, though, like for like ought to be determined by the status of the person offended, where that person is different from the victim—a principle used by Aquinas to justify eternal punishment for temporal sins. Perhaps, too, penal measures ought to be mitigated where the morbidity of individual conscience (as with Raskolnikov) inflicts a high degree of self-punishment. After all, is it fair that the conscientious suffer in excess of those who fail in conscience?

These are but a few of the conceptual disputes plaguing application of a retributive like for like. Add to them the enormous practical difficulties that would arise if, by magic, one of the alternatives *could* be agreed on, and the picture is that of the thorough collapse of an ideal.

Part III—"Breaking the Spell"—atones for the skeptical thrust of Part II. Chapter Twelve, "Retribution and Moral Theory," offers a constructive approach to moral reasoning about legal punishment by suggesting that we revise our views concerning the nature and application of moral theory. In particular, we need to abandon the idea that moral theory provides a grid of objective moral truth, with answers, in principle, to every case. Such a view of moral theory can only be sustained by invoking an implausible value monism. Once we abandon value monism, we find that the question of what an offender deserves is subject to a different set of constraints from the question of what any nonoffender, even when acting as an agent of the state, is morally entitled to impose. Much of the chapter is taken up with exploring deficiencies in a duty-bound logic of moral justification. It recommends, instead, a more flexible logic of permission. This position offers a flexible concept of tentative sanction far better suited to the problems of legal punishment than the inflexible, on–off logic of justification.

Chapter Thirteen, "Permitting Legal Punishment," argues for the permissibility of legal punishment, insofar as it coheres with acceptable retributive practices of blame and criticism. This basis for morally authorizing legal punishment requires supplementing because the controversial aspect of legal punishment is its infliction of retributive hard treatment *in addition to* the stigma of blame and censure. After adopting a logic of permission, our burden is to prove that institutions of legal punishment are not morally *im*permissible. The chapter thus argues, second, that retributive criminal sanctions are a unique and irreplaceable means of reinforcing the seriousness with which we view certain moral values.

Finally, Chapter Fourteen, "Legal Punishment and Moral Standing," shows how we may give a retributive answer to the question, What sort of hard treatment does a legal offender deserve? while still allowing nonretributive values to influence the question, What sort of hard treatment may agents of the state permissibly apply? Ameliorating considerations of a consequentialist nature may attach to the second question, irrespective of the retributive answer we must, morally must, give to the first question. The dimensions of desert and permissibility should be kept separate in evaluating varieties of morally authorized hard treatment. A major portion of the chapter is devoted to clarifying the manner in which these two dimensions affect, in general, the moral authorization of hard treatment. Placing legal punishment in relation to other authorized varieties of hard treatment shows how a permissive retributivism freed from the spell of like for like can defend against temptations to punish innocent persons. In addition, though failing to provide an exculpatory solace of duty, permissive retributivism focuses due attention on the state's maintenance of sufficient moral standing to allow its agents, in good conscience, to administer institutions of legal punishment.

The preceding outline suggests an underlying hubris in my undertaking. I paint on a sprawling canvas with a broad brush, and to add color I have poached from a variety of literatures far afield from my main discipline of philosophy. Without doubt, my efforts will provoke a just measure of criticism from specialists with a more detailed knowledge of these literatures than I possess. Without doubt, I am occasionally guilty of eccentric interpretations; certainly I am guilty of skating past controversies that specialists will regard as essential to a detailed understanding of their subjects.

Such, however, are the risks of an integrative approach—one that tries to achieve three related objectives. The first is to propose a unifying (and, as it happens, naturalistic) perspective on the persistence of retributive thought. The second is to offer a historical study of diverse retributive webs spun from the principle of like for like. The third is to contribute constructively to the philosophy of legal punishment. Though I do not ask to have my mistakes excused, I hope that specialized scholars will be mindful of the need, in a work such as this, to stress broad themes and overall tendencies at the expense of detail, however interesting in its own right.

I close with a word about the perils of writing for a broad scholarly audience. Not wanting to try the patience of nonphilosophers with an excess of the fine-grained, technical argument found in most philosophical journals, I have preferred directness to caution and qualification, thereby courting the evil of appearing dogmatic about fundamental issues in moral theory. I trust that anyone interested in such issues will consult the endnotes, finding there ample reference to a contentious literature on legal punishment that I could fully engage only in a very different kind of book.

I

Justifying the Ways

ONE

The Scope of Retributive Thought

Like the weather, retribution is an everyday topic of conversation; unlike the weather, however, men and women actually do something about it. Such maxims as "Don't get mad, get even" provoke guilty smiles of self-recognition. In ways both large and small, in grand schemes and in petty bickering, human beings find means of retaliating against those who have injured or offended them. A psychic economy of resentment and indignation underlies practices of blame, censure, and social ostracism. To see retribution only in terms of punishing legal offenders is to view it narrowly, concentrating on the analytic content of a few skeletal ideas. The body of retributive thought consists less of bone than of a flesh vivified by vigorous arguments aimed at sanctioning or disapproving wide-ranging cultural practices of returning evil for evil.

The full scope of retributive thought must await disclosure in Part II via the study of various cultural niches. For now, we explore its breadth within a framework of evolutionary naturalism. The character of retributive thought is a function of two dimensions: its pervasiveness across different historical eras, different cultures, and different institutions within a single culture; and its persistence in the face of criticisms that, on an analytical plane, seem sufficiently devastating that we wonder at the survival of morally retributive thought, let alone at its continuing robust health. The second section of this chapter takes up the pervasiveness of retributive thought, the third its persistence. Before proceeding to the dimensions of pervasiveness and persistence, however, we must first establish a meaning for the word "retributive" in such phrases as "retributive thought" and "retributive practice." This effort at definition will simultaneously examine the role of metaphor and metaphysics in articulating retributive aims.

Meaning, Metaphor, and Metaphysics

Etymologically, the word "retribution" derives from the Latin *re* + *tribuo,* literally, "to pay back." Ordinarily, of course, paying someone back is a good thing, a matter of settling debts to everyone's satisfaction. The debtor is relieved of a moral burden, whereas the creditor is given something of value. Despite these positive implications in its etymology, however, the concept of retribution has a largely negative cast. Though some old-fashioned uses of the word encompass the return of good for good as well as evil for evil, retribution has come almost exclusively to signify the latter. For our purposes, then, the unqualified word "retribution" refers solely to a deliberate return of evil for evil. In the few instances where it is necessary to use the word in its positive sense, we speak of "kindly retribution." For the more general concept of good for good as well as of evil for evil, we use the term "reciprocity."

Retributive thought, broadly conceived, is any body of deliberate reflection aimed at providing solace in the face of intentionally imposed human suffering. A retributive practice is one that, consciously or unconsciously, strives to guarantee a return of evil for evil. Suffering is the currency of retribution, the means by which one evil "pays for" another. If the object of a body of thought is to induce Stoic resignation in the face of suffering, that body of thought will have little or no influence on retributive practice. The emphasis will be on changing one's response to suffering, not on trying to inflict added suffering on others.[1]

If the point, however, of a body of thought is morally to authorize deliberate infliction of suffering on others, the implications for retributive practice are enormous. A second concept comes to the fore—namely, that of a moral *limit* to the evil returned within a practice. Critics of retributive thought often argue that retribution is indistinguishable from revenge, but it is exactly the search for limitation that separates the two. Retribution is a measured return of evil according to some notion of what an agent (or group) is perceived to deserve. Revenge, on the other hand, is an unmeasured return of evil that may or may not connect to desert.[2]

Two distinct precepts are thus embodied within the traditional idea of retribution. The first is the insistence that evil demands to be requited by evil. To many who embrace retributivism as a moral theory grounding legal punishment, this axiom is self-evident, a given. When the question arises of how much evil is deserved in return, the second precept of retributivism comes to the fore: The deserved evil to be "paid back" the evildoer must be the moral equivalent of the original. It is, alas, lamentably easy to conclude that these two precepts are actually one, for the most popular retributive slogan—the biblical "eye for eye"—combines them. This well-known *lex talionis,* or law of exact retaliation, stipulates evil returned for evil done, while also providing a criterion of moral equivalence. *One* eye for *one* eye, the slogan tells us, combining two conditions in an apparently inseparable whole.

But separate them we must. Properly conceiving of retribution requires seeing it in all its parts. Though these parts come as a package in many arguments for retribution as a putative grounds for legal punishment, we must resist the temptation to treat the concept in one guise only. Such an emphasis neglects literatures in which retributive thought serves very different ends. I refer in the first instance to a literature of warning and admonition, generally under a religious heading, which attempts to influence people's behavior for the better. Repent, reform, change now, this literature counsels, to avoid greater suffering to come.

Related to but distinct from a literature of warning and admonition is a dramatic literature of vengeance, of "evening the score" outside the proper channels of civil authority. This genre is enormously popular in our own age (witness the appeal of the lone-avenger figures in the *Death Wish* or *Rambo* films) and may well, over time, wax in inverse relation to popular satisfaction with public institutions of justice. This literature tails into yet a third kind, one of moral development in which retribution is viewed as a foundation for conscience and self-control irrespective of whether men and women fear a reckoning beyond this present life.

The ideal of the doer suffering what he does may or may not explicitly feature in a given retributive literature. Though measured, the evil returned can still be in excess of the evil done. It may be distributed collectively to a whole people for the crimes (or sins) of a few. It may be imposed irrespective of desert or culpability, so that the doer suffers, but not for what he does so much as for what happens to involve him. In all these instances, however (whether they involve excessive hard treatment, collective punishment, or strict liability), the idea of the doer suffering what he does lurks in the shadows. Even where an original literature may contain no hint of the idea, later apologists are prone to introduce it. In the West, at least, the history of retributive thought is partially a history of reinterpreting collectivist precepts in light of developing canons of individualism.[3]

In the metaphor of repayment at the heart of retributive thought, a collectivist mentality finds no difficulty in the idea that one person's suffering pays for the debts of another. Here, the economic metaphor is apt, for creditors are more than happy to accept cash from anyone. According to the moral spirit of individualism, however, the retributive debtor must pay with her own suffering. Vicarious suffering (payment from another) will not satisfy. This stipulation eliminates one source of ambiguity in the repayment metaphor only to introduce another. When the idea of repayment is applied to the sanctioned punishment of an individual, an ambiguity arises as to who owes what. It is easy enough to say that an offense creates a debt, but to whom is payment to be made? Do offenders owe their suffering to us nonoffenders, or do we owe infliction of suffering to them?[4] As often as not, unreflective uses of the metaphor want to have it both ways, but this is nonsense. What kind of "debt" is paid by the same currency passed in each of two directions simultaneously?

Other familiar retributive metaphors suffer from similar vagueness and ambiguity. Frequently, for instance, we say that a just measure of suffering "restores balance." The picture is often that of a balance-beam scales leveled by equal amounts of suffering on either side. Given the historically ancient use of such scales in economic transactions, it is hardly surprising that the metaphor of balance supplements the repayment metaphor.[5] One finds how much he is to pay for a quantity of flour or spice by leveling the scales against a known weight, whose units are translated into units of a currency. The just price is determined by the equilibrium point of the scales. Any tampering with the scales, mislabeling of the units used in weighing, or tampering with prices is a source of injustice.

Well and good, except that the metaphor of restoring balance also invokes pictures other than that of a scales. When multiple elements exist within a system, the idea is more abstract: A proper balance among musical notes produces harmony, a proper balance of the four humors in ancient medicine produces health, and a proper balance among the various plants and animals of an ecosystem produces stable populations over time. Each of these pictures differs from that of a scales in its implications for the retributive metaphor of restoring balance. Where the balance beam suggests equality, the other pictures suggest order or stability as the aim of justice. If a scales tips in one direction, we restore balance by adding weight to the opposite tray until the two sides are equal. If, on the other hand, an ecosystem is out of balance, we may restore it in a variety of ways. Perhaps the numbers in a certain species—rabbits, let us say—have exploded, threatening other species. Different routes may lead to the same end of reducing and stabilizing the rabbit population. Perhaps we introduce a microorganism known to produce a high mortality among rabbits. Perhaps we introduce wolves or eagles, or both. Perhaps we introduce plant species that compete with the rabbits' forage, cutting into their available sources of food.

Whatever we do about the rabbits, we are unlikely ever to return to an original point of balance. Instead, we produce an altogether new balance. Whole elements may be missing from this new order as compared to the old, yet we have readjusted to produce stability over time. This possibility shows that the metaphor of restoring balance is ambiguous not only between aiming at equality and aiming at stability, but also between returning precisely to a prior point of balance and introducing a new point of balance consistent with ineradicable changes in the system. Finally, there is an ambiguity in deciding between hydraulic and homeostatic processes of restoration. If an element in a system is out of place, perhaps a hydraulic push or pull—the application of an equal but opposite reaction—will return it where it belongs. If, however, its original place is gone, no amount of pushing or pulling will restore the prior order. What may be called for is homeostatic readjustment of other elements into a new equilibrium.

Metaphors of retributive thought serve the propagandistic end of concealing or distracting from the nonmetaphorical kernel of returning evil for evil. We may say that this return "pays a debt" or "restores balance," but what is more fundamental is that we ourselves *want* evil returned for evil done. The constitution of this desire, and not its metaphorical expression, is what ought to concern us. Resentment is the retributive emotion par excellence, causing us to desire that evil be visited on others irrespective of any benefit to ourselves. Resentment, however, meets with opposition. We are as constituted toward feeling sympathy as toward harboring resentment, and sympathy so colors our perception of suffering in others that we wince at their pain, whether we think it justly inflicted or not. We are troubled by our own administration of evil, and, to relieve its burdens, retributive thought invites a metaphysical turn. Human retributive practice, we yearn to believe, is part and parcel of a larger metaphysical whole. Perhaps retributive strife lies at the center of the cosmic process, as one interpretation of a fragment from Anaximander suggests: "Destruction comes to existing things from the same source from which existence comes to them in accordance with destiny; for they pay each other penalty and retribution according to the assessment of time." [6] Or perhaps a personal God commands that we adopt a retributive aim, a view attested to in varying degrees by Judaism, Christianity, and Islam. Whichever metaphysics we embrace, our retributive desires receive supernatural sanction. Human beings, it appears, are not originators of but rather slaves to the return of evil for evil.

Appealing as a transcendent grounds for retribution may be, we must look not to the cosmos but to human nature in our quest for understanding. To survey retributive practice is to explore the ways of human beings. It turns out that these ways are both widespread and variable.

The Pervasiveness of Retributive Thought

The ideal of "paying back" a fitting evil to a person or to a group pervades human thought and discourse. Exclusive of any ties to legal punishment, retributive thought is at home in discussions of child development, moral education, and the founding of conscience; in trade negotiations and diplomacy; in war and nuclear strategy; in theology and religion; in drama, literature, and film; in magic and superstitious belief; and finally (though certainly not most profoundly) in advice columns to the abused and lovelorn.[7]

When looking at the idea broadly, we resist focusing too soon on legal punishment. Instead, we conceive of retributive thought as authorizing hard treatment—the deliberate infliction of suffering—whether defended as a matter of policy, tactical maneuver, or morally just deserts. Not all hard treatment is punishment, though all punishment is hard treatment. The wider concept is necessary to capture, among other things, instances of poetic and cosmic justice. A stage malefactor is enmeshed in her own malicious design. Good—her hard treatment is a source of satisfaction to the audience. A man dies of a heart attack during his vicious attack on an innocent. Good also—his hard treatment produces satisfaction, whereas in other circumstances (had he, for example, been stricken while swimming to save a drowning child) we would commiserate.

Though few instances of poetic or perceived cosmic justice may be described as punishment, they sound a retributive chord in all but the most angelic of human onlookers. One measure, in fact, of the pervasiveness of retributive patterns is our tendency to project them on only the slimmest of pretexts. People suffer heart attacks with a roughly predictable frequency across a given population. A victim must be doing *something*, if only sleeping, at the time a heart attack occurs, yet we ignore the thousands of incidents without retributive content and give prominence to the few with such content. Perhaps because we find the idea of unmerited suffering intolerable, we allow its many instances to slip unperceived into the background.

Worse, we often seek to impose a retributive pattern where even pretext fails. A disease or ailment, we suspect, is deserved—connected to some personal trait or moral failing of the sufferer. Cancer is the visible manifestation of pent-up anger and hostility; those who suffer from it "merit" their fate. AIDS is a just token of God's vengeance against homosexuals and intravenous drug users. For any human disease, it seems, there lurks a retributive basis for blaming the sufferer.[8] Even where these views are rationally rejected, a taint of suspicion lingers. We assure victims that their ailments have an organic cause, but persist in shunning them. One result is isolation of the ill to an extent unjustified by the objective danger of contagion. Given so much time to themselves, they may end by blaming themselves for falling ill. Outward physical deformity hints at inward moral deformity: We *tell* ourselves it is not so, but we *feel*—or perhaps *fear*—differently. The greater the void in our understanding of a disease, the more likely it is that retributive explanations will fill that void.

Most of us, fortunately, are embarrassed by the retributivism haunting the corridors of modern medicine. Earlier ages, lacking the germ theory of disease and having little appreciation of sanitation, made no apologies for thinking of illness as a vengeful scourge. Plagues were signs of God's disfavor, epilepsy a mark of demonic possession. Indeed, the sufferings of the visible world could be most plainly rationalized by assuming retributive schemes involving an invisible world of sorcery and witchcraft. Spells, curses, oaths, and anathemas were the microbes of the world from antiquity to the Middle Ages and beyond.

One of the more bizarre applications of belief in retributive demonic possession is that resulting in the judicial trial and capital punishment of animals.[9] The history of animal prosecution, whether for the purpose of anathematizing locusts or hanging swine, provides a fascinating testament to the pervasiveness of retributive thought. The subject is of interest for the particular reason that, if ever there were a possibility for humans to embrace purely nonretributive aims, animals would seem to be the beneficiaries. Destroying a dangerous beast is one thing, but performing the costly rituals of public trial and execution is quite another. The evil of a single dangerous beast ends with its death, but the enormously larger evil of a beast possessed by a demon requires mustering a correspondingly larger counterevil. Only a ritual of public vengeance is sufficient to this task.

Animal trials in Europe reached a peak in the sixteenth and seventeenth centuries. Quite apart from viewing the phenomenon, as we would today, as misplaced superstition or, more charitably, as the need for punishment to serve expressive and symbolic ends, contemporary observers sought rational accounts for the increase in the number of animals called to justice. A Jesuit, Père Bougeant, writing in 1739, speculated that Christianity's success in baptizing infants and converting pagans had produced a shortage of human bodies for demons to inhabit. Given that the demons needed to be somewhere, they had taken to possessing animals in increasing numbers.[10]

The retributivism inherent in prosecuting and executing animals is far from rational; hence, to some extent it resists analysis. Nonetheless, we can venture a brief account of contributing factors, keeping in mind that they may not be consistent with each other. First and foremost is the retributivism of God's casting Satan from heaven and of Satan's dominion over lost souls. Second is belief in the ability of living human beings, primarily witches, to tap occult powers. A witch might summon a demon to inhabit an animal as easily as a human. Third (and related to the second) is fear of the direct efficacy of spells and curses; words in the right incantatory order could invoke or prevent disaster. Spells had to be countered by other spells, or conjured up to anathematize the offending animal or animals. (Lest the cursing of dumb beasts be thought pointless, Christian proponents of the measure had a ready example in Jesus' cursing of the fig tree.)[11] Taken together, these factors contribute to an atmosphere of ignorance, fear, and suspicion in which the easiest explanation of evil is to personalize it. A purely natural evil must be borne, but a personal evil may be resisted, and active resistance, however ineffectual by objective standards, always seems preferable to agents facing the sole alternative of doing nothing.

From the vantage of injustice perpetrated in the name of justice, the criminal prosecution of animals is but a footnote to the larger drama of witchcraft. Here

too a misidentification of the real evil invokes a retributive response that succeeds, from our modern perspective, only in compounding evil. Keith Thomas
cites evidence linking the rising prosecution of witches in England to the increasing numbers of women forced into begging by the periodic failure of local poor
relief.[12] After refusing a woman beggar, a farmer or an artisan might suffer a
reversal—for example, his daughter might sicken and die, or a debilitating accident might befall his son. In the search to explain his ill fortune, the man might
review his enemies to decide which of them might have cast a spell against him.
The begging woman, aggrieved at being turned from his door, comes to mind—
especially if rumor already has it that she is a witch. A guilty conscience having
given undue prominence to an innocuous event, the accusation is lodged and the
woman is brought to trial. To her accuser the case is simple: An intolerable wrong
has happened; there must, morally *must,* be a reason for it. Such is the pervasive
unconscious appeal of retributivism.

We could explore this appeal even further,[13] but to do so might suggest that
retributive practices are wholly nonrational. Were this so, their scope would be
vastly reduced. But in fact, we find varieties of retributivism rationally defended
as efficient and effective means of communicating attitudes and intentions in trade,
diplomacy, and defense policy. We cannot end discussion of the pervasiveness of
retributive thought without scrutiny of these practices.

Think, for instance, how the language of retribution suffuses diplomatic and
trade negotiations, where the measured retaliatory response is a time-honored
tactic.[14] One country excludes our goods, we exclude theirs; one country expels
five of our diplomats, we expel five in return. Such measures are retributive
exactly to the degree that they sanction—indeed, raise to the level of principle—
the deliberate infliction of evil. They would not be effective, nor would they be
employed, if one's opponent viewed them as advantageous.

We tend to accept retaliatory tactics in international trade and diplomacy for
a variety of reasons. First of all, the parties in such talks are subject to no higher
authority. There is no world government to compel abandonment of policies that
may lead to a mutually destructive sequence of retaliatory measures. Second,
the like for like of exact retaliation grabs headlines and communicates emphati-
cally. It is a well-understood sign of patience worn thin, alternatives exhausted.
As such, its threat—unmentioned—can pervade even the earliest stages of nego-
tiation. The language of exact retaliation also communicates to a domestic as
well as to an international audience. At the threat of retaliatory trade sanctions,
workers in domestic export industries are forewarned of possible sacrifices in the
national interest. Finally, retaliation in diplomacy and trade is generally preferable
to the claims and counterclaims of saber rattling, and it is undeniably preferable
to all-out war.

Abstracting from the preceding considerations, a rational defense of exact retaliation may be said to consist of the following conditions: The parties must be roughly equal and subject to no higher authority; the resort to a threat of retaliation must come only after other options have failed; and the resort to exact retaliation must preclude a greater evil—possibly that of unmeasured retaliation. These conditions look reasonable enough when we think of trade and diplomacy, but, as we shall see in the historical studies to follow, they are the same conditions cited by adherents of the blood feud and its latter-day descendent, the duel.

The extreme of exact retaliation is embodied by the nuclear strategy of mutual assured destruction.[15] Such a policy is unstable to the degree that one side suspects the other of lacking the will to retaliate in case of attack. There are, after all, strong moral grounds for arguing against actual retaliation, for once the policy has failed to deter it is useless. Invoking it only adds to the sum of suffering, for the side attacked will save none of its citizens by retaliating. Given that the gap between intention and action fuzzes communication, a doomsday device triggered automatically the moment any side attacks is theoretically the most stable option (presuming, of course, that nuclear arsenals are maintained).[16] The doomsday device renders both a first strike and retaliation against it irrational by subjecting all parties to a higher power. The first of the conditions in the preceding paragraph no longer applies.

Yet, even where these three stipulations do pertain, a policy of exact retaliation appears to clash with the moral imperative of forgiveness. Is it not better for both sides in a dispute to abjure retaliation altogether?

The Persistence of Retributive Thought

The previous section has shown that retributivism pervades both rational and nonrational human practice. In its nonrational guise, the desire to return evil for evil is the product of ignorance and a correspondent quest for simple remedies and simple explanations. Human wishfulness seeks magically to transform suffering into satisfactory patterns. Victims are blamed for their diseases, animals hung for demonic possession, and witches persecuted without so much as the blink of an eye. Where ignorance reigns, the persistence of nonrational retributivism seems assured. There is little more to say.

With rational—that is, philosophically defended—practices of retributivism, however, the case is different. Despite all manner of enlightened criticism, these practices persist. Why? Why, despite thousands of years of criticism by partisans of an ethics of forgiveness, does retributivism flourish? Why, despite a two-century onslaught of utilitarian-inspired reform, does the language of just deserts fail to wither away? Though these are questions without easy answers, they are equally questions that cannot be avoided.

Two accounts of the persistence of retributivism immediately suggest themselves. The first holds that retributivism endures in the face of moral criticism for the same reason that any species of immoral behavior continues. Murder is a demonstrable moral wrong, yet it persists despite stern censure and severe legal sanction. The trouble with this answer, of course, is that it begs the question. No one save a fanatic defends murder as a moral response, yet all manner of thoughtful people defend exact retaliation, not merely as *a* moral response, but as *the best* moral response to deliberate wrong. For this reason alone the persistence of rational retributivism cannot be assimilated to the persistence of clear-cut immorality.

The second answer holds that the endurance of rational retributivism is a spillover from the persistence of nonrational varieties. Men and women can be rationally persuaded that a nonretributive ethics captures the moral high road, but at this point nonrational factors intrude. Resentment, spite, and indignation give the nod to a return of evil for evil—this despite our better selves, our rationally "higher" natures.

Though there is a portion of truth in this second answer, it presupposes an oversimplified division between our emotional and cognitive natures. Resentment and indignation are not as blind and unreflective as we are inclined to assume. Conversely, the canons of rationality are not as clear and unambiguous as we are inclined to assume, especially when we ponder the clash between the moral imperatives of forgiveness and exact retaliation.

Nowhere is this clash better demonstrated than in the command of Jesus in the Sermon on the Mount: "You have heard that it was said, 'An eye for an eye and a tooth for a tooth.' But I say to you, Do not resist one who is evil. But if any one strikes you on the right cheek, turn to him the other also." [17] These words may be taken as a complete repudiation of retributive ethics, with Jesus commending a contrary ethics of love and forgiveness—of returning only good for evil. Yet few Christians act on the injunction to offer the other cheek as if it were an absolute return of good. Psychologically, in fact, it is tempting to understand Jesus' advice as retributive, the return of evil for evil. A stout refusal to defend oneself heaps odium onto the aggressor, who may be deterred from further blows only because he feels shamed by his unearned advantage. Whether or not the aggressor feels morally guilty is another matter, but shame—dishonor in the eyes of others—may be an evil sufficient to keep the other cheek from being struck.

This view heavily interprets the words of Jesus, and many readers will object to my adding assumptions that make offering the other cheek a return of evil for evil. Let us, however, reverse the question, asking what assumptions must be added to interpret the response as nonretributive. There are two possibilities: Either Jesus intended offering the other cheek to be morally neutral, or he intended it as a return of good for evil. The first need not concern us, for the context is too highly colored to suppose that Jesus could have recommended the response without believing it to have moral implications. So we concentrate on the second option, asking what assumptions are necessary to interpret turning the other cheek as a return of good for evil.

One traditional answer is that the gesture is a good to the one who is struck, even if he is struck again. He preserves his purity of soul irrespective of what happens to the striker. This answer, however, does not settle the issue, for the good in question is not returned but kept for the private spiritual consumption of the injured party. He may indeed feel blessed, superior, or even triumphant, he may indeed earn his reward in heaven, but he hasn't done anything—good, evil, or morally neutral—to the doer.

Not so, says the Christian—the offended party *has* done something good to the striker. He has shown the proper way to behave, and if the aggressor could only learn to imitate this response there would be fewer blows struck in the first place. By commending his followers to offer the other cheek, Jesus would have them return the greatest possible good in exchange for evil. He would, that is, have them demonstrate the means by which human beings may obtain eternal life.

We should observe several things here. First, note how heavily this response relies on interpretation. Multiple assumptions, many as controversial as those needed to understand offering the other cheek as the return of an evil, are required to transform the striker into the recipient of a good. Second, note how the suspension of a retributive aim by one who offers his other cheek is warranted primarily on the assumption of a larger retaliatory nexus—that of God's ultimate retributive standard.[18] Finally, following on the second point, note how God's ultimate retributive standard entails that, for an aggressor who does not get the message, an offering of the other cheek still constitutes return of an evil. The striker who fails to imitate the Christian finds himself eternally damned. The problem becomes less one of demonstrating how a good has been returned than of demonstrating how the evil returned (eternal damnation) is proportionate to the evil done (a blow struck).

The last point is tendentious to the extent that it is not the devout Christian, but rather God, who delivers the ultimate evil of damnation. But our purpose here is not to adjudicate at the highest level of generality between a retributive ethics and an ethics of forgiveness. Instead, the point is that such adjudication is hopelessly misconceived. Retribution and forgiveness do not engage each other as absolute antagonists pitted in eternal strife. More frequently, they complement each other. Much depends on which is the more general, or higher, aim. If it is forgiveness, it may well be achieved only if, at a lower level, retribution has been served. What better way, for instance, to account for our reluctance to forgive someone who commits a deliberate evil but does not suffer in the least on its account? Perhaps he is oblivious or lacks a conscience, and we say, "If only he felt the slightest bit guilty, I could forgive him." This response, it seems to me, is far from a piece of irrational vindictiveness. On the contrary, it expresses an important point about the sometimes complementary natures of retribution and forgiveness.[19]

Similarly, suppose we interpret offering the other cheek as a forgiving response. The striker knows not what he does, and the point of forgiveness is to indicate a higher path. We have seen, however, that one way—indeed, the traditional Christian way—of making sense of this higher path is to presuppose a more general retributivism. Forgiveness is more than simply blanking out the past, for its characteristic words and gestures frequently contain a warning as well as a dispensation. Once may be forgiven, but twice is another matter. As human beings have only two cheeks, there is nothing in Jesus' words to suggest that he counseled his followers to receive blows ad infinitum.

It is hardly accidental that Jesus' command to offer the other cheek is vague about the extent of one's obligation. Nor is it accidental that a Christian ethics of forgiveness finds an equivocal home within a larger metaphysical retributivism. Such areas of vagueness and equivocation are inherent in the foundations of retributive thought. Its protean ideals change to fit changing circumstances. What is more, the command to return evil for evil, simple as it may sound, is itself complex and equivocal when invoked in moral argument.

Recall that moral retributivism seeks not only to "pay back" evil, but to limit the amount of repayment according to some accepted standard. Accordingly, the retributive impulse has both a reactive and an epistemic component. The former consists of the raw return of evil for evil. In it we find the basis for Francis Bacon's calling revenge a kind of "wild justice." [20] If we stop here, we rest with those who insist that "retribution" is only a polite synonym for revenge. For this reason, defenders of retributivism add to the reactive component a second element designed to measure and to limit the return of evil. Because the favored means of limitation is imposition of a like for like formula, I call it the epistemic component.[21]

In reviewing the etymology of the word "retribution," we noted that despite some archaic uses denoting the return of good for good the predominant coloration of the word is negative. The plain linguistic fact is that most hearers automatically think of evil for evil when invoking the concept of retribution. Though "retribution" occupies the logically negative side of the concept of reciprocity, there is in English no single word or convenient concept occupying its positive side. When one reflects on this linguistic asymmetry, a deeper asymmetry suggests itself. One need not be an inveterate pessimist to read Western culture as preoccupied with punishment far more than with reward. Even in the hands of authors of genius, the themes are unfairly pitted against each other: *Paradise Lost* is poetically more engaging than *Paradise Regained*, the *Inferno* read far more often than the *Paradisio*. In our own age, it seems inevitable that second-rate fiction devoted to criminality will continue to outsell first-rate fiction devoted to moral exemplars.

Psychologically, satisfaction derived from learning of evildoers suffering a deserved harm far surpasses satisfaction from learning that the virtuous have earned a reward. Explaining this disparity requires a look at the biological basis of the retributive impulse. Chapter Two argues that, for social mammals, the disparity in power and generality between a reactive retributive impulse and a kindly reciprocal impulse confers selective advantage. The reason is not far to seek. Even the most devoted partisan of an ethics of forgiveness must admit that for any given individual of a social species the world is more full of enemies than of friends. Because enemies employ stealth and concealment, any animal with a half-chance of survival will reflexively regard other creatures as ill-disposed. To overcome this innate suspicion, members of a common social species perform elaborate behavioral rites to demonstrate and to reinforce nonthreatening intent. In exploring the naturalistic basis for the asymmetry between retribution and kindly reciprocity, we gain a refractive lens through which more clearly to view retributive thought in the cultural niches of Part II.

TWO

Retaliatory Genes

Few areas of speculation engage the passions more than efforts to link human behavior to the genetic endowment of our species. People long comfortable with the thought that genes account for the distinguishing features of human anatomy and physiology may still balk at complementary accounts of human behavior.

Two main factors underwrite this uneasiness. First is the tendency of human consciousness to define itself by stressing discontinuity, rather than continuity, with the rest of nature. Much of the vehement reaction against evolutionary thought is grounded in a vague sense that to emphasize continuity with animal nature is to demean our human nature. Ironically enough, the idea that *Homo sapiens* is demeaned by comparison with "lower" species stems in part from gross ignorance about the lives of animals other than ourselves. Scientific investigation of animal behavior is of recent vintage. Before the last century, we humans painted "beasts" not as they are, but as a projection of the way our fear and foreboding would have them be.[1] Before we object to comparison between ourselves and other animals, we should make sure that the far term of the comparison (the behavior of the other species) is drawn from fact instead of fiction.

If the excessive zeal of those intent on claiming a unique status for *Homo sapiens* is one factor underlying the reluctance to entertain genetic hypotheses about human behavior, a second factor is the excessive zeal of those who seek to vindicate such hypotheses. The crudities of social Darwinism are well known and require no examination here.[2] More problematic, however, is a subtle intermingling of biological explanation with moral justification. Pervading some of the contemporary literature of sociobiology is an uncritical assumption that biology is moral destiny. Once an arguably genetic basis for a human behavioral tendency is disclosed, the "naturalness" of that tendency may be thought to settle the issue of its moral evaluation. The reasoning goes roughly as follows: If a tendency is natural, it is inevitable; and if inevitable, there is no point in a moral practice or pronouncement meant to discourage it. A moral *ought* implies a biological *can;* and whenever we confront a biological *cannot*, we waste precious time and energy in lamentation and handwringing, misled by an unrealistic impression that things ought to be different.

Stephen Goldberg provides a prime example of the confusions lurking in this version of biological determinism. He argues that because human males produce, on average, larger quantities of testosterone than human females, patriarchal social systems are inevitable.[3] Elevated testosterone levels account for the greater aggressiveness of human males over human females. To march under a banner of gender equality, encouraging human females to compete head-on with human males, is, Goldberg maintains, an exercise in futility. Worse, the pursuit of equality is actually morally objectionable, for it leads many women to disappointment and excessive suffering as they fail to compete successfully.

The problem, of course, is that natural biological facts do not constrain judgments of moral value in the simple way Goldberg assumes. In an age of genetic engineering, for instance, the fact of elevated testosterone in males may, morally speaking, be as much an argument for genetically reengineering human males (or females) as it is an argument for dismissing the moral ideal of equality. In addition, there is nothing surprising or unusual about moral values standing in opposition to human tendencies or dispositions. Whenever such tendencies or dispositions are judged to be wrong, it is the role of morality—however unlikely the prospect of success—to oppose them.

This last claim is as true for natural as for culturally induced bad tendencies. A second example from sociobiology helps make the point. There are grounds for believing that human males may have an inherited genetic tendency to be promiscuous in sexual relations.[4] Such a trait has the effect of maximizing a male's chances of reproductive success. Human females may, by contrast, have a tendency to favor sexual exclusivity, for their chances of reproductive success are enhanced if, among other things, they can induce a mate to share in the labor of rearing offspring. Presuming these opposing tendencies to be matters of biological fact, neither one nor the other speaks directly to why most cultures sanction monogamy rather than promiscuity in sexual relations. The moral justification of monogamy entails more than the relatively narrow dimension of reproductive success. It involves ideals of love, fidelity, honesty, and integrity. These may in their turn have a naturalistic basis, but they are in largest measure products of human culture. Most people, male or female, who engage for the first time in an extramarital affair are liable to be surprised by the degree to which the ideal of fidelity—tarnished though it may be in their conscious minds—provokes deep, unanticipated promptings of guilt and shame.

None of the preceding is to suggest tossing genetic explanations of human behavior from the court of moral judgment. Quite the contrary. So long as the role of naturalism in ethics is the modest one of providing an informed perspective on human culture, we would be foolish to ignore the insights of modern biology and ethology. The suggestion, for instance, of a genetic basis for human males to be sexually more promiscuous than human females sheds interesting light on the double standard of sexual morality so rampant across diverse human societies. Our cultural institutions speak with mixed voices when it comes to promiscuity in males. Formal institutions of church and state condemn promiscuity, whereas less formal cultural practices may condone it—or at least cast a blind eye in its direction. Think how easily public moral teaching is undermined by a joke, a wink, or a slap on the back as young men are encouraged to "sow their wild oats."

Critics of sociobiology complain that it offers explanations that are reductionist and unidimensional, tending toward rationalization of the status quo.[5] Sometimes, as with Goldberg, such criticism is warranted. However, there is nothing intrinsic to a genetic perspective on human behavior that necessitates reductionism. On the contrary, the perspective may provide a deeper, more complicated, and truer vision of the mix between human nature and culture than existed prior to its adoption. Such, I believe, happens when we adopt a genetic—and hence evolutionary—view of the emergence of the retributive emotions.

Evolution and the Retributive Emotions

Charles Darwin's evidence for the biological evolution of species has stirred all manner of speculation linking evolution with the foundations of ethics. Much of the simple reductionism and naive biological determinism attendant on this enterprise might have been avoided had later writers on the subject heeded the caution of one of the earliest, T. H. Huxley:

> The propounders of what are called the "ethics of evolution," when the "evolution of ethics" would usually better express the object of their speculations, adduce a number of more or less interesting facts and more or less sound arguments in favor of the origin of the moral sentiments, in the same way as other natural phenomena, by a process of evolution. I have little doubt, for my own part, that they are on the right track; but as the immoral sentiments have no less been evolved, there is, so far, as much natural sanction for the one as the other.[6]

This caution that all human sentiments, moral and immoral, are rooted in an evolutionary past is taken seriously by Edward Westermarck,[7] one of the most profound authors seeking a naturalistic foundation for the origin of moral ideas.

For Westermarck, whose work has recently been called to attention by J. L.

Mackie,[8] the basis of moral sentiment is resentment on the one hand and gratitude on the other. Westermarck summarizes his perspective as follows:

> As for the origin of the retributive emotions, we may assume that they have been acquired by means of natural selection in the struggle for existence; both resentment and retributive kindly emotion are states of mind which have a tendency to promote the interests of the individuals who feel them. This explanation also applies to the moral emotions in so far as they are retributive: it accounts for the hostile attitude of moral disapproval towards the cause of pain, and for the friendly attitude of moral approval towards the cause of pleasure. Our retributive emotions are always reactions against pain or pleasure felt by ourselves; this holds true of the moral emotions as well as of revenge and gratitude.[9]

The self-regarding sentiment of resentment, Westermarck argues, turns into the quasi-moral sentiment of indignation thanks to the transforming power of sympathy. Via sympathy, someone else's hurt can become my hurt, and I am indignant. Similarly for the positive side of the equation: Sympathy turns gratitude (appreciation of benefit to ourselves) into a quasi-moral, kindly retributive sentiment that approves of benefits even when others enjoy them. Via sympathy, someone else's pleasure can become my pleasure, and I feel kindly toward its source. Even so, indignation and kindly retributive feeling can be either nonmoral (that is, narrowly focused) or moral (that is, impartial, disinterested, and generalized to include others).[10]

Westermarck's ethics, then, are in harmony with those of David Hume, falling under the general heading of what is today called emotivism. As with Hume (who calls justice a "cautious, jealous virtue"),[11] Westermarck's ethics are ambivalent: That resentment could in any guise be moral is doubtless hard for some to swallow. At the same time, however, the view is more robust than purely rationalistic accounts of morality. Take, for instance, loyalty and unremitting enmity. The former (gratitude toward those with whom we sympathize) accounts for our divided moral intuitions about such phenomena as honor among thieves. Condemn theft how we will, we still harbor respect for selfsacrificing loyalty among persons dedicated to it. As for unremitting enmity (resentment of those for whom we feel antipathy), we need only look at countless sordid histories of racial and ethnic hatred to see how mixed our attitudes are. On the one hand, stirred by the reverence men and women evince toward their heritage, we admire the devotion to "my people." On the other hand, we shrink at the accompanying narrowness of vision, the intolerance, that so often leads to carnage in the name of protecting ethnic solidarity.

Hume could know nothing of the principle of natural selection, which lends an emotivist ethics additional credibility in the hands of Westermarck. In his turn, Westermarck could know little of genetics, the mechanism of natural selection. We may thus update his views with a look at the emergence of "reciprocal altruism" in social species.

Evolutionists have long debated at what level, individual or group, the selection of species occurs.[12] (Westermarck, missing the rise and fall of the theory of group selection, assumes unproblematically that selective advantage must always work through the individual.) In cases of close kinship, of course, the debate need not arise, for we may view devotion to offspring as both "selfish" and conducive to species survival. If so-called altruistic behavior were confined in animals to the protection of near relatives, the problem would not be acute. The fact is, however, that some behavioral traits subject an individual to risks that seem, from its own standpoint or the standpoint of near relatives, patently unwarranted. Many birds, for instance, issue warning cries at the advance of a predator—cries that, however much they may benefit others, subject individuals to greater risk than if they remained silent. Presuming a genetic split between individuals with a tendency to issue warning cries and those without such a tendency, how could the former gain selective advantage over the latter? Criers, after all, would seem subject to a higher rate of predation.[13]

To indicate both the slipperiness of the slope on which such debates occur and to point toward a possible answer, we must first indicate how the argument changes if we shift the language characterizing the birds' behavior. Let us not, that is, think of a "warning" cry, but of a "distress" cry. Suddenly, as by magic, the problem of selective advantage is resolved both in favor of the individual and of the group. It is easy enough to see how a "distress" cry issued across a wide variety of dangers is advantageous to the individual, for the description implies calling for help. (Some bird species drive predators away by mobbing them.) The problem with the previous description is that "warning" cry gives the misleading impression of a "cry intended to warn" when birds may have no such intention. However complex in other respects, bird communication does not accommodate the anthropomorphic nuances of language we humans impose when describing it.

Enter Richard Dawkins, who argues that the primary unit of evolutionary selection is neither the individual nor the group, but the gene.[14] Despite disavowing the kind of anthropomorphizing I have just criticized, Dawkins nevertheless chooses to call genes "selfish" for exhibiting a blind imperative to reproduce themselves. Actually, of course, he means nothing more than that genes are fundamentally self-replicating, a neutral terminology that might have avoided a lot of needless acrimony.[15] Here, I take it, we can all agree: If genes were not self-replicating, none of us would be here to contemplate the matter.

The shift to regarding genes as the primary unit of natural selection is, it turns out, especially productive in explicating a biological basis for the retributive emotions. A focus on successful genes forces us to look at nonhuman species which share either a common ancestry or common life circumstances. Given a common ancestry, genes conferring advantageous traits might be expected to be shared homologously *among* as well as *within* species. The content of what particular genes encode for is crucial to their success at self-replication. Think, for instance, of coding for sexual dimorphism. Because of the advantages sexual reproduction confers,[16] once it is hit on in an ancestral species, genes for sexual dimorphism are likely to pass to countless numbers of descendent species. Even so, not all morphological or behavioral similarities among species can be explained by common ancestry. Sometimes analogous adaptive innovations occur independently of each other. In these cases of convergent evolution (e.g., eyes of octopuses versus eyes of vertebrates),[17] common features shared among different species stem from similarity of life circumstances.

Updating Westermarck, then, we have grounds to think that natural selection has blindly engineered a genetic substratum for the emotions of resentment and gratitude—that is, for retributively hostile and retributively kindly feeling. If so, we can further postulate that there is nothing distinctively human about the genetic basis of these sentiments. Other species with common ancestry or with life circumstances similar to ours may be expected to be genetically coded in like fashion. The path may be one either of evolutionary homology or of convergence. Following Robert Trivers, I characterize the relevant life circumstances for adaptability of retributively hostile and retributively kindly feeling as (1) a need to care for one's young, (2) a relatively long life, and (3) occupation of a territory in conjunction with other members of the species.[18] Any such creatures, facing multiple interactions with unrelated members of their kind, need to minimize conflict within the species while maximizing security from predators.

We must keep in mind that the genetic emergence of behavioral traits, like the genetic emergence of physical traits, is a nonconscious process. Only very recently with human beings has the prospect of planning a genetic endowment made any sense at all. In an article corroborative of a genetic basis for the evolution of retributive emotion, Robert Axelrod and William D. Hamilton make unfortunate use of the term "strategy" to describe a genetic blueprint for regulating interaction among individuals occupying a common territory.[19] Though the concept of a "nonconscious strategy" is paradoxical, we are stuck with it as a technical sense of the word "strategy" throughout the following section.

TIT FOR TAT as Optimal Social Strategy

Axelrod and Hamilton view the constraints of nature on social beings as a prisoner's dilemma. Mutual cooperation provides mutual advantage, mutual noncooperation (defection by all) results in mutual disadvantage. So far so good—no dilemma yet. The rub comes when one individual can gain added advantage by inducing another to cooperate without having to cooperate in return. Cooperation,

PLAYER B

		C cooperation	D defection
PLAYER A	C cooperation	R = 3 Reward for mutual cooperation	S = 0 Sucker's Payoff
	D defection	T = 5 Temptation to defect	P = 1 Punishment for mutual defection

FIGURE 1: Prisoner's Dilemma

of course, is costly: One creature expends time and energy on behalf of another, courting risk in so doing. If we presume that, in a two-creature encounter, each is subject to a payoff giving the highest reward to eliciting a partner's cooperation while defecting in return, the second highest reward to mutual cooperation, and the least reward to mutual defection, we have our dilemma. In an iterated series of prisoner's dilemmas played between two individuals, cooperation is a precarious strategy, always on the edge of undermining by either individual's choosing to defect. Figure 1 gives a summary of Axelrod and Hamilton's version of the game. The choices and payoffs are with respect to Prisoner A; Prisoner B faces a similar matrix, with the "sucker's payoff" switched for the "temptation to defect."

Assuming these payoffs, Axelrod and Hamilton invited scholars to submit strategies to play against each other in two round-robin computer tournaments. Submissions could be as complex as the proposer liked, incorporating memory of all, some, or no previous moves in a particular round. The strategy accruing the most total points against all others was declared the winner. In both of the two tournaments, the winning strategy was TIT FOR TAT: Cooperate on the first move, then do what the other individual did on the previous move.[20]

Before citing the implications of TIT FOR TAT's success in the evolution of retributive emotion, we need first to say more about the equivocal use of the term "strategy." In setting up their computer tournaments, Axelrod and Hamilton invited others to submit strategies (in an unproblematic sense of the word). That is, the scholars were invited to propose rational means to a proposed end—namely, that of accruing the most points in round-robin competition against the other strategies submitted. However, insofar as TIT FOR TAT sheds light on social relations in nonhuman animals, the term "strategy" acquires a technical sense of "nonconscious basis of behavior." We must therefore keep this latter sense free from anthropomorphizing, exactly as with such a term as "selfish gene." Genes don't mean to be selfish; they simply are self-replicating. Similarly, nonhuman social mammals are not required to employ TIT FOR TAT in a conscious way; rather, if Axelrod and Hamilton are correct, they are genetically programmed to behave in conformity with it.

Using tournament results to speculate on the evolution of cooperation, Axelrod and Hamilton lay particular stress on evolutionary stability: "A strategy is evolutionarily stable if a population of individuals using that strategy cannot be invaded by a rare mutant adopting a different strategy." [21] For instance, the strategy "always cooperate" is highly unstable; a population employing it will be invaded immediately by a mutant employing "always defect." By contrast, "always defect" is highly stable; a population employing it resists invasion, because its adherents exploit every cooperative move of a mutant strategy, while never yielding points by cooperating in return.

Evolutionary stability, a simple matter when considering no more than two strategies at a time, becomes much more complex in an environment rich in strategies. Indeed, dominance of one strategy over others depends very much on the environment: TIT FOR TAT cannot, for instance, dominate in circumstances involving only itself and "always defect." Still, in richer environments, playing against strategies both "nice" (tending to cooperate) and "nasty" (tending to defect), TIT FOR TAT does well. It is a robust strategy, thriving "in a variegated environment composed of others using a wide variety of more or less sophisticated strategies." [22] Axelrod and Hamilton identify three reasons for success along this dimension:

> An analysis of the 3 million choices which were made in the second round identified the impressive robustness of TIT FOR TAT as dependent on three features: it was never the first to defect, it was provocable into retaliation by a defection of the other, and it was forgiving after just one act of retaliation.[23]

TIT FOR TAT, then, combines reflexive "retaliation" with reflexive "forgiveness." Because it has no memory beyond the previous interaction, extensive cognitive powers are unnecessary to its operation. That is why, stripping the term "strategy" of its implication of a goal to be achieved, TIT FOR TAT is an attractive candidate for explaining the emergence of cooperation among non-self-conscious social animals. It allows the fruits of cooperation to spread when individuals are disposed to cooperate, but resists invasion from those disposed to defect.

Given its genetically programmed emergence in an ancestral social species, we could expect TIT FOR TAT to be passed on in the genetic endowments of descendent species. Nature is parsimonious in this way with regard to physical features: Feathers, for instance, have not been evolved separately in each species of bird. Equally, however—presuming its advantages are as great as Axelrod and Hamilton suppose—we could expect TIT FOR TAT to evolve convergently, making it analogous between species rather than homologous.

The retributive pattern implicit in TIT FOR TAT characterizes much of animal behavior. Less advanced species may be served by a generalized vindictive impulse, but once animals recognize each other as individuals, they begin to interact rather than simply to range or to flock together. Dominance hierarchies and defense of territory produce social cohesion in part because the conflict that maintains these relations is restricted. Animals in dominant positions cannot squander energy, so hierarchy is maintained by responses short of actual physical conflict— by bellowing, pawing, posturing, and the like. These fit the pattern of TIT FOR TAT: Hostility meets hostility until, as usually happens, one animal yields. When pitched physical battle is the last resort of intraspecies fighting, a defeated animal is seldom killed. Typically, the loser is able either to flee (a stag deer bested by a rival) or to trigger forbearance in the victor by adopting a recognized gesture of submission (one wolf baring its throat to another).[24] At the next encounter the pair may cooperate or conflict, but in either case memory of the previous encounter is likely to be dim to nonexistent.

From an evolutionary perspective, then, memory and high intelligence are disruptive factors in maintaining a stable retributive order. TIT FOR TAT is robust in part because it "remembers" no more than the previous move. A being employing it is "satisfied with" retaliating once only; its next move is conditional purely on what is done to it. In addition, even among non-self-conscious animals, what counts as "cooperation" or "defection" is subject to both an objective and a psychic interpretation. Objectively, cooperation encompasses interaction tending to preserve the species. Mutual grooming, insofar as it reduces parasites and the chance of disease, is cooperative behavior. Psychically, however, cooperation will be measured by one individual as an act of the other that produces pleasure. Grooming again fits the bill. We thus get two different kinds of answer to the question, Why do social animals groom each other? The first points to relatively distant and unrecognized advantage in the control of disease. The second points to a recognized and pleasurable reciprocity.

Viewing another member of one's species as a potential source of pleasure requires relatively complex mental development. Such development likewise entails extension of an animal's behavioral repertoire. It is hardly surprising therefore that a behavior conferring mutual advantage in the objective sense comes to be reinforced, at the psychic level, by pleasure. Social animals failing to derive pleasure from mutual grooming would find the practice swallowed amidst the many other behavioral options open to them.

"Forgiveness" and Forgetting

When operating in a computer, TIT FOR TAT "forgives" all but the immediately prior defection of its opponent. Similarly, it only "retaliates" against an immediately prior defection. When applied to non-self-conscious animals, this restriction suggests reaction to present and particular stimuli. There is no generalization over past events, no thought devoted to the history of a relationship. To be out of sight is to be, literally and figuratively, out of mind. Such a condition imposes severe limitations on the extent to which "retaliation" is pursued. In both intraspecies fighting and the securing of one's group against predation, the blood is always hot. There are no deliberate preemptive strikes, no attention to security beyond the next few minutes.

Such limitations of intelligence are, in prey species, often accompanied by limitations on the ability to inflict damage. During most of the year, herbivores are hard-pressed to hurt a conspecific, and, when they are equipped to do serious injury (as with bull elk in full antlers during rutting season), their agonistic encounters frequently end in flight. For predator species, by contrast, limitation of intraspecies aggression must be accomplished in other ways. Possessing at all times and in all seasons the physical ability to inflict serious damage on each other, adult predators must minimize the threat of aggression by adopting solitary habits (e.g., mountain lions) or by developing an inhibitory behavioral repertoire (e.g., wolves).

TIT FOR TAT covers the "forgiveness" induced both by flight and by a submissive gesture, for in each case dominance can be maintained without causing the group to lose one of its number. There is some evidence that the two means of inducing "forgiveness" are incommensurable. Male roe deer, for instance, will fight to the death if penned together to make fleeing impossible.[25] Relying on escape in their natural habitat, deer have failed to evolve the inhibitory behavioral cues that limit internecine aggression among social predators.

Though the breadth of TIT FOR TAT's explanatory power is a strength from one perspective, it appears to be a weakness from another. After all, how could the same genes encode for such divergent reactions as flight, on the one hand, and inhibitory response to a submissive gesture, on the other?

The trouble with this question is that it imposes a reductionist scheme, presupposing a one-to-one correspondence between specific information coded in known locations in known chromosomes and the specific expression of certain physical or behavioral traits. Though single genes are known, for example, to control human eye color, certain aspects of nest-building behavior in birds, and seizures generated in mice by auditory stimuli,[26] such examples are exceptions. Even something as simple as a flushed face will be influenced by processes rooted in a variety of genetic loci. Some genes code for the production of adrenalin,

others for the conditions of its release, still others for its inhibition. It is the interaction of different processes, each possessing its own genetic locus, that accounts
for the majority of both behavioral and morphological characteristics. Because
environmental factors influence the kind and degree of interaction, there is great
potential for indeterminacy in the genetic expression of physical processes—a
potential made even greater when we move from an involuntary process like
flushing to an instance of cognitive behavior.

Supposing, then, that there is a specific genetic locus for the reactive tendency
to meet peaceability with peaceability and threat with threat, nothing requires
its expression to follow the same pattern in each species exhibiting it. The interaction of this tendency with other traits native to each kind of organism may
alter its behavioral implications. Different animals will telegraph a willingness
to be peaceable or a threat in ways that can be deciphered only by a member
of that species (or by a keen-eyed ethologist, usually after years in the field).
Amidst the multiplicity of different responses governing interaction among members of different social species, we may overlook the extent to which reciprocity
is characteristic of them all.

I have already referred to the presumed tendency of a social animal to meet
hostility with hostility as the "reactive" component of the retributive impulse. It
is coupled with an analogous component underlying patterns of kindly retribution. For animals lacking in memory and high intelligence, there is no need for
sophistication in the reactive component, for proportionality of response is more
or less guaranteed by the natural contingencies of their existence. Most species
either cannot inflict grievous bodily harm on each other or have evolved reciprocal
means of averting it. An attack on others within the group is thus fundamentally
nonserious—an extension into adulthood, perhaps, of the TIT FOR TAT inherent in
juvenile play. Distance provides one kind of safety, submission another. In both
cases the margin of safety is buttressed by short memory.

For all their other blessings, long memory, high intelligence, and complex
social organization are curses in limiting hostile reaction. Long memory allows
persistent resentment to develop from what would otherwise be a momentary
flare-up. High intelligence provides foresight and planning; complex social organization fosters group identity and solidarity. Under these conditions, blood must
no longer be hot for retaliation to occur: A hostile reaction may be delayed for
days, months, or even years. Time is no longer an ally of "forgiveness," distance
no longer a refuge. These implications are frighteningly clear from studies of wild
chimpanzee behavior undertaken over the past two decades by Jane Goodall and
her associates.

Goodall observed the chimpanzees of Gombe National Park in Tanzania for
seventeen years prior to what can only be called an organized campaign of war between two groups that had formerly constituted a single community.[27] The males

of the larger northern Kasakela group systematically searched out and killed all the males and some females of the smaller southern Kahama group. The aggressors' behavior differed radically from the usual boundary patrolling and exploratory excursion into rival territory characterizing relations between distinct chimpanzee communities. The males of Kasakela were not content with ordinary aggressive displays and opportunistic beatings; rather, they pursued members of the Kahama group with policy and deliberation. The fatal beatings they administered far exceeded in severity anything the researchers had seen before. Goodall, in fact, concludes that the beatings can only be described as undertaken with intent to kill.[28]

If the community had not happened to divide, Goodall and her associates would doubtless never have witnessed chimpanzees' pursuing a policy of calculated extermination. What seems to have fueled the intensity of this response is the simple fact of schism. The northern males were fiercely hostile because the southerners were more than mere rivals; they were former allies who had defected. This seems to have touched a nerve that simple membership in a nonallied rival group would not. The Kahama males were perceived as a noxious threat, and the Kasakela males possessed the intelligence and solidarity to do something about it.[29]

Chimpanzees are the nearest existing species to our own. So far as inhibition of intraspecies aggression is concerned, both chimpanzees and humans seem to lie somewhere between the roe deer and the wolf. Unlike the roe deer, we have developed some inhibitory mechanisms aside from flight, but, unlike those of the wolf, ours are weak and easily overridden. As Mary Midgley puts the point for humans:

> The preoccupation of our early literature with bloodshed, guilt, and vengeance suggests to me that these problems occupied man from a very early time. I would add that only a creature of this intermediate kind, with inhibitions that are weak *but genuine* would ever have been likely to develop a morality. Conceptual thought formalizes and extends what instinct started.[30]

One of the most intriguing things about TIT FOR TAT is the way it couples instinctive "retaliation" with instinctive "forgiveness." If the robust baseline reciprocity of TIT FOR TAT leads creatures reflexively to answer hostility with hostility, it equally leads them reflexively to seal a truce. Long memory, high intelligence, and complex social organization deliver, as the Goodall observations attest, one blow to the adequacy of TIT FOR TAT. Language, culture, and consciousness deal a second blow. Once aggressive behavior becomes a deliberate and culturally regulated policy, the question of its limitation grows a thousand times more complex. A creature seeking with foresight to harm another of its kind must at some point ask itself what degree of injury to inflict. The question is acute because along with language and culture comes a technology of destruction that renders escape into time and space even less secure than for the poor male Kahama chimpanzees. Whether one is flinging stones or guided missiles, weapons reach where fists and slashing teeth cannot.

Biological evolution could not, of course, anticipate the development of a technology of destruction. A new sort of limitation on the vindictive impulse must be devised. It will, following Midgley's account, deserve the name of a *moral* limitation, for, whatever grounds are adduced, they will be reflective rather than reflexive.

How is it possible for an intelligent creature endowed with foresight, language, and long memory to forgive an evil wrought by the deliberate will of its fellows? The time-honored answer makes forgiveness contingent on either repentance or a just measure of suffering. Forgiveness is something that an agent must earn, whereas its close allies, mercy and clemency, are simply given out, dispensed. It is clear that the human retributive emotion of resentment is inhibited in all but the hardest of hearts by a show of contrition. It is equally clear that a lack of due contrition is a main grounds for aggravation of resentment. Yet if resentment goes too far in imposing its measure of suffering on an offender, the result may be a burden of guilt for having exceeded the bounds of justice.

The ideal of justice governing the interplay of resentment, guilt, contrition, retaliation, and forgiveness presupposes what I have called the "epistemic" component of retribution. It too has a biological basis, though the main thrust of its interest and application is cultural. This second component of the retributive impulse discloses itself in a tendency to impose a formula of like for like onto our retributively hostile reactions. As Chapter Three makes clear, the like for like of retributive thought—familiar as a protean cultural ideal—strikes the same resonant chord in human nature as does the allied principle of sympathetic magic and primitive causal explanation. We are bewitched by a spell intrinsic to the way we think.

THREE

Justice and Causality

Many of humankind's attempts to control nature involve mimicry of the desired result. For instance, members from a group suffering prolonged drought might dip cut branches in water, then dance about, shaking the branches in imitation of the rain they seek.[1] Even admitting that interpretation of such rituals is a complex task, it is difficult to come up with one that does not involve, at some level, belief in the efficacy of like producing like.

Observing the parallel between retributive and causal invocations of like for like, we may ask whether one is the foundation, or original, for the other. Two possibilities at first present themselves: Either the causal like for like is the original for the retributive, or the retributive like for like is the original for the causal. The next section examines each of these views in turn, finding them both wanting. We thus prepare the way for a third view (elaborated in the section "*Like for Like* in Retribution, Causation, and Exchange")—namely, that both causal and retributive thought are rooted in a fundamental principle of the association of ideas—a disposition of the mind to favor like for like irrespective of its application or interpretation. This epistemic formula casts a spell over both retributive and causal reasoning. Even though projection of like for like onto human experience proves unsatisfactory both in explaining nature and in redressing wrong, the formula is difficult—if not impossible—to extinguish. Accordingly, the concluding section argues that moral progress cannot be measured by the degree to which cultures abandon retributive aims and institutions. Given the reactive impulse to meet hostility with hostility conjoined with the mesmerizing spell of like for like, our best hope is to substitute one retributive practice for another, doing everything in our power to render our new ways more humane than our old. Though the principle of like for like is the gossamer out of which various webs of retributive thought are spun, to rank these webs morally requires invoking values other than the return of evil, however apt its measure.

Cause, Consequence, and Control of Nature

The most common view linking the like for like of causality and retribution holds that belief in retribution derives from experience of the implacability of cause and effect in nature. Herbert Spencer, for example, plumps for the superiority of "natural punishments" in moral education by presuming exactly this thesis. He views the causal nexus as a great teacher whose precepts we should imitate since we cannot avoid them:

> When a child falls, or runs its head against the table, it suffers a pain, the remembrance of which tends to make it more careful; and by repetition of such experiences, it is eventually disciplined into proper guidance of its movements. If it lays hold of the fire-bars, thrusts its hand into a candle-flame, or spills boiling water on any part of its skin, the resulting burn or scald is a lesson not easily forgotten. . . .
>
> Now in these cases, Nature illustrates to us in the simplest way, the true theory and practice of moral discipline.[2]

For Spencer, causality operates as a moral teacher in a way that is already a sophistication of the like for like of sympathetic magic. In magic, both cause and effect are assumed to share a common identity. Water must be shaken from the branches to induce water to fall from the skies—another liquid will not suffice. In Spencer's example, however, things are more complicated. Pain, the natural sanction of the child's mistake, is nothing like its cause—nothing like fire bars, candle flames, or scalding water. Instead, the like for like formula holds across repetitions of the causal sequence. A second or third instance of grabbing the fire bars is presumed to have a consequence similar to the first. Already, then, like for like is an *interpreted* pattern, requiring the interposition of judgment based on experience. As will be demonstrated in later chapters, the retributive like for like is constantly subject to such interpretation, not only through judgment based on personal experience but also through the intervening medium of cultural expectation.

Spencer lauds another feature of "natural punishments":

> Let it be further borne in mind that these painful reactions are proportionate to the transgressions. A slight accident brings a slight pain; a more serious

one, a severer pain. It is not ordained that the urchin who tumbles over the door-step, shall suffer in excess of the amount necessary; with the view of making it still more cautious than the necessary suffering will make it.[3]

Not only is like for like an interpretation holding across two or more repetitions of a causal sequence, it may also be used to rank different causal sequences in order of magnitude—so long as their effects are alike, that is, productive of some degree of pain. Here, also, parallels to an overtly retributive like for like are evident, as in the demand for proportionality in criminal sentencing or the precisely measured retaliations of diplomacy.

Spencer's aim in observing that painful sanctions abound in the natural world is to forward a particular view of the proper punishment of children—namely, that "natural punishments" are to be vastly preferred to "artificial punishments." These latter are inflicted without connection to the causal origin of the offense, as when a parent spanks a child for breaking another child's toy. Spencer's preferred "natural punishment" is to require that the child buy a new toy out of her own allowance. In addition to efficacy in moral instruction, such punishments have the added benefit, Spencer believes, of being miniature scientific lessons:

> A child who finds that disorderliness entails the trouble of putting things in order, or who misses a gratification from dilatoriness, or whose carelessness is followed by the want of some much-prized possession, not only suffers a keenly-felt consequence, but gains a knowledge of causation; both the one and the other being just like those which adult life will bring.[4]

The trouble is that the uniformities "which adult life will bring" are anything but products solely of nature. Rather, they are very much social products, contingent on custom and tradition. An English child's lessons about the "natural" sanction on dilatoriness may be very different from those of a Navaho child, raised in a culture with a time sense radically at odds with that of most Europeans. If "natural" means anything in such contexts, the nod should go to the traditional Navaho, orienting himself by sun and moon, rather than to the clock-conscious Englishman.

Our objective, though, is not to take exception to Spencer's prescriptive theory of punishment, but to note its foundation in causal reasoning. Nineteenth-century social science was much taken by this idea, succumbing to its temptation in viewing the "savage" and the child through the same lens. Here is Spencer indulging in an embarrassing (to modern sensibilities) version of this parallel:

> Do not expect from a child any great amount of moral goodness. During early years very civilized man passes through that phase of character exhibited by the

barbarous race from which he is descended. As the child's features—flat nose, forward-opening nostrils, large lips, wide-apart eyes, absent frontal sinus, &c. —resemble for a time those of the savage, so, too, do his instincts. Hence the tendencies to cruelty, to thieving, to lying, so general among children—tendencies which, even without the aid of discipline, will become more or less modified just as the features do.[5]

Here, in kernel, is the odious myth of the Childhood of Man—an unquestioning confidence that past ages were more vicious, primitive, and morally insensitive than one's own. Twined with misapplied evolutionary theory, this myth wreaked havoc in nineteenth- and early twentieth-century theories of race and criminality.[6] Savages and children, the myth holds, share a common inability to restrain their impulses, with the child possessed of the sole saving grace that she lacks the physical power to harm those who oppose her. Just as children can be ranked by age and moral development, so also can cultural groups be ranked by their degree of distance from the barbaric Childhood of Man. In racially based theories of this sort, the Caucasian "naturally" comes out on top, with members of European cultures possessing the full powers of mature adulthood. (Logically speaking, of course, these cultures might equally be in their dotage, but this implication seems never to have been raised.) Non-Caucasians come off as more childish—that is, less evolutionarily developed. (Note the racist implications of Spencer's description of physiognomy: "flat-nose, forward-opening nostrils, large lips. . . .") In the hands of Cesare Lombroso, this theory became the basis of a complete criminal physiognomy—with the criminal, like the non-Caucasian, scientifically "proven" to be an evolutionary throwback.[7]

The Childhood of Man myth need detain us only for the sake of two further observations. The first is that resemblances, real or imagined, have an intoxicating power over the human mind. Like calls out to be joined to like, even when otherwise there is no shred of evidence that two entities are connected. It is ironic that Spencer, the great advocate of "natural punishment" because of its soundness in teaching about causality, should himself fall prey to an acausal view of the resemblance between children and "savages." The second observation concerns the serious difficulty that Spencer's reversion to the Childhood of Man myth points up for his thesis about the derivation of retributive thought. If "savages" are like children, vengeful and unappreciative of the advantages of measured retaliation, they must at some stage know more about causal principles than about punishing. Yet as Emile Durkheim points out, exactly the opposite is true: Most primitive and archaic cultures possess elaborate institutions for redressing wrongs on generally retributive grounds while possessing only rudimentary knowledge of the physical world.[8] Spencer lauds the causal nexus for its inexorable application of physical sanctions (fire always burns), but his "savage" may well believe in special categories of humans (shamans and witches) who are impervious to fire. This view comes to the same thing as believing that the fire "punishes," not through application of a uniform law but because of one's low social status; persons of sufficiently exalted rank might be thought immune from such "punishment."

Given that a primitive or archaic culture understands its social order far better than it understands nature apart from society, Hans Kelsen is led to exactly the opposite conclusion from that of Spencer. The causal principle projected onto nature, Kelsen believes, derives from a retributive principle universally embodied in human culture. This thesis, painstakingly supported by a review of both ancient and modern texts, hits nearer the mark than does Spencer's.

Kelsen begins by denying that the principle of causality is innate; it is instead a refined methodological achievement of the first order. In support of this view, he observes the preponderance of animistic and personalistic explanations for natural phenomena in primitive and archaic cultures. The actions of nature are lawlike and inexorable only to the extent of the personalities governing them, and as these personalities are in their turn modeled on human prototypes explanations of their influence are gusty and passionate rather than calm and apportioned. The birthplace of causal reasoning in Western thought, Kelsen argues, is the nature philosophy of the ancient Greeks as it "emerged from mythico-religious ideas which are in extensive agreement with the mentality of primitives as we know it, and in which the idea of retribution plays the decisive part." [9]

A review of Kelsen's evidence would take us too far afield, for his argument is only partially relevant to our concerns, and its useful portion does not require a detailed look at sources. Let us concentrate on his interpretation of Heraclitus fragment "the sun will not overstep his measures; otherwise the Erinyes, ministers of Justice, will find him out." [10]

Noting that the Erinyes are implacable retributors par excellence, Kelsen stresses that Heraclitus' words contain the striking idea that natural order is maintained, not by impersonal regularity, but by vengeance and the threat of vengeance. Thus,

> the inviolability of the causal law, so hotly contested in modern science, the absolute validity ascribed to it, are ultimately derived from the inviolability ascribed by myth, and by the nature philosophy which only gradually detaches itself therefrom, to the principle of retribution, as the content of a divine and thus absolutely binding will. The earliest science develops its natural law from this principle of retribution. [11]

In offering a historical generalization about ancient Greek culture, Kelsen is right to observe that ideas of natural order connect with ideas of retributive order. It is also perhaps true that ideas about the uniformity of retributive pun-

ishment precede and are the original for ideas of uniform causation—at least for
the ancient Greeks. The difficulty is that there is as large a gap between the like
for like of exact retaliation (the dictum of the Erinyes) and the conception of a
uniform legal order as there is between the like for like of sympathetic magic and
the conception of a uniform natural order. What closes the gap in each case is
cultural practice. A lawgiver attempts to make retaliatory sanctions uniform over
time, and from these practices the scientist–philosophers of a later age derive
their model of causality.

Because cultural practice is implicated in this manner, we might equally argue
that, for other cultures, the like for like of economic exchange serves as the prototype for ideas of retribution as well as for ideas of uniform causality. Indeed, as
Chapter Four attests, the ancient Near East provides evidence of economic exchange serving in place of physical retaliation as a foundation for a retributive
social order. Because voluntary exchange embodies the like for like formula in
the equality of satisfaction experienced by each party, it is far from obvious that
we should insist on the primordiality of exact retaliation over exchange. Rather
than claim that a retributive like for like is the foundation for allied principles of
exchange and causal reasoning, we do better to posit an uninterpreted like for like
as underlying all three spheres—the retributive, the causal, and the economic. In
its disposition to seek resemblances, the human mind projects like for like onto
experience, with the result interpreted according to context.

Like for Like in Retribution, Causation, and Exchange

One might try to save universal application of Kelsen's thesis by pointing
out that in ancient Greek culture restitution is not always clearly distinguished
from retribution. True enough—in the blood feud, material compensation is often
accepted as satisfaction for homicide. Even so, this concession does not make
physical retaliation the original of restitution as a variety of coercive economic
exchange. In asserting such a thesis, we are misled by a seductive common dimension of exchange and retribution: namely, the adherence of each to the formula of
like for like. It is this dimension that gives both certain kinds of retribution and
certain exchanges a claim to fairness. An exchange is fair when the satisfaction on
both sides is equal, when like value has been given for like. Only if the exchange
is somehow faulty, as when one party cheats another, do punitive considerations
apply. Thus when restitution exhibits a retributive dimension, it is not because
of some concealed retaliatory feature intrinsic to exchange, but because a wrong
has been committed. As a means of explaining uniformity of action over time, a
presumed retributive like for like lacks the fundamental status ascribed by Kelsen.
Instead of one concept underlying the other two, all three concepts (retribution,
causality, and exchange) have their source in the same native, but uninterpreted,

mental anticipation. Only when applied in a particular cultural practice does like for like appear to be retributive, causal, or economic.

This thesis has a variety of advantages over Kelsen's view. Think, for instance, of the like for like of sympathetic magic. Belief in sympathetic magic may persist despite evidence of its meager accomplishments. Poor results prove insufficient for its undermining because belief in sympathetic magic, unlike belief in the causal propositions of science, tends to be unfalsifiable. The appeal of like for like proves too strong for assault via observation and experience. The formula is especially comforting to those frustrated by a combined lack of understanding and an ominous sense that the complexity of things is out of hand. This phenomenon makes for an instructive parallel between the hankering of most persons for simplistic explanations of nature (especially when the accounts of science soar beyond their ken) and the increasing clamor for greater retribution when institutions of justice seem (as they will always seem to some people) too labyrinthine to do the job. If I am correct, both responses result from a deep satisfaction attendant on anticipation of like following like—a satisfaction of our biological nature and a basis for the several varieties of retributive solace. Unmerited suffering causes distress that cries out for solace metaphysically, vindictively, or judicially imposed.

Before leaving Kelsen to elaborate on the thesis that an uninterpreted anticipation of like for like is part and parcel of the human genotype, I point to a special advantage of this assumption with respect to his own view. Retributive thought, Kelsen maintains, can be presumed to be the original for causal thought because the former is so universally met with in primitive and archaic cultures, whereas the latter is a sophisticated idea with a traceable history. Kelsen posits an all-embracing "retributive ideology" from which the like for like of causality emerges. In the studies of Part II, however, we find that retributive institutions and practices are themselves subjects of particular histories. Their diversity suggests that, if anything, there are many ideologies of retribution. Where Kelsen and I agree is on the universality of retributive thought. In his account, however, this universality is an unexplained datum, a starting point; whereas in mine it is a necessity of our biological natures. As with causal reasoning, sympathetic magic, and the insistence on fairness in exchange, human retributive ideologies have their foundation in a genetic disposition to think and to react on the basis of *like for like*.

A similar advantage, mutatis mutandis, may be perceived in my account when contrasted to that of Herbert Spencer. Why should "natural punishment" enjoy an advantage over "artificial punishment" simply because the former derives from experience of causality and the latter does not? Spencer's answer lies in the impersonality of the sanction; the child may resent his parent, but resentment of implacable causality is irrational. If parents take pains to make themselves "vanish" from the punishment, the child not only finds it fruitless to bear grudges against nature, but a counterproductive grudge against the parent is likewise avoided.[12]

Whatever its other merits, this account begs the question in presuming as axiomatic the child's resentment of the parent. After all, resentment is retributive, issuing in a desire to punish the parent. If resentment is a lesson learned from the causal nexus, then Spencer's case in favor of "natural punishments" is undermined. If it is not a lesson learned from the causal nexus (as I believe Spencer must hold), then the best supposition is the one explored in Chapter Two—namely, that resentment stems from the reactive tendency to meet hostility with its like.

This reactive component of retribution is qualitative only. It pins one pole of our moral judgment to the intuition that evil deserves to be answered with evil. To do otherwise—to return good for evil—is to devalue reciprocity. Because this reactive component is so strong and so crudely qualitative, it pushes retributive thought toward strict and collective liability. Motives do not matter—a wrong of any stripe calls for redress. Moreover, the target of a hostile response may be diffuse and ill-defined, involving a group or an individual and including those innocent of the perceived offense.

As discrimination improves, however, only wrongs issuing from the defective will of others become the proper object of resentment.[13] At the same time, self-reflection leads to the realization that an excessively hostile response is grounds for further hostility in return. The search is on for a limit—a recognizable "equivalent" to the original evil. Like for like satisfies in part because it is a foundational principle in the association of ideas. Prior to its application in particular instances, the formula lies ready to order experience.

Ultimately, a naturalistic perspective on retribution explains the power and predominance of the retributive emotions. It further suggests that the longing for simple explanations of nature (like producing like) has the same root as the longing for retributive justice (ensuring that one's punishment is likened to one's offense). Though illuminating, these insights are a bare thousandth of the story. Our biological impulses are expressed in, subdued by, and channeled through cultural institutions of astonishing scope and varying degrees of proficiency. Culture cannot abolish human retributive emotion any more than it can prevent linkage between resentment and the mind's innate favoring of like for like as a formula for interpreting experience. But abolition is unnecessary—for a culture's power lies in sanctioning some retributive practices and denigrating others. The process is in some measure nonrational because human loyalties are bound as much to ritual as to reason. Purely analytic attempts to justify or to dismiss something called "the retributive theory of punishment" are doomed to failure. Analytically we are left with the bare formula that deliberate evil deserves to meet with an exactly equivalent evil. What counts, however, is not the formula, but the way it is elaborated—the way it is bound with other precepts and ideas into a variety of complex webs.

Retributive Webs

Retributive themes of punishment and moral learning are seldom far from each other. The appeal of both is summed up in the "perfect justice" of Rhadamanthus—the desire that a person suffer as his deeds warrant, no more and no less. This ideal is deep, pervasive, and time worn because it promises not only to dispense justice but to teach it. Like Siamese twins joined at the chest, the themes of just punishment and moral instruction have different faces flushed with blood from a single heart.

Still, for all the imaginative satisfaction it confers, the ideal of imposing suffering on an offender identical to what he has caused in others is intolerably vague. It may be depicted in numerous compelling but contradictory ways. To study them we must leave naturalism behind. It is true that we are disposed to meet hostility with hostility and to measure justice by the rod of like for like; but if nature disposes, culture channels and selects. Any particular evil that we suffer may be measured along numerous dimensions—for example, degree of suffering inflicted, social status of the victim or the offender, economic value of the loss, and the like. There is no *a priori* answer to which, if any, of these dimensions is most relevant in likening offense to sanctioned response. The shaping power of culture selects appropriate interpretations and applications of the retributive formula.

A picture of moral progress as the steady abandonment of retributive aims is thus illusory. Cultures may reform their institutions for redressing deliberate wrong, but they do so by developing more humane retributive practices rather than by abandoning altogether the aim of meeting evil with its like. To measure moral progress our scale must be sensitive to nonretributive values. The rhetoric of reform may obscure this need, for, in the scramble for good words, present practices of addressing wrongdoing may be censured as "primitive," "vengeful," or "retributive," whereas the retributivism inherent in the proposed reform passes unperceived. Take, for example, imprisonment as a substitute for flogging, hanging, or public humiliation via confinement in stocks.[14] While the former may be more humane than any of the latter, the difference does not lie in its degree of retributivism. Whatever eighteenth-century reformers may have thought about the "penitentiary" as a place of reform rather than of punishment, it was not long before the institution was enmeshed in the familiar trappings of retributive thought—for example, determining a "fit" response to each category of offense, ensuring proportionality of sentencing, and so on. Today, of course, the evils of incarceration are cited with the same vividness as past ages cited the evils of flogging and mutilation. Today's reformers still search for better methods of dealing with legal offenders, yet to the extent such methods are touted as nonretributive, experience will show otherwise. An evil in hand always appears worse than alternatives as yet unrealized.

Why, though, is dissatisfaction with the retributive status quo the rule rather than the exception? Part of the answer lies in the gap between expectations raised by the like for like formula and the reality of punitive institutions. Justice seems, inwardly, so simple, so easily measured; yet cold reality demonstrates that to liken punishment to offense in one way is to decrease its likeness in some other way. If we impose on an offender a measure of pain commensurate with her social status (perhaps she has enjoyed a special trust and is arguably deserving of harsher treatment because of her abuse of it), we violate the like for like of causing only so much suffering as she caused her victim. In the cultural studies of Part II, we find that the spell of like for like is as bound to disappoint in our reflective judgments about justice as it is bound to dominate in our prereflective anticipations of it.

We are, I have argued, biologically and psychologically disposed to impose retributive patterns onto our experience. This disposition is far from a simple and blind rage for vengeance, for even at the prereflective level it can be blunted by an apology or a gesture of submission. Accordingly, forgiveness is a complement rather than a contradictory of the impulse to retaliate. We are most disposed to forgive in circumstances where wrongdoers have suffered in some measure, if not by the hand of formal justice then at least by the reproach of conscience. As a result of the complications involved, we should not expect a naturalistic perspective to do more than provide a framework for interpretation. We must beware of exaggerating the claims of biological determinism, even when focusing on unidimensional tendencies and dispositions.

Take, for instance, a biologically deterministic explanation of the incest taboo. Genetically, of course, there is a clear case against incest, for it substantially increases the chance that lethal or debilitating alleles carried by each parent will match, resulting in less viable offspring. Selective pressure will favor spread of an innate disposition to avoid mating with near relatives. There are thus good prima facie grounds for holding that the moral prohibition against incest is rooted in a natural disposition of our species. Even so, it is difficult to translate this insight into the thesis that our "real" or "foundational" reason for avoiding incest is that our genes constrain our behavior in determinate fashion.

Three observations support this point. The first is that expression of a natural disposition in all but the most rigidly programmed of social species is likely to be opposed by other natural dispositions. Jane Goodall's chimpanzee studies show that matings between presumed brothers and sisters, as well as between known mothers and sons, occur less frequently than nonincestuous matings.[15] This said, however, incestuous matings *do* occur, for males are also disposed toward extreme cognizance of females in estrus. Even prepubescent males poke and probe at the swollen behinds of sexually receptive females. We must thus complicate the picture of a natural disposition in favor of a certain behavior by also citing natural inclinations that oppose it.

Second, even when no innate dispositions oppose behavioral expression of a given trait or tendency, culture may intervene to provide its own opposition. It is hard, for instance, to imagine a more natural disposition than picking one's nose, yet the behavior is suppressed—if not universally, then at least in our culture at most dinner tables.

Third, cultural norms may speak with mixed voices in respect to a particular natural disposition. Among those, for instance, who oppose the trappings of class and privilege, picking one's nose at the dinner table may be de rigueur—a means of giving deliberate offense. Culture channels and selects, leaving scope for social irony, spottiness, and inconsistency. These in turn produce a kind of moral indeterminacy, for a disposition will be opposed in some contexts, applauded in others. (Recall the discussion in Chapter Two of the presumed natural disposition of human males toward sexual promiscuity.)

It is thus difficult, if not impossible, to distinguish the boundary between culture and nature in explaining a given piece of behavior. In most human societies, for instance, marriage forges ties among potentially rival groups. A sociologist of power relations thus accounts differently for the incest taboo than does the geneticist: Marriage within a family is discouraged for reasons of policy and strategic alliance, and it happens that an effective means of enforcing this policy is to prohibit sexual coupling of near relatives. In arguing from either biological or cultural fact to moral practice, we must distinguish between reasons for the existence of a practice and reasons for believing in it. Grounds for the existence of a practice may well be nonconscious—the stuff of revelations by detached biologists, historians, sociologists, and others. Reasons for believing in a practice cannot, of course, be nonconscious, but they may have scant relation to the causes for its existence. Most people who avoid incest have little knowledge of genetics and would count the need to encourage marriage among potentially rival families as beside the point. To the extent they give reasons for their forbearance, they are likely to say that incest violates divine law or destroys the fragile good of familial intimacy.

The hope of discerning the "real" or "foundational" reason for a particular cultural practice—even of something as well-nigh universal as the incest taboo—rests on the supposition that one explanation trumps all others. In the crudest versions of biological determinism, it does not matter what cultural role incest avoidance plays, or what reasons agents give for believing in it. People observe the incest taboo, the biological determinist holds, because of a basic and nearly irresistible aversion.[16] But this picture is implausible. Why cannot the various reasons from various good explanations be cumulative in effect? Why must one trump the others when all are conducive to the same end? If we allow for reasons to be cumulative, the picture emerges of a biological impulse channeled into cultural practice and supported by a web of belief that, though perhaps wide of the mark in accounting for the origin of the practice, still gives agents palpable grounds for compliance.

In focusing on the reactive component of our presumed retributive impulse, the story is enormously more complex than for the incest taboo. A given response may combine retaliation and forgiveness in such a way that we judge each to be retributive. When the more powerful party in an agonistic encounter accepts the submissive posturing of his rival, a cycle of kindly reciprocity may ensue, but the question of who is dominant has been settled, at least temporarily. Given the urge among most individuals of a social species to rise to a higher position, affirmation of the old order is overtly retributive—the return of an evil. His challenge overcome, the defeated individual must content himself with a lower than desired social station until such time as he succeeds in changing places with his rival. Social hierarchy complicates what would otherwise seem an easy matter— namely, identifying a response as either "retaliatory" or "forgiving." One may not simply measure pains or count gashes to judge whether an evil has been inflicted.

Even in species lacking an elaborate language and culture, retaliation and forgiveness are imbued with social meaning. How much more this is so for *Homo sapiens* will become evident in the studies to follow. Divergent cultural practices channel the retributive impulse in a variety of ways. Exact retaliation and dispensation of forgiveness acquire social meaning according to their mode of interpretation. Despite our tendency to think that there exists in nature some raw baseline, some foundational like for like to serve in ultimately justifying retributive practice, we shall find that all likeness, all "fit" between offense and punitive sanction, is in the eye of the beholder. What is more, each eye is conditioned to perceive as it does by a web of belief sanctioning some retributive practices and rejecting others.

To capture the diversity and extent of these culturally sanctioned responses, the image suggests itself of a variety of webs spun from the reactive and epistemic components of our retributive human nature. As with any web of belief, retributive webs do not collapse if a few strands are destroyed or a corner disturbed. They are elastic and, while viable, subject to continuous maintenance and repair. Moreover, their description entails more than listing materials and citing a formula for composition. Each web is unique and must be patiently observed for its characteristic size, shape, configuration, and mode of suspension.

Some elements are common between webs, others not. It is often thought, for instance, that retributivism makes sense only on the supposition of human free will.[17] Throughout the studies to follow, it is evident that the claim of a logical link between retributivism and free will fails to appreciate the protean nature of retributive thought. The connection is far from analytic, and the best we can say is that certain retributive webs insist on the doctrine of human free will, whereas other such webs reject it. Ultimately, acceptance or rejection of an allied doctrine or idea is determined by coherence with the web as a whole, not by *a priori* compatibility or incompatibility of discrete parts.

The chapters of Part II show how retributively hostile sentiment and the spell of like for like are spun into diverse precepts for the redressing of deliberate wrong. Some of these precepts reflect actual retributive practice, whereas others are proposed for the sake of reform. Some are backward looking and nonconsequentialist, others forward looking and consequentialist. Some espouse equality as a primary value, others are acutely sensitive to upholding differences in social station. Some speak to hard treatment by an external force or agency, others to the internalized hard treatment of a guilty conscience. Some insist on life as the ultimate value for setting the measure by which evil is to be returned, others insist on honor or self-respect as that value. Whatever selection is made among allied doctrines, values, or ideas, each retributive web must be examined as a whole if we hope ever to understand it.

We must not, however, forget that retributive webs are deployed to solace human suffering. One or more of four kinds—metaphysical solace, vindictive solace, the solace of self-control, or the solace of duty—is patterned into each. Though we introduce our studies according to the prominence given each kind of solace, we find—in concert with our tragic thesis—that none suffices in its aspiration. Distress at unmerited suffering remains our constant companion.

In this respect the thrust of Part II is skeptical. Its intent is to break the spell of like for like by showing the degree to which retributive ideals are culturally relative. At the same time, the skeptical results of Part II are brought constructively to bear in Part III. In addition to showing the protean nature of the like for like formula, Part II indicates the extent to which nonretributive values supplement the weaving of retributive webs. This insight positions us to investigate retributive thought as a portion of a larger value pluralism, paving the way for an excursion into moral theory.

II

The Spell of
Like for Like

FOUR

Lex Talionis

Part I provided a naturalistic perspective on retribution. We saw that the retributive impulse in human beings consists of two basic components. The first, or reactive, component (which human beings share with other social mammals) is a reflexive striking out against a cause of pain, coupled with a reflexive kindliness toward a cause of pleasure. The former is the basis of vindictive retribution, the latter of kindly retribution. Insofar as they are purely impulsive, both reactions lack limitation or constraint. A hostile reaction will persist as long as necessary to rid an animal of its pain, a kindly reaction as long as pleasure ensues. In social interactions among creatures with short memories, these reactions are self-governing. When the source of pain is another member of the same species, a hostile reaction will provoke flight, result in physical battle, or evoke a submissive gesture to blunt the dominant individual's aggression. Grievances are quickly "forgotten" among creatures for whom "out of sight" literally entails "out of mind." Time and distance each provide escape.

For human beings the impulsive component of retribution is no longer self-regulating. Our longer memories allow the bud of vindictiveness to leaf into persistent resentment. Worse, technology extends our abilities to maim and to kill, supplementing the native power of the body with weapons, many of which—for example, stones, spears, or guided missiles—act at a distance. For one who flees, memory negates time as a refuge, even as technology negates the safety of physical separation. The world becomes an altogether more dangerous place.

At this stage the second, or epistemic, component of retribution operates on the reactive component. Its foundation is an uninterpreted like for like in the association of ideas. This formula underlies the allied quests to explain nature and to establish justice. One of its guises is the like for like of sympathetic magic and its later descendent, causal reasoning. Another of its guises is the vindictive solace of dishing out like for like in punishment and reward.

For the remainder of the story, culture is vastly more important than biology. Like for like is open textured, protean. The constraints it imposes on our administration of suffering are subject to an enormous variety of interpretations. By itself, uninterpreted, the formula of like for like bears no tincture of morality. It is simply an instinctive means of preserving the species—and a precarious one at that, ever subject to being overridden by powerful vindictive reaction.

The first historical, sanctioned, and arguably moral version of like for like in Western culture is the *lex talionis,* or law of exact retaliation. Readers will be familiar with the *lex talionis* in the "eye for eye, tooth for tooth" language of three separate passages of the Jewish Torah, or biblical Pentateuch. Probably less familiar is the historical context of the law and its relationship to the practice of pecuniary compensation for harm. The protean nature of like for like is nowhere more evident than in the breadth of interpretation to which the *lex talionis* is subject. Ranging from insistence that "eye for eye" mandates physical retaliation to the idea that it serves only as a metaphor for pecuniary compensation, these interpretations raise strong passions. Some scholars proclaim retaliation to be "barbaric," "primitive," and "undeveloped"; others apply the same adjectives to compensation. The danger is that we may persuade ourselves of a favored rational reconstruction of the development of retributive institutions more on the basis of moral predilection than on genuine historical evidence. In surveying a variety of ancient Near Eastern codes, we discover that solace for the grief of death or the suffering of bodily injury may take a variety of legal forms. We likewise discover that the better part of wisdom lies in declining to rank these forms on a scale of moral progress or development.

Retaliation versus Compensation in Ancient Near Eastern Law

Hubert J. Treston offers an instructive scheme for outlining the relations among different retributive practices in archaic and primitive cultures.[1] Taken as a reconstruction of moral progress or a descriptive generalization of historical laws governing actual development across cultures (both or neither of which Treston may intend),[2] the scheme has its deficiencies, but it serves admirably as an analytic grid to identify varieties of retributive social order.

The first such system described by Treston is the unrestricted blood feud between warring nomadic clans. The blood feud is essentially a war of attrition: A loss to the clan weakens the clan; to "get even," it must inflict at least a similar (and preferably a greater) loss on the rival that weakened it. If there is any "balance" to the blood feud, any giving of measure for measure, it is purely negative and defensive, innocent of a sense of justice. If a clan contents itself with life for life rather than two or more lives for one of its lives, expediency is its motive. The aim is to put the feud on hold, strengthen the clan, and strike back on a more advantageous occasion.

Against the backdrop of unrestricted vendetta, stage two (the adoption of strict retaliation), looks very much like a piece of moral progress. Presuming an interest in minimizing cruelty, an eye for an eye is better than two eyes for an eye. This stage is reached, so the argument goes, when clans group into confederations, giving rise to towns and cities. A nomadic existence buffers against the worst excesses of clan violence, limiting the opportunities for retaliation and giving time for blood to cool. Settling into confederations of clans presents new opportunities and new dangers. The blood feud is unsatisfactory because it threatens the body politic. Interclan warfare is intracity strife: The state has no need of a rival to weaken it, as it weakens itself all too effectively. The norm of life for life is enforced by public opinion, if not yet by a central authority. The state leaves the law of injury and homicide in private hands while consolidating its power in the religious sphere.

Eventually monetary compensation becomes acceptable in lieu of exact retaliation, giving rise to stage three—a wergeld system or a mixed system of wergeld and exact retaliation. Initially, the option of settling for monetary compensation is voluntary on the part of the aggrieved party. If the proposal for a monetary payment is refused, blood must be paid. Gradually, however, the authorities perceive the advantage of compensation over exact retaliation, enforcing it as the norm and abolishing the aggrieved party's right to refuse compensation. This transition occurs especially for injuries, and may or may not evolve to include homicide. Insofar as homicide is excluded, exacting vengeance remains a private matter.

The fourth and final stage arises with the perception that bodily injury and homicide are crimes against the state as much (or more) than they are private wrongs against individuals. State authority arrogates to itself the responsibility for punishing wrongdoers. In a mixed stage of this transition, the state may still use a relative of the victim as executioner, but execution occurs only on judicial authority. Later, an institutional executioner, unrelated to the victim, is appointed as a further step toward what now deserves the name of public justice, as distinct from private satisfaction for harm.

Ignoring the options of banishment and self-exile, Treston's scheme constitutes an enticing rational reconstruction of the evolution of retributive institutions. It has proven enormously popular in the scholarship on ancient law, and may properly be called the standard or conventional view.[3] There is no quarreling with its final stage, whether as a general historical tendency or as a desirable advance over the practices presumed to precede it. Punishment by state authority is an innovation in justice that we should be loath to abandon. When we assess the antecedents of state punishment, however, the preceding scheme proves untenable in both its historicist and morally developmental guises. The difficulty is that it cannot be assimilated to the historical record of ancient Near Eastern law.

We leave aside the problem of assuming the nomadic blood feud as the baseline institution, if not of justice, at least of a policy vaguely resembling it. To challenge this baseline would involve speculative reconstructions of prehistory based on a survey of modern anthropological evidence for cultures in which the blood feud is unknown.[4] This route is tenuous and, in any case, unnecessary, for the favored developmental scheme is vulnerable on a point for which historical evidence *is* available. We can, that is, rebut (or at least seriously question) the view that a system of exact retaliation precedes one of monetary compensation.

Supporters of the view that retaliation is foundational in ancient law point to the *Code of Hammurabi* (c. 1728–1686 B.C.E.)—the first written evidence for penalizing offenses with an exact talion. Their case is impressive. For personal injury, the code prescribes taking eye for eye (#196), breaking bone for bone (#197), and extracting tooth for tooth (#199). These "exact" or "identical" talions are supplemented by another kind—namely, "mirroring" punishments. Such sanctions might include cutting out the tongue of an adoptive son who has denied his adoptive parents (#192), cutting off the breasts of a wet nurse who, without informing the parents, contracts for another child to replace a child who has died (#194), and cutting off the hand of a son who strikes his father (#195). In mirroring punishments, a part of the body connected with the offense becomes the object penalized. Both identical and mirroring talions have a graphic element often lacking in the third and final category (not found in the Hammurabic Code)—that of the "equivalent" talion. In punishments of this kind, retaliation is confined within the limits of some presumed moral equivalent of the offense. As these equivalents are culturally and institutionally defined, they display enormous variety. For instance, life imprisonment as punishment for deliberate murder is, in many peoples' minds, the baseline-equivalent talion from which all others should be calculated. Other people, however, will only accept the death penalty as the relevant moral equivalent for murder.

The lack of anything but identical and mirroring talions in the Hammurabic Code is hardly surprising when we reflect on the difficulties of administering justice in the ancient world. With few standing institutions—no police, prosecutors, prisons, and the like—the enforcement of justice, like the provision of health care, was a private matter. The state might involve itself in the adjudication of disputes by encouraging parties to submit to a trusted arbiter, but limited resources dictated immediacy of punishment. Requiring nothing in the way of elaborate institutional apparatus, identical and mirroring talions have the advantage that they can be administered on the spot at little cost.

This same advantage inheres in penalties of death and mutilation, whether they are talions, and hence limited, or excessive in degree and kind. Accordingly, no fewer than thirty-two articles in the Hammurabic Code prescribe a penalty of death. Only a few of these involve the *lex talionis*. The remainder, mandating capital punishment for such offenses as theft of temple property (#6), kidnapping (#14), abetting the escape of a slave (#15), robbery (#22), hiring a substitute for military service (#33), adultery (#129), harboring outlaws (#199), and son–mother incest (#157), appear from our modern vantage to be both monstrous and capricious. Paradoxically enough, no article deals explicitly with homicide. G. L. Driver and John C. Miles interpret this omission to mean that murder was left to private self-help and did not come before the courts.[5] This view runs into difficulty when we consider that false accusation of murder is punished by death (#1). It seems unlikely that courts would have dealt with false accusation of murder but not with murder itself. After all, where might the false accusation occur to make it a state concern in the first place? The reasonable answer is the court, for if murder were left to the blood feud, why would accusation of murder be any different? What is more, the first application of the *lex talionis* in the Hammurabic Code prescribes death to anyone bearing false witness in a capital case (#3).[6] The governing principle is "as one would have done to another [see him put to death] so shall it be done to him." False witness in a capital case is viewed as an attempt to take life, and the attempt would not have been penalized by the state in greater degree than the act itself.

A more likely view is that the Hammurabic Code assumes, without need of explicit statement, a penalty of death for homicide. Other applications of the death penalty have to be spelled out because the link between crime and punishment fails to be obvious. Nontalionic death penalties must be specified, engraved in stone, for the very reason that their arbitrary nature makes them difficult to remember.

The inference of a state-sanctioned, identical talion for murder is strengthened by the prevalence of the *lex talionis* in a variety of other provisions of the code. Hammurabi legislates for the three classes of nobles, commoners, and slaves, as well as for their respective possessions, including women and children. (Neither king nor priests are mentioned as subject to penalty, their prerogatives presumably above the law or prescribed in a lost code.) Two cases in particular advance our study of the *lex talionis;* hence, we cite them in full. First case:

209: If a seignior struck a(nother) seignior's daughter and has caused her to have a miscarriage, he shall pay ten shekels of silver for her fetus.

210: If that woman has died, they shall put his daughter to death.
211: If by a blow he has caused a commoner's daughter to have a miscarriage, he shall pay five shekels of silver.
212: If that woman has died, he shall pay one-half mina of silver.
213: If he struck a seignior's female slave and has caused her to have a miscarriage, he shall pay two shekels of silver.
214: If that female slave has died, he shall pay one-third mina of silver.

Second case:

229: If a builder constructed a house for a seignior, but did not make his work strong, with the result that the house which he built collapsed and so has caused the death of the owner of the house, that builder shall be put to death.
230: If it has caused the death of a son of the owner of the house, they shall put the son of that builder to death.
231: If it has caused the death of a slave of the owner of the house, he shall give slave for slave to the owner of the house.[7]

The first item to note in these passages is their intermingling of retaliation and compensation, along with their acceptance of vicarious punishment. The seignior's daughter (#210) and the builder's son (#230) are innocent parties who suffer as a means of getting at the prime offender. Another item to note is how the like for like formula adjusts for differences in class and sex. In #210, the death of the woman is paid for by the death of the man's daughter; if a commoner's daughter (#212) or a female slave (#214) is killed by the seignior, money suffices as compensation. It is the status of the victim's father that determines the penalty: Some deaths are less equal than others. A third and final item to note is that the first statute suggests an effort to replicate the original injury as exactly as possible. Why not put the offender's wife rather than his daughter to death? The answer may be that only the daughter is likely to be of child-bearing age; hence the penalty involves deprivation of future offspring, exactly as in the offense.[8]

Defenders of the conventional evolutionary view of justice argue that these statutes prove the thesis that compensation gradually replaces retaliation as an aim of law. The most serious offenses in the eyes of the culture are punished by death, the less serious by compensation, exactly as the standard view would have it. Gradually, compensation becomes acceptable for more serious crimes also, especially as the manifold difficulties of exact retaliation reveal themselves—for example, what to do with a childless seignior who kills a pregnant daughter of another seignior.

One difficulty with this view is that it imposes on the texts a distinction between retaliation and compensation that may not exist. Taking daughter for daughter or son for son is, we tend to think, clearly retaliatory. Paying five shekels for a commoner's daughter is, we also think, clearly compensatory—or a gesture in that direction. But what of the provision in #231, where a slave killed in the fall of a house must be replaced by a slave from the builder? Objectively considered, it is an example of restitution: The slave that was lost is replaced. Still, that slave for slave in #231 follows hard upon the death of son for son in #230 suggests that retaliation, compensation, and restitution are not clearly distinguished. The appeal of like for like is emotionally so compelling as to override distinctions. This interpretation is buttressed by a later article (#252), where a slave gored and killed by a seignior's ox commands a price of one-third mina of silver, with no mention of replacement by another slave.

Inconsistencies of this sort are common in the Hammurabic Code. Theft, for instance, is penalized by death in some parts (#7, #9, and #10), and in other parts by fine (#259, #260). We can explain this phenomenon by assuming that the written code builds on oral law from many sources and centuries. The method, then, of reading provisions within their immediate context makes more sense than attempting to rationalize the body of law as a whole.

One might, of course, argue that there is little difference between actually yielding up a slave and paying a fine that would be sufficient for purchasing one. In both cases the objective is restitution. This claim, however, falls into the trap of reading back into the Hammurabic Code a distinction between compensation and retaliation—the very difference that is missing in the slave-for-slave exchange of #231. Still, if we insist on the distinction, then a better case can be made that #231 has a retaliatory as opposed to a compensatory aim. A signal difference between the builder's case and the ox-goring case is that the latter comes about between two members of the aristocracy, whereas the former transpires between an aristocrat and a commoner. We might expect a class-conscious law to impose a punitive sanction in the builder's case while failing to do so in the other case, the aristocrat considering his honor assailed by the delicts of a commoner, but not by those of a peer.

Speculation aside, there remains an even worse embarrassment for the view of compensation as a distinct and morally advanced institution emergent from a retaliatory nexus. If true, we would expect older codes to have less of compensation and more of retaliation than the *Code of Hammurabi*. In fact, though the evidence is scanty, exactly the opposite seems to hold. The *Laws of Eshnunna* (c. 2000 B.C.E.) evidence remarkable restraint when it comes to physical injury:

42. If a man bites the nose of another man and severs it, he shall pay 1 mina of silver. For an eye he shall pay 1 mina of silver; for a tooth ½ mina; for an ear ½ mina; for a slap in the face 10 shekels of silver.

Fragments from the even earlier code of Ur-Nammu (c. 2100 B.C.E.) also provide for purely pecuniary damages in three cases of serious personal injury.[9]

Moving forward in time brings further embarrassment for the conventional developmental view of retributive institutions. Two codes roughly contemporary with each other (1500–1200 B.C.E.), *The Middle Assyrian Laws* and *The Hittite Laws*, are radically at odds in the tenor of their punishments. *The Middle Assyrian Laws* prescribe death, mutilation, and flogging without apparent rhyme or reason. There is little exactness in the mutilations prescribed: a finger from a woman who has crushed a seignior's testicle; both her eyes if she has crushed both testicles (Tablet A, #8). When there is, presumably, an attempt to prescribe a talion, the results are grotesque mirroring punishments. Castration is prescribed for spreading rumors of a neighbor's sodomy (Tablet A, #19), while for a seignior who illicitly kisses another seignior's wife "they shall draw his lower lip along the edge of the blade of an ax and cut it off" (Tablet A, #9).

It is a relief to move to *The Hittite Laws*, where fines alone are exacted for physical injury (Tablet 1, 9–16). More remarkably, no death penalty is imposed for cases of inadvertent homicide. Instead, the offender must compensate by yielding up four slaves if the victim was a free person (Tablet 1, 1), or two slaves if the victim was a slave (Tablet 1, 2). There is even a hint that compensation likewise covers instances of deliberate homicide, for when anyone kills a Hittite merchant "for his goods" (Tablet 1, later version of 5) he is fined. Its amount is reduced "if only the hand is doing wrong," a phrase that in the preceding articles connotes striking out in anger.

Some scholars are wedded to the conventional view that retaliation simply *is* primitive, even when their tone suggests a grudging respect for it; thus C. H. W. Johns, in arguing that the *lex talionis* predates the Hammurabic Code:

> Now the aristocratic *amelu* or patrician of Babylonia was very sensitive to a personal injury. He would accept no compensation for a blow as might a commercial plebeian. The exact retaliation "eye for eye, tooth for tooth, limb for limb" was his sole satisfaction. The *mushkenu* or commoner had to be content with a money payment. . . . We say that the proud patrician was conservative of a more primitive type of law, which we find to be that of a nomad Semitic folk, the Bedawin Arabs, still.[10]

J. J. Finkelstein directly contradicts this view with an assertion that "the idea of physical punishment for physical injuries was an *innovation* in Hammurapi's laws." [11] Compensation rather than retaliation is the more primitive system, he argues, for inflicting physical injury—however bad in other respects—at least recognizes assault as a morally reprehensible "criminal" act rather than as a mere pecuniary "civil" harm. Moshe Greenberg mounts a similar defense for the insistence in Hebrew law that compensation not be accepted for the life of a murderer.

He credits ancient Hebrew law with discovering the principle of the sanctity of life, contrasting the severity with which it treats homicide (applying the *lex talionis*) with its leniency toward crimes against property.[12] In this view, too, exact retaliation is an advance over compensation, marking as it does the important moral insight that life and property are incommensurable.

Who, then, is right—those who adhere to the conventional developmental model, viewing exact retaliation as the more primitive system, or those who, still developmentalists, introduce the wrinkle of seeing compensation as more primitive? Both parties stretch the textual evidence, and both neglect the likelihood that retaliatory and compensatory systems of redress were distinguished differently from the way we distinguish them today. Compensation need not be pecuniary, and retaliation may be inferred where it does not belong. Life for life may connote slave to replace slave as easily as dead daughter to satisfy for dead daughter. The real "advance" (if we must use developmental language) may lie less in the fact of one system's superseding its rival than in the simple perception that retaliation and compensation—though sometimes difficult to disentangle—possess different implications for the legal system as a whole.

Even if wrong on this score, however, we must keep in mind that both compensation and retaliation for harm are retributive institutions. Because compensation involves exchanging money (or a commodity), there is a tendency to assimilate it to other economic exchanges. This tendency can be misleading. Two parties in an economic exchange enter voluntarily and with a sense that each is getting what he or she wants. Compensation for harm, however, is typically involuntary on the part of at least one of the parties. Thus, like physical retaliation, pecuniary compensation for harm has an essentially coercive dimension. The threat of vindictive reaction, along with the belief that certain offenses warrant such reaction, drives a wergeld system every bit as much as a system of exact retaliation. If it did not, there would be no motive for redress of damages.

Whatever our personal predilection for retaliation over compensation or vice versa, a reluctance to endorse one developmental scheme over another must follow from our ignorance of the degree to which the prescribed penalties in ancient law were actually imposed. We must guard against assuming that a dead culture's written laws were administered efficiently (every offender captured) and inflexibly (no mitigation of penalty). Think, for instance, what a misleading picture of modern criminal justice would be derived from reading criminal statutes apart from a study of suspended sentencing, plea bargaining, and other mitigating institutional factors. Even the harsh Assyrians doubtless tempered justice with mercy. We must not always credit what we read, and we must be wary of telescoping the centuries together. The inherently conservative nature of law means that a penalty can be "on the tablets" or "in the (oral) tradition" for centuries after it has fallen into disuse. This problem is especially acute when law becomes a fixed portion of holy writ, as with the three versions of the *lex talionis* in ancient Hebrew scripture.

Yahweh and the Redeemer of Blood

Missing from the codes we have so far examined is the doctrine of blood guilt. As a result of this principle and the allied belief that blood guilt is dangerous to others—polluting [13]—the ancient Hebrews were hostile to wergeld (*kofer*) for homicide, whether deliberate or intentional. Shedding of blood is an abomination that must be expiated, "for blood pollutes the land, and no expiation can be made for the land, for the blood that is shed in it, except by the blood of him who shed it" (Num. 35.33).[14] In the case of homicide, human beings are commanded to take an active hand in alleviating blood guilt: "Whoever sheds the blood of man, by man shall his blood be shed; for God made man in his own image" (Gen. 9.6). If the shedding of blood goes unexpiated, the consequences may be disastrous to the collective body of Israel. To prevent pollution in the case of rural homicide by an unknown person, the law commands the elders of the nearest city to perform a ritual for obviating blood guilt. They must testify:

> "Our hands did not shed this blood, neither did our eyes see it shed. Forgive, O LORD, thy people Israel, whom thou hast redeemed, and set not the guilt of innocent blood in the midst of thy people Israel; but let the guilt of blood be forgiven them." (Deut. 21.7–8)

In addition, the elders must cleanse their hands in fresh heifer's blood (Deut. 21.6). Only blood has the magical potency to wash away blood—a belief illustrating the connection between rituals designed to ward off portended evil and the epistemic component of retribution. In deed as in word, like for like shadows the attempt to govern or propitiate forces beyond human control.

Equally important as the inspiration for a piece of sympathetic magic (or for a form of words embodying the *lex talionis*) is its mode of transmission. In the case of the ancient Hebrews, of course, that mode is as a command of Yahweh—jealous protector-cum-punisher of his chosen people. Along with several of the Ten Commandments, the *lex talionis* is easily the best-known precept of ancient Hebrew scripture. Thanks to its graphic imagery and its mnemonic simplicity, the precept transcends context to resound without restriction or qualification. Careful analysis, however, suggests that we should not speak of "the" *lex talionis*, but of several. Not only are its scriptural tokens highly contextual, but later interpretations at the hands of rabbinical authority remove all but a vestige of whatever exact retaliation it may once have prescribed. Clemency, never completely absent, slowly expands its portion of the retributive web represented by the ancient Hebrew law of physical injury and homicide—a process worth examining in order to appreciate the protean nature of *like for like*.

Despite an impression of overwhelming scriptural authority, the *lex talionis* appears in only three passages of the Torah. In order of probable antiquity, they are Exod. 21.22–25, Deut. 19.19–21, and Lev. 24.17–21. Each is problematical, for none can be safely generalized and all have affinities to other Near Eastern codes. Far from insisting that any injury or death (or even any *intentional* injury or death) should be requited *like for like,* bodily member for bodily member, the three passages address specific concerns: hurting a pregnant woman, perjury, and guarding Yahweh's altar against defilement. Short, then, of begging to be spun into an all-encompassing retributive web for every person guilty of physical injury or homicide, the scriptural *lex talionis* begs to be dissociated and shrunk, fashioned into three smaller webs confined to remote corners in the governance of human affairs. Historically, this tendency is reflected in the treatment of the *lex talionis* by the rabbis (third to fifth centuries, c.e.) responsible for compiling the Babylonian Talmud. Surveying the law and its Talmudic interpretation provides a case study in the dangers of focusing on retaliation apart from an understanding of conditions for excuse and mitigation.

The first and, in most parts, oldest version of the *lex talionis* is Exod. 21.22–25:

> When men strive together, and hurt a woman with child, so that there is a mis-carriage, and yet no harm follows, the one who hurt her shall be fined, according as the woman's husband shall lay upon him; and he shall pay as the judges deter-mine. If any harm follows, then you shall give life for life, eye for eye, tooth for tooth, hand for hand, foot for foot, burn for burn, wound for wound, stripe for stripe.

Similarities between this passage and the one already cited from the *Code of Hammurabi* are sufficiently striking to suggest that the Hebrew scriptures, like the Hammurabic Code, originally prescribed a vicarious talion: In the case of harm (death of the woman), the offender's daughter is to be put to death. The presumption is that in a culture where women are chattel, taking a male life for a female life would be viewed as excessive rather than as exact retaliation.[15]

There are, however, several problems with transferring the vicarious punishment of the Hammurabic Code to the Exodus case. First of all, *The Middle Assyrian Laws* (#50) makes clear that the male is to be put to death in such an instance, and the Assyrians were no more inclined to treat women equally than were the Hebrews. Second, the Exodus passage lacks much of the class bias of the Hammurabic Code, for the next provision (Exod. 21.26–27) is for the free-ing of a slave if his or her master gouges out an eye or knocks out a tooth. In general, memory of their own enslavement in Egypt rendered the Hebrews more enlightened in their treatment of slaves than were the ancient Babylonians. The forced miscarriage of a female slave would have, in Hebrew law, resulted in her freedom, whereas in the Hammurabic Code she is paid a sum of money. With class prejudice diminished in the Exodus passage, why not the grosser manifestations of sexual prejudice along with it? Finally, the Hebrews possessed the overarching doctrine of blood guilt, which the Babylonians lacked. The Exodus context makes the "harm" look accidental (thereby arguably subjecting the culprit to exile rather than to death), but insistence on blood guilt may explain why someone (presumably the one who hurts the woman) must pay with a life.

So much for the case of who is to suffer. It is left to consider the problem of what most scholars agree is a clear interpolation of later material into the Exodus version of the *lex talionis*. The idea of "harm" is enigmatic. How can a miscarriage fail to be "harm," which apparently blossoms only if the woman herself dies? The parallel passage in the Septuagint appears to distinguish between miscarriage of a fully formed versus unformed human fetus.[16] Death only of the formed fetus, being in the image of God, invokes blood guilt. Accordingly, A. S. Diamond argues that the original and more ancient law prescribed compensation alone, but that a later priestly interpolator imported the "harm" idea to make clear Yahweh's opposition to *kofer* if innocent blood has been shed.[17] (Diamond is a partisan of the view that compensation is more primitive than retaliation.) David Daube, on the other hand, thinks that the older text is the one prescribing exact retaliation, which he interprets in light of an ancient superstition of "taking back" the blood—and hence magically capturing the powers—of a dead person.[18] On this view the interpolated material would be that specifying compensation for the fetus, introduced to mitigate the harsh talion.

Elaboration on Daube's view gives reason to suspect that for the ancient Hebrews, as for their Near Eastern predecessors, retaliation and compensation failed to be distinguished as we would differentiate between them today. To set Daube's argument before us, we need first to examine the role of the "redeemer of blood" (often translated "avenger of blood") in the administration of the Hebrew law of homicide.

Most authorities agree that the redeemer of blood (*go'el ha-dam*) was a close male relative of the person killed: father, son, brother, or uncle. As early law confines redress of homicide to the sphere of private relations, the typical Near Eastern redeemer of blood sought either to avenge the loss or to exact blood money (*kofer*) as restitution. For the Hebrews, Yahweh's clear prohibition of *kofer* in the case of homicide foreclosed one of these options. For deliberate homicide, no mercy could be shown: Yahweh closed off his altar as a sanctuary for anyone with innocent blood on his hands (Exod. 21.14). If, however, the homicide were inadvertent, a killer could protect himself by fleeing to one of six cities of refuge (Deut. 19.7–10; Num. 35.6; Josh. 20.1–9). The redeemer of blood had no right to enter such a city to avenge his relative, though if the murderer were caught outside the city limits the redeemer of blood could slay him without blood guilt. Those who killed unintentionally were confined to the city of refuge until the death of the high priest in office at the time of sentencing.[19]

Beyond the open-ended charge of looking after a slain relative, the duties of the redeemer of blood are murky. Scholars agree that Hebrew law gradually relies less and less on blood kin in administering the penalty for homicide, but details are much disputed. In the Talmud, R. Jose argues that it was the duty of the redeemer of blood to slay the intentional homicide, and optional for all others, whereas R. Akiba holds that vengeance was optional in the case of the redeemer of blood and a capital crime for others.[20] Mayer Sulzberger insists that the redeemer of blood was not a relative at all, but an impartial representative of the state, a kind of sheriff–executioner.[21] Johns, on the other hand, thinks that the redeemer was always a relative, but with his role shrinking to that of participating in the execution—and this only in cases where a court sanctioned a finding of deliberate murder.[22]

Fortunately we need not adjudicate in this debate, for following Daube our attention turns to the affinities between the redeemer of blood and two other instances of biblical redemption, both in a legal context. The first is the right of buying back property (or persons) lost to another as surety for unpaid debt. Hebrew law allowed a man to redeem his property at any time, and Hebrew custom obligated relatives to aid his endeavors. The second relevant instance of redemption is "taking back" into the family a widow via marriage with her deceased husband's brother. The law even prescribed that the first son born of such a union belonged to the dead man in case he had not produced a son of his own.

Daube believes that the legal practice of redemption predated and gave rise to the religious concept. In two of the three biblical invocations of the *lex talionis,* Exodus and Leviticus, the phrase "life for life" is *nefesh tahat nefesh,* literally "life in place of life." Only in Deuteronomy does the phrase *nefesh be-nefesh* suggest taking a life rather than replacing it. How, though, could the idea of redemption, "taking back," be the original for literal retaliation, as even the Talmudic rabbis who deny the talion for physical injury insist that the law prescribes for homicide? Daube speculates that the idea of "taking back" in the case of the redeemer of blood is grounded in the superstition, already mentioned, that a manslayer won magical possession of his victim's powers. In order to "take back" those lost powers, relatives felt obliged to pursue and kill the manslayer.[23]

We need not endorse Daube's hypothesis about this particular superstition to appreciate that his more general thesis suggests a mode of thought in which compensation and retaliation fail to be clearly distinguished.[24] Independent evidence for this view comes from the Assyrians, for whom the equivalent phrase for "redeemer of blood" is translated "owner of the blood" or "owner of the dead person."[25] It would be fascinating if archaeological evidence allowed us to trace the relationship between the concept of exact retaliation and a culture's favored mode of economic transaction. We can speculate, for instance, that a barter economy would be more susceptible than a money economy to confounding compensation with retaliation. For a barter economy, every compensation is a literal exchange of one good for another, encouraging the habit of thought that "life for life" might constitute a similar substitution.

Let us turn next to the version of *lex talionis* preserved in Deut. 19.16–21:

> If a malicious witness rises against any man to accuse him of wrongdoing, then both parties to the dispute shall appear before the LORD, before the priests and the judges who are in office in those days; the judges shall inquire diligently, and if the witness is a false witness and has accused his brother falsely, then you shall do to him as he had meant to do to his brother; so you shall purge the evil from the midst of you. And the rest shall hear, and fear, and shall never again commit any such evil among you. Your eye shall not pity; it shall be life for life, eye for eye, tooth for tooth, hand for hand, foot for foot.

The perjury context is, of course, the signal feature of this version of *lex talionis*. A special odium surrounds perjury, such that harsher talionic penalties may cling to it after they have been abandoned for other offenses. After all, people typically injure others by accident and in fits of rage. To lie under oath, however, is to pursue an evil course with calm intent. Under the assumption that people are more culpable the more opportunity they have to deliberate, forgiveness and mercy have greater appeal in cases of direct physical injury than in cases of invading another's interests by lying. The special loathing reserved for the perjurer invites elastic application of like for like. What one "intends" in a case of bearing false witness derives its content from the penalty associated with the alleged offense. Even for cultures that have abandoned identical talions (or never possessed them), simple reference to the prescribed penalty, however arbitrary, establishes the fittingness of doing to the perjurer "as he intended."

Sometimes, of course, the punishment could not be matched—for example, where the defendant falsely accused was exiled to a city of refuge. According to the Talmud, the perjurer was in these cases to be flogged.[26] But if intent had to be ignored for certain categories of noncapital crime, this necessity did not prevent the Talmudic rabbis from focusing narrowly on intent as a route to de facto elimination of the death penalty. Following an argument first broached by the Pharisees, the Talmud concludes that the perjurer in a capital case must be made to suffer only what he intended, not what he in fact caused to happen. Hence he could only be put to death between the time of sentencing and the time of execution of his victim. As this interval was short, seldom longer than noon to dusk, the penalty was rendered impractical.[27]

The final and historically most recent version of the *lex talionis* in Hebrew scripture is Lev. 24.17–21:

> He who kills a man shall be put to death. He who kills a beast shall make it good, life for life. When a man causes a disfigurement in his neighbor, as he has done it shall be done to him, fracture for fracture, eye for eye, tooth for tooth; as he has disfigured a man, he shall be disfigured. He who kills a beast shall make it good; and he who kills a man shall be put to death.

Because no offense is mentioned, this version seems a strong candidate for espousing a generalized talion for physical injury and homicide. May we thus infer that the passage endorses exact retaliation for all cases of physical injury and homicide?

Only at great risk, for the concern with bodily integrity, reinforced by other laws in the immediate context, suggests a more limited application. Anyone with an injury or deformity is prohibited from approaching Yahweh's sanctuary (Lev. 21.16–21). A permanent deformity (given the sorry state of medicine, many injuries must have been or become so) prohibited one from entering or compelled one to leave the priesthood. Exchanging "fracture for fracture" may be no more than a convenient expression to convey the idea that Yahweh's altar must remain as secure from evil deeds as from evil appearances. Alternatively, to the extent the talion is literally intended, there is no reason to conceive of it as applying to injuries among the populace at large. Whatever its previous history, the talion in Leviticus smacks of priestly concerns and priestly rationalization. Loss of the privilege to approach Yahweh's sanctuary is no great loss to the layperson, who would fear to tread there under any circumstances. The hurt beyond physical injury falls only on the priest, who might thus endorse a harsh rhetorical sanction out of special sensitivity to his own vulnerabilities.

In the case of death, the Leviticus passage invokes both compensation and retaliation. Life for life connotes replacement in the case of a beast, the death penalty in the case of a human being. The drawing of this distinction, combined with Yahweh's abhorrence at the shedding of innocent blood, leads some scholars to credit the ancient Hebrews with discovering the principle of the sanctity of human life.[28] By implication, then, ancient Near Eastern cultures that tolerated *kofer* are morally inferior for setting human life on a par with economic commodities. Attractive as this argument may be to partisans of ancient Hebrew culture, equally plausible counterarguments suggest that we should be chary of evaluating different retributive webs on a scale ranging from "morally higher" to "morally lower." The case for such skepticism parallels that of associating "historically later" with "better developed" and "historically earlier" with "less developed."

Retributive Metaphysics and Moral Development

Talmudic commentators on the *lex talionis*—save for one R. Ezra who insists on its literal application—argue that it prescribes compensation in the case of physical injury. The Talmudic objections to the letter of the law pay tribute to the emotive appeal of identical retaliation while denying its practicality.[29] What if one man's eye is larger than another's? What if one man has lost an eye already? What if the gouging out of the eye cost a man his life through loss of blood? The law is undermined for physical injury, not because its aim is misguided, but because human beings are all too clumsy in administering it. The practice is forbidden because the aim, appropriate in its own right, is likely to be overshot.

In later Jewish tradition, then, the *lex talionis* is restricted to deliberate homicide. Its invocation in other contexts is interpreted as metaphorical, signifying that all injuries, from the slightest (loss of a tooth) to the most grave (loss of an eye), are subject to adjudication, with the victim deserving monetary compensation. This traditional view, however, is the product of a later age looking back with mixed reverence and embarrassment on the sanctions of its ancestors. To argue that exact retaliation for physical injury is completely alien to Hebrew scripture is as misguided as to argue that the *lex talionis* was, in its origins, generalized to include all injuries. It is true that physical mutilation of a talionic nature is for the most part missing from the historical narratives of Hebrew scripture (see Judg. 1.7 for an exception), but any argument from silence is unconvincing, for recording ordinary crime is of scant interest to writers preoccupied with crime writ large—for example, with Israel's persistent violations of Yahweh's covenant.

Given the fragmentary nature of the evidence and the tendency of surviving codes to preserve laws without documenting their degree of neglect, the wisest course is to acknowledge a plurality of Near Eastern retributive webs woven from the strands of retaliation and pecuniary compensation for suffering. Against this backdrop, we may ask what proof for the antiquity of compensation over retaliation (or vice versa) would actually tell us in the case of a particular Near Eastern legal tradition. The most obvious lesson is that one practice preceded the other only in the experience of a particular culture. We would still be as far as ever from establishing the universality of this experience for other Near Eastern cultures, let alone for all cultures in general. Even so, the rhetoric of the various developmental schools would have us postulate that its reading of the legal experience of ancient peoples illuminates a dark childhood through which we—history's "adults"—have, thankfully, passed.[30] (Counterexamples may be discounted when applying this framework, for we simply proclaim that some cultures are still in their childhood, others in arrested adolescence.)

Ultimately, I think, the desire to establish temporal priority for retaliation or compensation in the development of retributive practice derives from the application of naive evolutionary thinking to cultural studies. All too frequently, evolution is conceived as a march toward perfection rather than as blind adaptation to circumstances based on random genetic mutation. Our age is inheritor of a reflexive faith in progress, leading us to equate *earlier* with "primitive" and "morally deficient," and *later* with "less primitive" and "morally improved."

In truth, we should separate our moral evaluations from our judgments about cultural influence. To draw on earlier examples, one motive of some who deem compensation a later development than retaliation (Sulzberger, et al.) is that they view wergeld as more humane than, an obvious advance over, the "insecure foundation" of the literal *lex talionis*. Contrarily, those, like Greenberg and Finkelstein, who insist that exact retaliation is a later practice than pecuniary compensation exhibit a distaste for systems that treat human beings as possessions. They thus judge Hebrew law to be "more developed" in light of its alleged recognition of humanity's special status.

When all is said and done, the parties to this debate fail to engage each other, for they apply different measures. The first emphasizes the moral good of minimizing suffering, the second bestows on human beings a unique dignity. Both aims are laudable; but they do not, together or apart, resolve the issue of moral development. This failure is only worsened when we reflect on the variety of other factors affecting retributive institutions: for example, degree of centralized administration, societal wealth, tendency toward nomadic life, and tenacity of religious dogma.[31]

Behind developmental speculation about the origin of retributive institutions lurks the intuition that, deep down, lies the bedrock in which all penology is grounded. In our digging, however, we sift through bedrock that has eroded into soil. We scrape away the last of the fine particles, then complain at finding nothing. If "bedrock" exists, it is biological rather than cultural, and we should abandon the project of imposing an invariant scheme on retributive webs spun for requiting physical injury and death.

Let us close with a word about an issue touched on in Chapter One: the desire to dress ideas about punishment in metaphysical garb. Morally reflective human beings are sensitive about the imposition of deliberate suffering on others. The quest for more humane forms of punishment may wax or wane; but in waxing, it is driven as much by dissatisfaction with the status quo as by a realistic hope of improved alternatives. In returning evil for evil, one individual does to another what, objectively speaking, he would not want done to himself. This creates such a dilemma for the conscientious person that the evil of suffering must be transformed rhetorically into a good. A larger story unfolds—the sanction of deliberately inflicted evil is grounded in something more substantial than human nature. In the case of the ancient Hebrews that "something" was their warlike and jealous protector, Yahweh. This stroke bequeaths to the world the simplest and most enduring metaphysics of retribution: Human beings must accept retributive practices because such punishments are embodied in and commanded by a personal God. Even today, inscrutable though it be, this assertion is sufficient to settle the minds of millions of Jews, Christians, and Muslims.

Pursuing further ramifications of this metaphysics must be deferred to Chapters Six and Seven. For now, in Chapter Five, we turn to another world entirely—that of the ancient Greeks, who produced their own assorted twists in rationalizing the infliction of deliberate suffering.

FIVE

Suffering unto Truth

Among the products of human invention linked to the inevitability of suffering, none shows greater genius than the ancient Greek Erinyes. Even Satan, archfiend and intractable opponent of good, is too rational a concoction to rival the Erinyes in suggesting the mystery, misery, and sublimity of suffering. Satan's motives are too plain, his quest for dominion too explicable, to do justice to the murkier haunts of the human psyche. The black, impalpable, shrieking, Gorgon-coiled Erinyes have no peer when it comes to prefiguring the old law of blood for blood in all its inexplicable malignity. Even so, the Erinyes possess a dram of reason, for, rather than visit their torments at random, they are provoked only at the shedding of blood.

The Erinyes thus do for the Greeks of the seventh to fourth centuries B.C.E. what Yahweh does for the ancient Hebrews—they demand the blood of homicides. On closer analysis the Erinyes exhibit a peculiar taste for slayings within the family. Ixion, the first Greek homicide and the first to be plagued by the Erinyes, is reputed to have killed a kinsman and sought sanctuary from Zeus, who consented to his purification.[1] In outline the tale of Ixion anticipates that of Orestes, whose story we examine in this chapter.

The noncompensatory retributive webs of ancient Near Eastern law emphasize the epistemic component of retribution: When outraged by personal suffering or the loss of a loved one, we are urged to ponder exact retaliation. Despite its practical deficiencies, the *lex talionis* constitutes a powerful ideal (some would call it the sole ideal) of justice. Familial homicide, however, places this standard under enormous strain. Instead of constituting a limitation on revenge, exact retaliation for slayings within the family injects one into a hall of mirrors. The blood feud cannot achieve stasis (both sides content at an equal loss), nor can the state provide disinterested solace to relatives of the person slain. These deficiencies arise for the simple reason that a familial avenger, on shedding kindred blood, himself becomes an appropriate object of vengeance. We are thrown back into the contradictions of the purely reactive component of retribution. We fervently wish evil to befall the offender, yet we cannot hold him at the same psychic distance as a stranger or other nonkinsman. The blood of a relative avenging against other relatives is an outrage, whether coursing through his veins or staining the ground in requital of his deed. That blood is our blood, leading love to intertwine with hate and obligation to shade into obsession.

Later in the chapter we examine two diametrically opposed treatments of this conflict. The first is that of Aeschylus. In it we discover a parallel to the Judaic assertion of vengeance as a divine prerogative. Familial homicide is a contradiction resolvable only by taming the Erinyes, claiming their power on behalf of an institution suffused with the majesty of Apollo. The second treatment, that of Euripides, is less sanguine. It is a story of familial retaliation remaining in the sullied, irresolute hands of human beings. In telling it, Euripides casts doubt on all presumptive stabs at justice. His Erinyes prefigure, in madness, the pangs of conscience—a perspective suited to introducing the discussion of Plato in Chapter Six.

Before contrasting Aeschylean optimism with Euripidean pessimism,[2] we need first to place the Erinyes in the context of the ancient Greek doctrine of pollution, which gives a characteristic shape and suspension to the conflicting views woven by the two playwrights. That Aeschylus makes pious use and Euripides skeptical use of belief in pollution suggests a retributive web that is gleaming white when viewed from one direction, pitch black when viewed from the other.

The Erinyes, Pollution, and the Metaphysics of Retribution

Hesiod attributes the Erinyes' origin to blood spattered from the testicles of Uranus during his castration (and attendant killing) by his son, Cronus.[3] Sounder if less dramatic accounts are given by Erwin Rohde and Lewis Richard Farnell. Rohde argues that the Erinyes were originally and literally spirits of the ancestral dead crying for vengeance from the grave.[4] Woe to any person failing to avenge a slain kinsman, for the wrath of a dead person could palpably affect the living. Farnell attributes the Erinyes, partly by etymology, to belief in the potency of curses, especially those of a murder victim.[5] Both accounts explain the Erinyes' taste for hounding kin, and both suggest a basis for the Greek preference for exiling deliberate homicides.[6] (This preference, of course, contrasts sharply with the ancient Hebrew prescription of death as befitting murder.) The more distant the bloody hands of a manslayer from the grave—and hence from the curse—of his victim, the less the Erinyes are inflamed.

A link to the grave is likewise consonant with another of Hesiod's derivations in which the Erinyes are associates of Ge, archaic Earth goddess and precursor of Demeter.[7] Here are imported mystical ties to fertility and to the regularity of the seasons, and ties to Themis, daughter of Ge, who personifies the concept of order fundamental to the ideal of justice. The Erinyes become generalized spirits zealously maintaining order, as in the fragment from Heraclitus (also discussed in Chapter Three): "The sun will not overstep his measures; otherwise the Erinyes, ministers of Justice, will find him out." Werner Jaeger and others following him attribute to the pre-Socratic philosophers—especially Anaximander, Heraclitus, and Parmenides—a metaphysical view of retributive justice as inherent in the cosmos.[8] Critics of this reading, notably Arthur W. H. Adkins, Eric A. Havelock, and Michael Gagarin, see it as too sophisticated for the time.[9] In these critics' view the Erinyes are amoral, their anger as susceptible to placation by ritual purification as by conscientious atonement or measured reciprocal suffering. Shame is the great motivator of the pre-Platonic, pre-Aristotelian Greeks, whom Adkins sees as consumed by a competitive success ethic.

There is no need to adjudicate between these views, for the Erinyes are a triumph of imagination precisely because they embody both reason and unreason, both the demand for justice and the howl for vengeance. Likewise, the doctrine of blood pollution, from which the Erinyes cannot be dissociated, testifies to a similar wedding of opposites. Though at first glance it may seem a product of ignorance and superstition, belief in pollution is a cogent means of achieving retributive deterrence. At least as applied to manslaying, the doctrine provides a basis for the quasi-rational administration of justice.

Homicide pollution entails the following. One guilty of murder, deliberate or accidental, contracts a metaphysical stain, invisible save to the Erinyes and to the gods. Like a deadly disease, pollution renders the agent a danger to others, for until the stain is purified or the polluted person exiled the public at large stands threatened. Crops may be blighted (witness *Oedipus Rex*) as incentive for the populace to seek out the murderer. Liability to suffering, then, is collective; and in its nearly allied form of the curse, pollution can be hereditary as well as collective, visiting each generation of a single family with renewed suffering. Finally, the doctrine of pollution imposes strict liability for its offenses. No excuse, justification, or mitigation of penalty is allowed: The accidental manslayer must seek purification equally with one who kills out of greed or passion.

This doctrine is so at odds with our contemporary spirit of individualism that we see it as the product of ignorance and superstition—a view amply reinforced by the favored method of ritually purifying the manslayer. The blood of a sacrificial animal was poured over the hands of the polluted person,[10] "driving out murder with murder" as Euripides puts it.[11] Despite such dissenters as Heraclitus, who scornfully compares the practice to a vain attempt at washing mud away with mud,[12] the ritual enjoyed widespread assent. From what has already been demonstrated about the mesmerizing spell of like for like, note its invocation here as a means of avoiding rather than of advancing a retaliatory aim. If hands defiled by blood pose a vicarious danger to others, why should not the blood of others (in this case animals) satisfy in lieu of the blood of the polluted person?

The graphic nature of this ceremony, the literal use of blood for blood, seems atavistic. If so, the doctrine of pollution ought to be stronger in Homer than in Aeschylus. However, exactly the opposite is true, leading E. R. Dodds to assert that "the haunted, oppressive atmosphere in which Aeschylus' characters move seems to us infinitely older than the clear air breathed by the men and gods of the *Iliad*."[13] Dodds views the doctrine of pollution as a development of the unlettered and presumably lawless "dark ages" of Greece (c. 1000 to 750 B.C.E.). Purification in Homer, he notes, is entirely personal, with no hint of infectious or hereditary pollution.[14]

Accordingly, pollution is a signal innovation in the transition from a Homeric shame culture to the incipient guilt culture of archaic and classical Greece. Homeric man concerns himself with reputation above all else, with how he appears in the eyes of others. If shameful facts can be hidden, so much the better for one who thus avoids being shamed. By contrast, according to Dodds, a fully "modern" moral person concerns himself with the purity of his own motivation, with how he appears to himself. Guilt rather than shame provides the basis for conscientious self-control. Fear of pollution seems transitional between shame and guilt. In common with guilt, pollution drives the polluted person to confess and be purified, but, in common with shame, there is nothing intrinsically moral about the disclosure. The "guilt" of pollution is a generalized brooding, in which the consciousness of the polluted party involves itself in the same way as the consciousness of the public at large.

In criticism of Dodds, Hugh Lloyd-Jones argues that the absence of a collective doctrine of pollution in Homer could as easily arise from its not fitting the narrative purpose of the poet(s) as from its being unknown.[15] Lloyd-Jones outlines the gradual weakening of the doctrine of pollution from the epic through the archaic and into the classical age. Hubert J. Treston offers yet a third perspective, suggesting that the concept was neither of indigenous ancient lineage nor developed indigenously to cope with the lawlessness of the eighth century B.C.E. Instead, the doctrine was imported via contact with Semitic peoples from the Near East, and embraced for the same reason as it found welcome there: as a means of combating a barbarous system of unrestricted vendetta between feuding clans.[16]

The true origin of the Greek belief in pollution, so dominant in the literature and law of the fifth and fourth centuries B.C.E., is unlikely ever to be known. Even if one of the conjectures from the preceding paragraphs happens to be true, we lack sufficient evidence to disprove its rivals. Nonetheless, our review has positioned us to show how, despite its air of mystery and superstition, the doctrine may play an important role in the orderly administration of justice.

As with the ancient Hebrews, enforcement of homicide law in fifth-century Athens was left to the family. Only a relative of the slain could bring action against the accused.[17] (It is tempting to see this prerogative as the remnant of a more extensive, earlier right of self-help.) The more inflexible a relative's known disposition to press charges, the greater the deterrent value of the penalties imposed by the state. The objective of ridding the state of pollution gives neighbors a powerful incentive to urge prosecution on a slain man's reluctant relatives, whose inclinations otherwise might be to let things slide. In this way, even though enforcement remains private, the administration of justice benefits from a preoccupation with public welfare.

The threat of hereditary pollution introduces yet another deterrent, this one acting on the mind of the homicide or prospective homicide. A man's descendants were thought to be vital to his welfare after death, easing his way through the impalpable gray of Hades. Though in several generations his shade would be no more, the evidence of elaborate and costly funereal observances (which Solon attempted to repress)[18] indicates that fifth-century Athenians were haunted by the potential horror of existence beyond the grave. Pollution endangered one's own proper funereal rites, for descendants suffering the dire consequences resulting from an unpurified ancestor are unlikely to pay him homage. The message is clear: Refrain from homicide and, if one happens to kill inadvertently, seek purification prior to death.

We again see that it is an oversimplification to declare deterrence to be a nonretributive, purely consequentialist concern. This is especially so when retribution is generalized to incorporate collective liability for harm. It is a grim but unavoidable axiom that deterrence is maximized as the odds of effective retaliation approach a certainty. Paradoxically, therefore, it is rational to put retaliation beyond the bounds of reason, to make it both implacable and unavoidable, as with the doomsday device in strategies of nuclear deterrence. Such is the role of the Erinyes, emboldened by a widely shared belief in the pollution of homicides—to serve as doomsday devices of a different kind, assuring retaliation.

We have outlined the deterrence in retributive deterrence, but one may justly ask, Where is the retribution? Exactly as innocents are liable to suffer at the hands of a nuclear doomsday device, so also do innocents suffer when the Erinyes blight crops to reveal an undisclosed homicide. If retribution entails anything, a critic might insist, it entails the administration of measured punishment to the guilty alone. To the extent suffering diffuses beyond these bounds, some other policy is at work.

This objection makes good sense in a metaphysics of retribution like that of the ancient Hebrews, where an angry but just Yahweh ultimately disavows the doctrine of hereditary punishment. The ancient Hebrew metaphysics of retribution is hydraulic: Yahweh administers an equal and opposite reaction to each crime or sin. (This, at least, is the refined ideal, if not the practice, in every text of scripture.) In addition to this hydraulic metaphysics, the ancient Greeks possessed a different metaphysics, which we have already labeled homeostatic, after the analogous concept in ecology.[19] As with the hydraulic metaphysics of retribution, the restoration of "balance" is crucial to a homeostatic metaphysics, but the means by which balance is achieved may differ in important respects. The homeostatic is a holistic view, intent on the equilibrium among numerous elements at once. Place and relative position are crucial; if one element is misaligned, balance may either be restored by putting it back into place or by adjusting the other elements into a new pattern of equilibrium. Because it encompasses the first option (along with the second), a homeostatic metaphysics is sometimes consistent with a hydraulic metaphysics. In these cases the difference between the two views is undetectable. Only when elements other than the one disturbed are rearranged for the sake of renewed balance does the homeostatic metaphysics become distinct.

Nowhere is the homeostatic metaphysics of retribution better illustrated than in the fatalistic belief that good fortune must be followed by bad: "If a man has some good fortune he receives Nemesis by way of compensation," as Aesop puts it.[20] The pattern, if we insist on forcing it into a hydraulic metaphysics, departs from a retributive like for like, proposing instead a baffling unlike for like, evil for good. Farnell suggests that this idea originates in the crude belief that the gods are enemies rather than benefactors of humankind.[21] Jealous even of innocent success, the gods stand ready to requite success with suffering. Later moralizers added the insistence that, appearances aside, the successful are struck down, not for their innocent success, but for the hubris engendered by it.[22] In the final analysis, then, evil *is* returned for evil.

We need not, however, force this doctrine into a hydraulic pattern. There remains an alternative, homeostatic source for the idea in the cyclical regularity of the seasons. It is a commonplace for humans to remark that an expanse of fair weather will be "paid for" by foul weather to come (or, alternatively, that fair weather is "deserved" after an expanse of foul). Despite the language of compensation frequently employed, people are committed in such utterances to nothing more than that in the larger order of things fair frequently follows foul: Sunny days succeed cloudy days just as spring and summer follow winter. Weather is a homeostatic system par excellence—one element disturbed shifts the remainder into a different balance, a different equilibrium.

Once we unmask the homeostatic metaphysics, we find it at the root of the pollution doctrine. Homicide pollution is too specific an instance to disclose these roots, for homicide is generally susceptible to a hydraulic response, the application of an equal and opposite reaction to the deed of the killer. When we consider the fuller range of things for which a person can be polluted, however, we disclose a deeper source of anxiety. As Adkins notes, pollution could be contracted by having a bad dream, by contact with death or with a particularly repellent disease, or by childbirth. He supposes that these cases have nothing intrinsically in common with each other, or with homicide pollution. Instead, he locates their mutual dimension in the mental attitude of people toward them: Each is regarded as "queer," unnatural.[23]

Why, though, are "queer" things dangerous in the way that polluted things are dangerous, not just to the polluted person, but to others as well? The answer is that a "queer" thing is a thing out of homeostatic balance; if it is not addressed by punishment or purification, other elements of the system will be affected, probably adversely. In this way, the infliction of suffering on apparently innocent parties becomes a part of the retributive panorama. What is more, the homeostatic metaphysics of retribution is what gives punch to the narrower, hydraulic metaphysics. Why must evil be requited with evil, or purification be performed? Answer: to prevent an overall readjustment in which things are shaped by a new and perhaps grimmer necessity. In the homeostatic view, evil will trail good, inevitably creating a kind of equilibrium, but some equilibria are preferable, containing on the whole less evil than others. Both measured retaliation and like for like propitiation (as in cleansing blood with blood) serve as instruments to prevent a homeostatic system from deteriorating.[24]

One may, of course, be either an optimist or a pessimist about the overall balance of elements needed to achieve cosmic justice. In the matter of homicide pollution, nothing challenges the optimist more than a slaying within the family. The killer is guilty of causing death and simultaneously charged with avenging it. The Erinyes cannot sleep: The very act that satisfies them provokes them to merciless pursuit of the agent who has done their will. Such is the grip of the story of Orestes on the Greek mind. If the problem of retributive justice can be solved here, it can be solved everywhere; but if it cannot be solved here, it may not be soluble.

In broadest outline, the preceding alternatives are endorsed by Aeschylus and Euripides, respectively. Though Sophocles also tells Orestes' story, his account so downplays the element of pollution as to sidestep the theme of assimilating vengeance to cosmic order. We thus consider only Aeschylus' *Oresteia* and Euripides' *Electra* and *Orestes*.

Orestes in Divine Hands

Homer tells the story of Orestes' slaying of Aegisthus and Clytaemnestra, usurpers of Agamemnon's throne, as an exemplary tale of revenge foreshadowing

the justice awaiting Penelope's suitors on the return of Odysseus.[25] There is no
mention of a family curse, no special cognizance that one of the killings is matricide, and no story of Agamemnon's slaying his daughter to unleash the Greek
fleet at Aulis. The ethics of the story in Homer are those of the restricted vendetta.
Honor requires Orestes to avenge his father, and anyone sharing the same sense
of honor will let matters rest, seeing that Orestes has taken his just measure and
no more.

How different the story is in Aeschylus. The family of Agamemnon lies under
a curse stemming from Atreus' tricking his brother Thyestes into feasting on the
flesh of his slain children. The net of blood relationship in the *Oresteia* is thick
and tangled: Agamemnon is the son of Atreus, Aegisthus the son of Thyestes.
Clytaemnestra is the sister of Helen, cause of the Trojan War and wife of Agamemnon's brother, Menelaus. At one level, then, the trilogy examines bitter fruits
peculiar to enmity within the family. With blood ties existing between avenger
and victim, the purity of restricted vendetta—honor satisfied with life for life—
proves untenable. At another level, however, the plays may be read as generalizing to all homicide. The pattern of consanguinity metaphorically suggests blood
ties among all Greeks, and the emergent homicide court under protection of the
Eumenides serves for adjudicating all cases, not simply those of kin slaying.

Agamemnon begins in darkness with a watchman learning from a blaze of
light (part of an ingenious system of beacons established by Clytaemnestra) of
the fall of Troy. Agamemnon returns to his palace, importing a warrior's pride
that he refuses to temper or to accommodate to civic order. The retributive aim
of war is the same as the unrestricted vendetta: Whatever measure one's strength
can command is the measure one may take. Legally speaking, then, Aeschylus'
vision of the Trojan War is also a vision of the dark ages prior to the rule of law,
a Greek version of a Hobbesian state of nature.

Only suffering can guide humans toward something better, an assertion made
twice by the chorus early in the play:

> Zeus, who guided men to think,
> who has laid it down that wisdom
> comes alone through suffering.
>
> (176–78)

> Justice so moves that those only learn
> who suffer.
>
> (250)

To teach wisdom, suffering must be comprehensible—otherwise it merely brutal-
izes. Aeschylus offers multiple explanations for Agamemnon's suffering. His fate
is a reflexive consequence of the hereditary curse, retaliation for slaying his inno-

cent daughter, and a fitting recompense to overweening pride. Returning with the princess Cassandra as his spoil, Agamemnon blithely expects Clytaemnestra to take her in. When offered the chance to tread into his palace on a crimson carpet, he at first demurs, paying lip service to the sentiment that such a prerogative belongs to the gods rather than to man (918–24). But his conqueror's arrogance runs high, allowing Clytaemnestra to seed the question that induces him to overstep his bounds: What would Priam have done (935)? The Trojan king would have tread on the carpet, so how could anything less befit Agamemnon, Priam's conqueror?

In the overstepping of bounds, Agamemnon finds his match in Clytaemnestra. A female usurper of rights customarily reserved to men, she embodies her husband's own misplaced ethics of war. Odysseus proved at Troy that subterfuge is as much a part of the warrior's code as strength, and Clytaemnestra raises the art of subterfuge to the level of genius. She lies unashamedly, telling of her fidelity during Agamemnon's absence (605) and professing only love and contentment at his return (856)—all this as a ploy to strike him down, unwitting, in his bath.

The world of *Agamemnon* is thus one whose native order is profoundly disturbed. Aegisthus, who by ancient right ought to be the one to shed Agamemnon's blood, leaves everything, including the death stroke, to Clytaemnestra, then afterward boasts of his daring (1604). Cassandra foresees the impending doom but is powerless to be believed. (The most ironic misconstruing of her prophecy occurs when she is understood to mean that a *man* will slay Agamemnon [1251].) The Chorus of Elders, who ought to protect Agamemnon's prerogatives, are won over to Clytaemnestra's view that her husband was fated to die for the sacrifice of Iphigenia:

> The spoiler is robbed; he killed, he has paid.
> The truth stands ever beside God's throne
> eternal: he who has wrought shall pay; that is law.
> (1562–64)

So things might end—except that, outraged by the pretension of Aegisthus, the chorus recognizes a further implication of this law. It is a net for snaring Clytaemnestra and Aegisthus at some future date (1615). The play closes with Clytaemnestra's chiding the old men for their impotence, boasting that she and her consort possess sufficient power to restore civic order. Theirs, however, is an order founded on deceit; and to deceit, in *The Libation-Bearers*, it will fall.

In this second play of the trilogy, Aeschylus adheres to a retributive motif that marks Clytaemnestra for death by treachery, precisely as she slew Agamemnon. The touch is one of several mirroring devices that exploit the mesmerizing spell of like for like. A second, purely visual example is created by juxtaposing images as the palace doors open onto separate but interconnected scenes of slaughter.

In *Agamemnon* (1371), Clytaemnestra stands over the bodies of Agamemnon and Cassandra. In *The Libation-Bearers* (971), Orestes strikes an identical pose over the bodies of Clytaemnestra and Aegisthus, while his attendants display the same bloody robe in which his mother entangled and killed her Agamemnon. Lest we overlook the fierce symmetry of the doer suffering what he does, the chorus provides reminders:

> The spirit of Right
> cries out aloud and extracts atonement
> due: blood stroke for the stroke of blood
> shall be paid. Who acts, shall endure. So speaks
> the voice of the age-old wisdom.
>
> (310–14)

Though Aristotle correctly dismisses as impractical the ideal of a doer suffering what he does,[26] the world of the dramatist is different from that of the philosopher. It may be impractical offstage for the doer to suffer the fruits of his act, but the stage world of *The Libation-Bearers* is magical, deliberately archaic, allowing Aeschylus to exploit the retributive anticipations of his audience.

Confident that the "age-old wisdom" of blood for blood lies, first and foremost, in the hearts and minds of those watching the *Oresteia*, Aeschylus is free dramatically to locate that wisdom in the Erinyes, who jealously guard, by divine right, the prerogatives of the slain. The chorus deliberately recalls the ancient belief that the shades of the ancestral dead lie in their graves, crying for vengeance (37–41). Dead Agamemnon demands more than the libation of oil that a nightmare-haunted Clytaemnestra has ordered Electra to administer (90). He demands the older, more graphic purification of blood to wipe out blood:

> It is but law that when the red drops have been spilled
> upon the ground they cry aloud for fresh
> blood. For the death act calls out on Fury
> to bring out of those who were slain before
> new ruin on ruin accomplished.
>
> (400–404)

It is no accident that the play opens with Orestes at his father's tomb—there to pay his respects, yes, but also to harness the outraged power of the dead in assuring his revenge. Fearful of this power, Clytaemnestra has mutilated Agamemnon's corpse (439–44). She acted as much prudentially as vindictively, for ancient superstition connected the effectiveness of vengeance from beyond the grave with the physical wholeness of the body presumed to seek it.

In addition to the outraged spirit of his father, Orestes has a second, more powerful protector. This is Apollo, youthful god of reason, sky-borne Olympian certain to raise the ire of the earth-bound Erinyes. At least twice (270–75; 555–59) we hear that Apollo has commanded Orestes not only to slay his mother, but to employ deceit and thus replicate the duplicity of her own crime. (Orestes wins entrance to the palace by pretending to bear news of his own death.) We might dismiss the specificity of Apollo's command as poetic finery were it not for the final play of the trilogy. In *The Eumenides* we learn that the new order represented by Apollo must win over the Erinyes. What better way than to challenge their own harsh precepts, ultimately proving that, torn by strife and contradiction, they cannot hope to stand alone against the future?

The Eumenides celebrates Orestes' liberation from the Erinyes of his mother. This effect is achieved in part by ritual purification, which releases him from the standard of strict liability. An earlier, nonritual effort to achieve this aim has proven futile, but the motivation for it warrants mention. In *The Libation-Bearers* Orestes, sword in hand, tells Clytaemnestra: "It will be you who kill yourself. It will not be I" (923). Orestes does not speak in the hope of evading his own guilty conscience; he wishes instead to avoid pollution. In a strict liability system, pollution for bloodshed must fall somewhere; and Orestes' sophistry, if accepted by the Erinyes, would render his mother the polluted one. The attempt has parallels elsewhere in ancient Greek thought. Antiphon, for example, argues that a young boy accidentally (from our point of view) impaled by a javelin has killed himself by running in front of it.[27] Such a view absolves the thrower of blame, and hence of pollution. In a similar vein, Demosthenes argues that a wrestler killed in the Olympic Games died as the result of his own weakness.[28] Given a world of pollution and strict liability, there are no accidents, no unavenged slayings: The Erinyes must have a body to pick over, even if it is the body of the victim.

For all its ingenuity, the claim that Clytaemnestra slays herself cannot stand. Orestes, after all, strikes the fatal blow. Besides, were he somehow to evade credit for the deed, the Erinyes of Agamemnon would plague him for letting Clytaemnestra escape her apportioned end (*Libation-Bearers*, 285–90). His mother's Erinyes torment him even in exile, but can these be the same creatures who earlier sought Clytaemnestra's blood? Aeschylus is ambiguous on the point, sometimes suggesting that certain Erinyes are partisans of specific persons (Clytaemnestra's ghost awakens "her" Erinyes at the opening of the play), and sometimes suggesting that the Erinyes have the generalized function of pursuing all homicides (as when the Chorus of Erinyes argues (*Eumenides*, 490–98) that Orestes' release will give crime a free reign). From the standpoint of exacting vengeance, there is little to choose between these two pictures, the first suggesting clans of Erinyes warring among themselves, sharing the grievances of those whose causes they advocate, the second suggesting a unified horde with a nose for blood, the fresher the spill the greater their arousal. In terms, though, of conversion into the

Eumenides—kindly ones—the second picture wins favor, for these new, civilized Erinyes must unite in protecting the innocent and despising the guilty.

The Eumenides gives evidence (416) for Farnell's derivation of the Erinyes from curses. This ancestry makes everyone in the play, including the Olympian gods, Athena and Apollo, wary of naming the Erinyes, for once uttered curses were thought to be inexorable. Failing to find their intended mark in a victim, they rebounded against their originator.[29] Yet the play also gives continued evidence for Rohde's thesis that the Erinyes derive from the spirits of the ancestral dead. In one of their moods, acting as partisans of Clytaemnestra, the Chorus of Erinyes argues that it has no stake in Agamemnon's slaying, for the killing of husband by wife is not the shedding of kindred blood (212). This argument later proves fatal to their cause when Athena votes for Orestes' acquittal on the same grounds. By a sophistry surpassing even his attempt to paint Clytaemnestra's death a suicide, Orestes is declared to be unrelated to his mother, who merely provided a place of nourishment. As "the parent is he who mounts" (660), only patricide is kinslaying; matricide is not.

In vexation over this demeaning of the woman's contribution to procreation, today's reader of *The Eumenides* may overlook the significance of the Erinyes' haste to focus on the narrow significance of blood relationship. Like Demosthenes' wrestler, they are slain by their own weakness, their own shortsightedness. The court arrayed in Athens to hear Orestes' case is a new testing ground, distinct from the usual haunts of the Erinyes, as described by Apollo:

> Where, by judgment given, heads are lopped
> and eyes gouged out, throats cut, and by the spoil of sex
> the glory of young boys is defeated, where mutilation
> lives, and stoning, and the long moan of tortured men
> spiked underneath the spine and stuck on pales.
>
> (186–90)

For all its differences, the court has two important things in common with the Erinyes' former empire: The stronger wins, and the loser is a fit subject of vindictive anger. Without this pair of ingredients, the Erinyes would never convert into the Eumenides.

In the new order, of course, the weapons are words and arguments rather than swords and stones, but this should not obscure that the most telling arguments are retributive—lines of attack that, like curses, sometimes find their mark and sometimes turn on their propounders. Nor should it obscure that the new order is founded on the will of the stronger. Persuasion wins the day, even with the Erinyes, because all-powerful Zeus "guides men's speech in councils" (973). After their transformation, the Eumenides turn to a rhetoric of kindly retribution, disavowing hereditary punishment and the use of their powers to blight the earth (940–44). If we are careless in scrutinizing their closing paean to community and to the returning of good for good, we may miss a crucial vestige of their former nature:

> Let
> not the dry dust that drinks
> the black blood of citizens
> through passion for revenge
> and bloodshed for bloodshed
> be given our state to prey upon.
> Let them render grace for grace.
> Let love be their common will;
> let them hate with single heart.
>   (978–86)

Like the big stick prudently carried by those who walk softly, enmity is retained to scourge violations of the new order. Hating with a single heart is, Aeschylus suggests, a moralized passion capable of taming the impulse toward private vengeance; and if state authority is too blind to give proper scope to this passion, the old law of blood for blood surges to the fore. More than two thousand years before the thesis favoring a persistent retributive aim in criminal law could be dubbed "the channeling argument," [30] Aeschylus places it at the center of his solution to the problem of justice. The idea preserves the inexorable ferocity of the Erinyes, presuming as it does that vindictive passion cannot be repressed. Ever lurking beneath the veneer of civilization, this passion will burst into dangerous channels of its own unless other, socially productive conduits are kept open. By granting the Eumenides a home beneath the Areopagus, most prominent of Athenian homicide courts, Aeschylus signals his faith in the genius of suffering to turn the meeting of evil with its like into a ritual and institutional good.

Orestes in Human Hands

In Euripides' *Electra* the story of Orestes' revenge is, in outline, much the same as for Aeschylus. The family lies under a curse, Agamemnon has been slain, Clytaemnestra has taken Aegisthus as her husband, and Apollo commands Orestes to exact vengeance. Though not themselves depicted, the trial at Athens, Orestes' pursuit by the Erinyes, and his acquittal on a tie vote are all recapitulated in the epilogue. This Aeschylean packaging is deliberate, for Euripides turns the pious hope of suffering unto truth into the gritty reality of suffering unto depravity. The honor-bound like for like of divine retribution may be well and good for Apollo, who does not suffer, but when lodged in the human heart, Euripides asserts, the formula makes for stunted lives and barren wishfulness.

Nowhere are these qualities more apparent than in the character of Electra. She has been forced to take a peasant farmer as her husband, and, though he treats her well, Electra is consumed with humiliation at her lowly status. Aegisthus has commanded the marriage, reasoning that any son born to Electra will have enough of the farmer's base breeding to be a coward, and hence no threat in taking revenge (34–42). The king's precautions prove unwarranted, for Electra's marriage is unconsummated. She remains a virgin, hysterically jealous of her mother's open sexuality. She broods on vengeance, pretending to grieve for Agamemnon as cover for a narrow obsession with her own suffering and indignity.

Though Electra speaks the language of Apolline justice, her actions reveal the extent to which the jealous side of this virtue has consumed her. She speaks of noble endurance, but courage and patience have no place in her. On meeting her unrecognized brother, for instance, fear immediately gets the better of her; she conceives without evidence that he is a criminal waiting to ambush her (215–19). She claims to admire her husband's humble virtue, but when that virtue translates itself into hospitality (an invitation for Orestes to enter their hut) all she feels is shame, angrily dispatching the farmer to procure food worthy of such a visitor (408–14). When slain Aegisthus is brought to her, she harps on his stupidity in failing to perceive his subservience to Clytaemnestra (907–55). This harangue, however, betrays itself: In scorning Aegisthus, Electra assimilates herself to him. Both have been cowed by Clytaemnestra, but in Electra hate and envy intertwine to produce an incredible accusation: Aegisthus has wronged her, Electra, by failing to keep the apportioned domestic order. The implication is that a Clytaemnestra kept humbly in her woman's place would have diminished Electra's own suffering. Fed on invidious comparison of herself to others and abandoning everything to a fixed idea of vengeance, Electra has no core. How apt that her harangue to Aegisthus falls, literally, on dead ears.

In Aeschylus, Clytaemnestra strikes her own blow to fell Agamemnon, but Euripides alters the telling to make Aegisthus the slayer (10). Accordingly, Orestes enters the story determined on vengeance against Aegisthus (85). He is won over to include Clytaemnestra only as the result of Electra's badgering. True to her self-infatuation, she shapes the imperative of killing Clytaemnestra by a warped appeal to Orestes' sympathy, insisting that if only he could feel her distress he would be moved to act (300–38). There are no Erinyes in the play, for Electra herself has become one, dressing in rags and never washing. Nor is pollution mentioned prior to the hollow tidying up of the epilogue. In Euripides' human world, pollution is the inward cause rather than the outward consequence of homicide. He reminds us that killing, even in the name of justice, is still the taking of human life. The results are mixed, the glory never pure: For all his imputed treachery, Aegisthus is slaughtered as a charitable host, innocently receptive to the stranger whom he fails to recognize as Orestes (773–843).

Against this muddy, irresolute human world Euripides juxtaposes the world of cosmic justice, not to celebrate but to cast suspicion on it. The chorus tells how Zeus is alleged to have changed the course of the stars and the sun on learning of Atreus' tricking his brother into cannibalism. Here, in an offense so horrible as to untune the cosmos, is the homeostatic metaphysics of retribution at its grandest and—given faith in the justice of Zeus—most solacing. The chorus, however, refuses to endorse the fable:

> I am won only to light belief
> that the sun would swerve or change his gold
> chamber of fire, moved in pain
> at sorry and sin in the mortal world,
> to judge or punish man.
>
> (737–42)

The sanction for killing in revenge, Euripides insists, cannot be read from off the heavens. It is found in one place only: the spite of a heart blinded by its own exaggerated wrongs.

Whereas Aeschylus employs a formulaic rhetoric of exact retaliation to construct a moralized unity of civic hatred, Euripides uses the same rhetoric to shock and to alienate. When Orestes, still in disguise, questions Electra's boldness in aspiring to kill her mother, the affirmation "Mother by the same ax that cut Father to ruin" signifies nothing save blind malignity. In Aeschylus, Apollo insists that Clytaemnestra must die by deceit, a strategy designed for winning over the Erinyes. Euripides adheres to the same idea, but without the divine command and its patina of rationalization. The deceit is all Electra's, a plan hastily cobbled together at Orestes' suggestion that Aegisthus may be preparing a sacrifice to celebrate the birth of another child (625). Taking the suggestion, Electra resolves on enticing Clytaemnestra to her hovel (and away from bodyguards) by a false report that she, Electra, has given birth. In this weaving of a web to capture Clytaemnestra, the symmetry is dark, the strands repellent. There is no hint of noble purpose—only of frantic expediency spiked by Electra's envy of her mother's sexuality.

In searching for watchwords to sum up the vision of *Electra*, one cannot improve on these, uttered by the chorus to Clytaemnestra: "Justice is in your words but justice can be ugly" (1051). Even the divine Dioscuri, dispatched by Apollo to impose Aeschylean order, see the futility and falseness of their task, speaking thus of the death of Clytaemnestra:

Justice has claimed her but you have not worked in justice.
As for Phoebus, Phoebus—yet he is my lord,
silence. He knows the truth but his oracles were lies.
Compulsion is on us to accept this scene, on you
to go complete the doom which fate and Zeus decreed.

                                                      (1244–48)

Lest we still might hunger to believe, with the eye of faith, that divine decrees are
a source of solace tailored to human good, Euripides follows bleak *Electra* with
an even bleaker *Orestes*.

However, it is not a sequel, for the play wholly abandons the Aeschylean
framework. No longer a dim figure from the mists of time, Orestes is presented
as a contemporary of the audience, a pathetic coward who has slain his mother
rather than pursue justice in the courts. He is plagued by Erinyes, but they are
phantoms of his own mind, invisible to others. There is no shift in scene from
Argos to Athens, and the trial is a public assembly in which passionate rhetoric
rather than quiet reason carries the day, resulting in Orestes' condemnation rather
than acquittal.

The whole of the surviving family is gathered: Orestes, Electra, Menelaus and
Helen, their daughter Hermione, and Tyndareus, father of Helen and Clytaemnestra. Not a jot of nobility survives: Menelaus is a fence straddler, unwilling to
involve himself in the dispute between Orestes and the Argives; Helen is a vain
and fading beauty, fretful about her safety and little affected by her sister's death;
and Electra is a whiner to match her brother, Hermione an insignificant reflection
of her mother. Tyndareus possesses the sole wisdom of the play, but he bruits it
with an old man's spite, raging against the degeneracy of the present in a way
that rightly confirms the other characters in a policy of ignoring him.

Apollo has again commanded Orestes to slay Clytaemnestra (160–64), but
as a consequence of the contemporary setting he in effect commands murder.
Euripides suggests that such heuristic tales as the *Oresteia* can have the perverse
effect of giving unintended sanction to self-help whenever courts are thought to be
unjust or inconvenient. Brave Orestes, our revered ancestor, did not shrink from
revenge and was purified, the argument goes—so why not the same recourse for
ourselves? The character to whom this argument appeals is, naturally enough,
the contemporary Orestes of the play: shallow, spiteful, and self-aggrandizing.
To ennoble violence on stage, giving it divine sanction, is to encourage it as a
remedy elsewhere. Euripides' strategy is to divide the violence from the divine
order, showing each for what it is—violence a resort of criminals, divine order a
fantasy of those with no stomach for reality.

It is tempting to interpret Orestes' phantom Erinyes as the pangs of conscience, for their attack is inward and selective, inflicting a measure of suffering

on Orestes alone. The best we can say, however, is that the Erinyes of the play adumbrate conscience, taking only a halting step toward the idea of an inwardly just retributor. When Orestes emerges from a bout of madness, he blames Apollo for his plight (285). He refuses to place himself at the heart of the crime, and when asked about his sickness names it thus:

ORESTES: I call it conscience. The certain knowledge of wrong, the conviction of crime.
MENELAUS: You speak obscurely. What do you mean?
ORESTES: I mean remorse. I am sick with remorse.

(395–98)

This answer is even more shallow than it seems. What Orestes means by remorse is that he laments being trapped in a palace surrounded by an angry mob demanding his blood. His standard of conscience is as variable as his fear, which in the event causes Orestes to vacillate as he contemplates various means of escape.

First he tries to barter with Menelaus, his appeal a cynical twist on the familiar retributive formula:

When my father mustered an army for the siege
of Troy, he also did a wrong—and yet
that wrong was generous. He did that wrong for you,
to right the wrong that your wife Helen did.
And wrong for wrong, you owe me that wrong now,
Menelaus.

(648–51)

Orestes, of course, refers to Agamemnon's sacrifice of Iphigenia. Even apart from his ludicrous twisting of words, Orestes lacks the moral standing to barter, for he has done nothing and suffered nothing to merit an exchange. The proposal is a brilliant satire, turning on its head the pretense of redeeming family honor. As with the curse of a murdered ancestor, the debt Orestes mentions is hereditary, its repayment conveniently vicarious.

Menelaus does not reject the proposal, but rather pleads enervation of his forces (684–90). Orestes proceeds to more desperate measures. He and Pylades slay Helen on the presumption that Argive's hatred of her will rebound in their favor: The mob will forgive Orestes' matricide in a glut of celebration over Helen's death (1131–53). But the killing goes supernaturally awry; no sooner is Helen struck than she is transported into the air, vanishing (1495). The two desperate men next seize Hermione as a hostage, holding a sword to her throat and, in company with Electra, confronting the others with a demand for safe passage.

As Orestes orders Electra to set the house on fire (1618), Apollo descends *ex*

machina to impose divine order on the whole squalid affair. Helen has been made
a goddess, Menelaus is to remarry, Pylades and Electra are to wed, and, strangest
change of all:

> Then,
> Orestes, you shall marry Hermione,
> the girl against whose throat your sword now lies.
>
> (1653–54)

Despite his evident shallowness and treachery, Orestes is to reign in Argos (1660).
Like counters rearranged on a gaming board, the characters rush to embrace
Apollo's edicts, and like the game board, too, the new order is a pale simplifica-
tion of life—at best a fitful distraction.

There can be no doubt of Euripides' desire to vitiate Apolline justice by
attaching it as an absurd finale to the melodrama of *Orestes*. But to what purpose?
The play may well be the product of exhausted hope, despairing misanthropy,
and a loss of political faith in Athens. Even so, the implications are far from
wholly corrosive. Deeper than any before or after him, Euripides peers into the
solace claimed for a homeostatic metaphysics of retribution. Through the voice
of Electra, he recalls (as in *Electra*) Zeus' supposed realignment of the heavens
at the crime of Atreus (1001–6). What solace, he asks, can even the eye of faith
derive from contemplating Zeus' intervention when suffering continues to follow on suffering as the result of brute will? Electra has already perceived this
possibility:

> Look at your lives,
> all those happy hopes
> cut down with failure and crossed with death.
> See, in endless long parade,
> the passing generations go,
> changing places, changing lives.
> The suffering remains.
> Change and grief consume our little light.
>
> (977–82)

For Euripides, the truth we suffer unto is that suffering has no larger pattern
beyond the inward impulse to retaliate. Though skeptical, this answer directs us
to examine ourselves rather than pious fables of cosmic order. As Orestes took a
half-step toward conscience in the mental visitations of the Erinyes, so Euripides
takes a half-step toward Plato's rich inward doctrine of suffering. Unlike Euripides, however, Plato's rage for order leads him to reimpose a heuristic pattern. This
plan falls only secondarily on the cosmos, for its primary locus is the human soul.

SIX

Order in the Soul

Euripides' view that deliberate infliction of suffering may as easily make human beings worse as better is answered by Plato, who argues that this deficiency applies only to suffering imposed in ignorance.[1] True philosophical wisdom makes it possible to impose a just measure of pain that will improve and reform character. Applying a medical analogy, Plato thinks of vice—the source of crime— as an ailment of soul in the way that physical illness is an ailment of body. He attributes vice sometimes to ignorance (*Protagoras*, 357e), sometimes to disorder among the elements of the soul (*Republic*, 444b), and sometimes to bodily fractiousness affecting the soul (*Timaeus*, 86b); but in each case, the object of punishment is the same: to restore order in the soul. A skilled legislator targets the source of evil in the soul with the same precision as a skilled physician targets the source of bodily disease. The physician seeks homeostatic balance among the elements of the body; so also must the legislator seek homeostatic balance among the elements of the soul. Ideally, this equilibrium is achieved by training and education (gymnastics for the body, philosophy for the soul), but when these devices fail punitive constraint is necessary. Suffering must be visited on the disordered soul, insists Plato, for the sake of its own improvement. To the extent, then, that such suffering worsens a person's character (as in Euripides' view), it bears all the trappings of poor medicine: a wrong dose administered to a misunderstood illness.

Diseases, of course, are cured for the sake of future health. In this respect Plato's curative view of punishment is forward looking and, apparently, a strange candidate for inclusion in a book on retribution. After all, in the classical retributivist view, punishment is inflicted for the sake of past crime, irrespective of future efficacy.[2] According to this understanding of retributive theory, Plato's position seems clearly nonretributive. Classical retributivism, however, is a late development, attributable in its purest form to Kant and Hegel. We have already seen how forward-looking considerations, especially of deterrence, are integral to the retributivism of the blood feud. Making similar allowances for Plato, we find his curative theory infused with retributivism. The epistemic component of retributive thought haunts his penology and eschatology for the same reason as it haunts other retributive webs—to provide solace in the face of suffering. The signal innovation in Plato is that the solace he envisions is intensely private, the repose of a soul in harmony with itself.

Pain and Cure

Platonic retributivism is primarily expressed in myths of the afterlife sprinkled throughout his dialogues. Each of these myths, however else it may differ from the others, involves some manner of postmortem punishment. The *Phaedo* contains both a moralized animal metamapsychosis (81d–82c) and a literal judgment of the dead (113d–114c), which is matched by the nearly identical eschatology of the *Gorgias* (523a–525d). In both dialogues, the wicked are judged by Rhadamanthus, Aeacus, and Minos, who divide their charges into curable and incurable. The former suffer appropriate punishment to earn their release, whereas the latter suffer eternal torment in Tartarus. In both dialogues, also, the blessed who have purified their souls through philosophy receive an appropriate eternal reward. The *Phaedrus* (249a) embraces a moralized animal metamapsychosis similar to that of the *Phaedo*. The *Republic* (614b–618b) combines the postmortem judgment of the *Phaedo* and the *Gorgias* with a mixed human-and-animal metamapsychosis, taking special pains to stress that the lives undergone in the latter process are fixed by the soul's own choosing (617e). In the *Timaeus* we learn that a mixed human-and-animal metamapsychosis is an inherent aspect of creation (42a–e). Finally, the *Laws* contains two references to unavoidable postmortem punishment for intentional homicide (870e) and for parricide (872e), along with a punitive eschatology that appears not to involve judgment by Rhadamanthus or Minos, but is automatic and self-regulating (905a).

These various eschatologies prove an embarrassment to reading Plato's theoretical penology as fundamentally forward looking and, hence, nonretributive. Thus, one reaction is to view Plato's retributive eschatology in isolation from his theoretical views on institutional punishment.[3] On this interpretation, Plato is among the first thinkers to come to grips with the disparity between divine or cosmic justice and the incapacity of human beings to realize it. We need not, therefore, assimilate Plato's eschatology to his curative theory of punishment, because each is meant for a separate sphere. The ideal justice of Rhadamanthus—

that the doer shall suffer what he does—is confined to the heavens; but for this world Plato endorses a more enlightened and humanitarian view, keeping foremost in mind the future welfare of the doer. Only for the incurably wicked, this view holds, does Plato slip back into retributivism, for on the curative theory they alone are put to death. Others are treated so as to awaken them to virtue.

This view of Plato's theoretical penology, however, confronts several difficulties. First, the curable–incurable dichotomy finds its place in the eschatology, as well as in the theory, of institutional punishment, suggesting that Plato did not view the two realms as entirely separate. Second, when it comes to robust examples, most of which are provided in the *Laws*, Plato's penology turns out to be conventionally retributive.[4] The Athenian speaks the language of cure, but dishes out the substance of traditional just deserts. Finally, the presumption that the death penalty is retributive in Plato's thought turns out to be mistaken. As a consequence, the fate of the incurables in both the human and divine spheres must be held to one side, and we must look at the treatment of the curably wicked for clues to Plato's retributivism.

This last point requires elaboration, for it runs counter to our contemporary sense that advocacy of the death penalty remains one of the last domains of pure retributivism. A murderer deserves death, the argument goes, because he has caused death. That is the heart of the matter; everything else, including deterrence, is a frill. In direct contrast to this view, Plato makes clear that the incurable are put to death solely for future benefit:

> But suppose the law-giver finds a man who's beyond cure—what legal penalty will he provide for this case? He will recognize that the best thing for all such people is to cease to live—best even for themselves. By passing on they will help others, too: first, they will constitute a warning against injustice, and secondly they will leave the state free of scoundrels. (*Laws*, 862d)

As for this life, also for the afterlife:

> But those who have been guilty of the most heinous crimes and whose misdeeds are past cure—of these warnings are made, and they are no longer capable themselves of receiving any benefit, because they are incurable—but others are benefited who behold them suffering throughout eternity the greatest and most excruciating and terrifying tortures because of their misdeeds, literally suspended as examples there in the prison house in Hades, a spectacle and a warning to any evildoers who from time to time arrive. (*Gorgias*, 525c)

Punishing as an example to others is criticized by classical retributivists precisely because of this tendency to treat human beings as instruments. According to classical retributivism, matching punishment to the crime preserves the inherent dignity of the individual by placing objective limits on the extent of punishment. On Plato's view, by contrast, once a soul is deemed incurable, there is no point in an objective measure of its offenses. The incurable are executed, not because they deserve it, but because execution is in the interest of society.

Thus if retributivism is to be found in Plato, it must lie elsewhere than in his treatment of the incurably wicked. One such place is the pollution-haunted atmosphere of the *Laws*, where ritual purification of manslayers is insisted on (865d, 868a), homicidal beasts are put to death (873e), and inanimate objects connected with a man's death are banished beyond the city's frontiers (874a). These laws may be illuminated by reference to the system of strict liability evident in the first two plays of the *Oresteia*: Polluted things must be purified to be rendered harmless. In keeping with the *Oresteia*'s horror at the shedding of kindred blood, the Athenian cites the authority of "ancient priests" who decreed:

> If ever a man has murdered his father, in the course of time he must suffer the same fate from violent treatment at the hands of his children. A matricide, before being reborn, must adopt the female sex, and after being born a woman and bearing children, be dispatched subsequently by them. No other purification is available when common blood has been polluted; the pollution resists cleansing until, murder for murder, the guilty soul has paid the penalty and by this appeasement has soothed the anger of the deceased's entire line. (*Laws*, 872e–f)

The view favored by those who insist on divorcing Plato's penal theory from his eschatology is that these retributive strains in the *Laws* stem from Plato's political conservatism. He is seen as a traditionalist unable to distance himself from the actual practices of his native Athens.[5] Thus, rather than systematically reform the laws of his Cretan city according to his curative theory of punishment, Plato merely tinkers on the fringes of contemporary Attic law, imbibing large retributive chunks without fully perceiving their inconsistency with his own theory.

That Plato did merely tinker on the fringes of Attic law seems indisputable, but there is no reason to judge his acceptance of traditional practice to be uncritical. Because Plato saw retributively painful punishment as essential to restoring order in the soul, he approved of contemporary punitive practices so long as they were guided by knowledge. This insight will be missed if we take it as axiomatic that retribution looks only to what has already happened. Relaxing this dogma allows us to see that retributive institutions may stand on something other than irrational attachment to past events.

Take, for instance, the execution of animals that have killed humans and the casting of homicidal instruments outside the city's borders. From one vantage, these practices appear driven only by an irrational belief in pollution, but from another they embody important considerations of future welfare. Beasts that kill once may kill again. As for the banning of polluted instruments, D. M. MacDowell suggests that the Athenian courts (Prytaneion and Phylobasileis) dedicated to such judgments may have "served some of the purposes of a modern coroner's court." [6] Learning the cause of death in one instance is often a means of preventing similar deaths in the future. The trappings of a formal trial and the ritualized casting out of "guilty" instruments may be, in part, devices for inducing people to participate in a civic proceeding they would otherwise be inclined to shirk.

Let us examine MacDowell's hypothesis more closely. It is not an explanation that would occur to anyone who believes in the doctrine of pollution. Such people would insist that polluted artifacts need to be banished for no other reason than that of their implication in an unnatural death. (Even here their concern would be both with the past event *and* with certain unspecified future dangers.) So long as such belief remains in force, further explanation is unnecessary. Only the mind of one who is skeptical of pollution begins to look for some additional meaning. The doctrine is now evaluated, not from the vantage of an inner psychology of belief, but from the vantage of its social efficacy, its role in forming allegiances and furthering communal bonds. MacDowell may be thought a "defender" of the doctrine of pollution because he reduces, for us skeptics, its apparent illogic and irrationality.

Plato, I believe, stands in an analogous position by embracing, at a practical level, conventional retributive punishments. He is critical, not of the dishing out of measured suffering, but of the usual reasons given for it. His earliest reservations are put into the mouth of Protagoras:

> In punishing wrongdoers, no one concentrates on the fact that a man has done wrong in the past, or punishes him on that account, unless taking blind vengeance like a beast. No, punishment is not inflicted by a rational man for the sake of the crime that has been committed—after all one cannot undo what is past—but for the sake of the future, to prevent either the same man or, by the spectacle of his punishment, someone else, from doing wrong again. (*Protagoras*, 324a)

Given Plato's views of the soul and of the involuntary nature of wrong, a curative approach to punishment emerges as a logical extension of Protagoras' criticism. We must be wary, however, of turning Plato into a supporter of a modern therapeutic view, willing to accept any course of treatment, punitive or not, that might better the condition of a wrongdoer's soul.[7] For all his emphasis on forward-looking considerations, Plato retains a retributive core in his thinking about punishment. His afterlife myths with their just measures of suffering are much more than exercises in wishful thinking: They express a connection that Plato never questions—namely, that pain is essential in restoring the disordered soul. As the old reasons for this connection will not do, Plato offers new ones. In criticizing the old version of retributivism, he replaces it with another, more enlightened one.

We may thus move in the direction of Trevor J. Saunders in reconciling Plato's retributive eschatology with his theoretically curative penology.[8] That Plato's view of punishment is simultaneously curative and retributive is easily missed because the main dialogues espousing cure, the *Gorgias* and the *Republic*, are bereft of examples. The interlocutors speak variously of "suffering punishment" or "paying the penalty," making it easy to overlook that Plato has in mind the deliberate infliction of *pain*. It might be thought that the pain is merely adventitious to the treatment, inessential in the way that the pain of an inoculation is inessential, playing no role in ridding us of illness. After all, if we press the medical analogy, we must conclude that the best physician is one who minimizes the pain of her treatment. The ideal physician might then be one whose treatments involve no pain at all.

Plato's curative theory does bear some of the implications of its medical analog, but these are by no means always humanitarian. The amount of pain inflicted in punishment need not be proportionate to any extrinsic measure of the gravity of a crime, but must instead be tailored to eradicating the cause of the offense. If a lesser pain than usually administered will eradicate the cause, then such pain is indeed a just measure. The converse holds as well: If restoring order in the soul requires greater pain than is usually administered, so be it. Importantly, however, Plato rejects any move toward an ideal legislator who would abolish all pain from his "punishment" in the way that an ideal physician might abolish pain from her practice of medicine. The clearest such rejection is from the *Gorgias*:

> Now, those who are benefited through suffering punishment by gods and men are beings whose evil deeds are curable: nevertheless it is from pain and agony that they derive their benefit both here and in the other world, for it is impossible to be rid of evil otherwise. (525b)

Far from being adventitious to just punishment, pain lies at its very heart.[9] It is Plato's acceptance of this retributive connection between pain and cure that explains why, in the *Laws*, he so disappoints those who anticipate great innovation in the treatment of crime. On Plato's view, conventional penology (aside from the death penalty) *is* therapeutic; it is simply that others have missed this dimension in their defense of traditional practice. Plato sees need for innovation, not in the practice of punishment, but in the view taken of it. Far from being an unreflective traditionalist, he is driven by his own curative theory to embrace the retributive sanctions of Book IX of the *Laws*.

This interpretation of Plato's theory of punishment may appear to run into difficulty when we consider the following passage from the *Laws*. The Athenian answers a question from Cleinias as to what a policy of cure involves:

> When anyone commits an act of injustice, serious or trivial, the law will combine instruction and constraint, so that in the future either the criminal will never again dare to commit such a crime voluntarily, or he will do it a very great deal less often; and in addition, he will pay compensation for the damage he had done. This is something we can achieve only by laws of the highest quality. We may take action, or simply talk to the criminal; we may grant him pleasures, or make him suffer; we may honor him, we may disgrace him; we can fine him, or give him gifts. We may use absolutely *any* means to make him hate injustice and embrace true justice—or at any rate not hate it. (862d–863a)

If we focus only on the latter half of this passage, we might think that Plato has changed his mind from the *Gorgias*. Pain, it would appear, is inessential to curing at least some disordered souls. The wise penologist will adapt his methods to the individual offender; and if bestowing pleasures, honors, and gifts are the best means to his improvement, then the curative theory endorses their use. It looks as if therapy is liberated from pain: The ideal legislator is free to follow the humanitarian model of the ideal physician.

Notice, however, that this reading of the passage neglects the first sentence, which insists on combining "instruction and constraint." The latter provides the punitive element that Plato believes is indispensable. All the assorted other measures, the bestowing of pleasures and the like, are insufficient to do the job in isolation. A measure of pain is required, though afterward it may be intermixed with whatever other means complete the cure.

Not only does this interpretation do justice to the passage as a whole, but it is consistent with the one extended example of a mixed penology provided in the *Laws*. Plato devotes Book X to the vexed subject of impiety, arguing that three general misapprehensions are the source of all punishable impiety: the belief that the gods do not exist; the belief that they exist but are indifferent to human affairs; and the belief that they can be won over to one's cause by sacrifices and supplications (885b). These misapprehensions may combine with one of two types of characters (908a–e). The first is naturally just, mitigating his impiety with a hatred of scoundrels and a loathing of evil. The second type is a born dissembler, full of cunning and guile. Both types are unrestrained by fear of divine retribution; but the latter, far more dangerous than the former, is incurable—and so deserves death as does any other incurable offender. By contrast, the atheist who combines impiety with a naturally just character is deemed curable. Plato prescribes for him a minimum of five years' imprisonment, with regular visits by the Nocturnal Council, who will admonish and instruct him in true religion. This is precisely the combination of instruction and constraint Plato had advocated in the passage cited above.

Imprisonment is rare in Attic law, and in the *Laws* is otherwise prescribed only for holding those awaiting trial, for metics and slaves, and for debtors unable to pay their debts.[10] On conviction most criminals are sentenced to death, banishment, fine, or flogging, depending on the laws governing the offense. Why, then, does Plato hit on imprisonment as appropriate to this single case? He conceives, I think, of the punishment as a retributive mirror of the crime. Impiety exalts the human will beyond its native sphere. A punishment that humbles the will,[11] causing it to suffer constraint, will both induce the proper discipline and stand as a constant reminder of the grounds for its imposition. Plato's matching of the cause to the cure of impiety is more sophisticated than the cruder versions of mirroring punishments exhibited in ancient Near Eastern law, but it stands as an example nonetheless.

In considering the dissembling atheist, Plato remarks that he "deserves to die for his sins not just once or twice but many times" (*Laws*, 908e). We have already seen that Plato imposes the death penalty for the sake of deterrence, but this remark about deserving many deaths makes sense only if retributivism is presupposed. The dissembling atheist is a threat to others, and the most natural gloss on this passage is that he deserves to die once for each soul he either endangers or actually seduces into sharing his misapprehension. The impossibility of such treatment only underscores the extent to which, for Plato, the death penalty is nonretributive.

To cinch the case in favor of Platonic retributivism, we turn finally to exceptions from the prescribed penalties of the *Laws*. The protean like for like of retributive thought so pervades his prescription of penalties that it sometimes spills over into his reasons for suspending punishment. The most notable example is Plato's provision (*Laws*, 869a) that a parricide who is personally forgiven before his parent's death need not be executed. As R. F. Stalley points out, this exception makes no sense on a purely curative theory, for there is no reason to think that a forgiven parricide is magically cured, whereas an unforgiven parricide is inherently incurable, requiring execution.[12] Because Stalley is committed to the view that Plato rejects retributivism, he fails to draw the proper parallel between Plato's exemption of the forgiven parricide and the conventional retributivism of Attic law. Forgiveness by the victim was long a grounds for suspending the prosecution of homicide, probably dating back to belief in retaliation as imperative to blunt the anger of the slain. If that anger is blunted by some other means, the imperative does not exist. Forgiveness initiates a cycle of kindly, as opposed to vindictive, retribution.

A second instructive example of mitigation on retributive grounds may be seen in the penalty for wounding with intent to kill (*Laws*, 876e–878b). As the penalty for voluntary homicide is death, the Athenian first notes that the element of intent, being no different in the case of wounding, would seem to justify making the attacker stand trial for murder. Yet as the victim did not die, this fact must ultimately be mirrored in the punishment, and so the Athenian prescribes exile rather than death. In the course of this reasoning, the Athenian stresses that luck has kept the victim's curse from falling on the attacker's head—a further echo of ancient retributivism, curses serving as the medium for the slain to manifest their anger.

Lest it still be thought that examples of retributivism in the *Laws* are the result either of Plato's confusion or his unreflective adoption of a mode of thought incompatible with his curative theory, we may note how intractable the problems become if cure is presumed to have no connection to a just measure of pain. Every criminal sanction in the *Laws* is punitive; on a nonretributive theory of cure, this fact must be either an accident or a reflection of the undeveloped state of the penologist's art. In light of Plato's explicit claims that pain and cure are inextricably linked, we are commended to the thesis that he conceived of cure as a means of rehabilitating rather than of eliminating retributive institutions. Only on this reading can Plato's retributive eschatology, his theory of punishment as cure, and the penology of the *Laws* be reconciled.

The Homeostatic Soul

Closer investigation of Plato's conception of the soul explains why a form of retributivism is absorbed into his curative theory of punishment. This examination further documents the degree to which retributivism pervades Plato's theoretical views on punishment, as well as his eschatology and conservative penology.

Plato's various accounts of the soul differ, and there is much debate over whether, fundamentally, the soul is unitary or composite.[13] We will content ourselves with the *Republic*'s tripartite account of the embodied soul, for it is this account that Plato seems to presuppose in the *Protagoras*, *Gorgias*, and *Laws*—the main dialogues concerned with punishment. Accordingly, we may ignore the issue of whether or not the soul is fundamentally unitary, for it is clear in the *Republic* that, while still in connection with the body, the soul appears as a composite of three elements: reason, high spirit, and appetite. After separation from the body, the soul (or some souls, at least) may be unitary, but this status affects only postmortem punishment, not the institutional punishment of criminals.

The *Republic* develops its theory of the soul by extended analogy with the well-governed state. Plato's overriding view of justice, the prime virtue of both state and soul, is conservative and nonegalitarian. Justice is the maintenance of an order in which each of the three main classes of citizens in the Republic fulfill their appointed tasks. Injustice arises when one class aspires or condescends to the prerogatives of another. Disorder is the result—tasks are incompetently done by people unsuited to do them. Similarly, the soul's three elements of reason, high spirit, and appetite attain justice only if each is confined to its native sphere. Reason must command, with high spirit as its ally. Injustice in the soul most commonly occurs when appetite plays the usurper, allying with high spirit to defeat the governance of reason.

Justice in both images—state and soul—requires a harmonious balance among elements. Because there are more than two elements in each case, the balance of Platonic justice cannot be conveyed in the familiar image of the scales: one element weighted against a discrete second element. Instead, the image is homeostatic: The elements are bound together so that disruption of one influences each of the others, but not necessarily in push-pull, hydraulic, or balance-beam fashion. A slight perturbation of one element might be resisted by the other two, maintaining a desirable balance—exactly as a healthy ecosystem overcomes a minor disruption or a healthy body a small infection. Nonetheless, a significant disruption of one element may produce major disruptions of the others. A new balance arises among them, one that is likely to be both unpleasant and undesirable. Chaos threatens—the chaos of disease, disorder, and disharmony.

In effect, Plato internalizes what in the previous chapters we have called a homeostatic metaphysics of retribution. Fundamental to this metaphysics is the idea of each element having a natural place in a dynamic system. Violent disruptions are never singular and solitary events, but rather percolate throughout the system. Restoring harmony may or may not involve responding to the cause of the disruption. Harmony may sometimes be attained by acting on seemingly unrelated aspects of the system, tailoring them to the demands of the whole.

The homeostatic view is thus plastic, its implications allusive and elusive. It can, as we have seen, comprehend a hydraulic or balance-beam metaphysics of retribution. Equally, it may disguise or even stand at odds with such a view. An ambiguity arises between two distinct homeostatic pictures—that of restoring the previous balance versus attaining a new and different balance among elements. The difference can be illustrated with a Rubik's cube. Any configuration of squares in which all surfaces are flush might be thought of as "in balance" in the second sense, but the object of the game is to restore the single privileged configuration with all surfaces flush and only one color on each side. When Plato considers the just ordering of the soul, it is not always clear which of these pictures we should have in mind. We might presume that his Theory of Forms inclines toward the restorative view, for the Forms would seem to lay down an eternal pattern with fixed relations among elements. The just soul would imitate this pattern, the unjust deviate from it. In the *Timaeus*, however, where Plato suggests that injustice is the result of bodily upset, the implication is that justice is relative to the individual. Each person must find a harmonious balance adjusted to his or her body's proclivities, and there may be no optimum suited to all individuals.

As far as curing a disorder is concerned, however, both of these pictures share the same implication—namely, that a return to harmony will be contingent on accurate diagnosis. Whether or not a specific justice is optimal for all persons, there can be no doubt that states of injustice are relative. As the clash of elements varies from case to case, disorder in the soul takes many forms. To attain (or restore) order, punishment must be tailored to the individual.

In his punitive eschatology, Plato at one point supposes that wicked souls are marked in such a way that the requisite kind and degree of correction can be read off from them (*Gorgias*, 524e). The automatic and self-regulating eschatology of the *Laws* (903b–905d) presumes a different but still objective standard for matching punishment to desert: Souls gravitate, on the principle of like seeking like, to their kindreds. Vicious souls congregate with vicious, virtuous with virtuous, so that punishment or reward consists of nothing other than that a person will "do and be done by according to the standards that birds of a feather naturally apply among themselves" (*Laws*, 904e).

For the human legislator, however, no such objective marks or self-regulating processes exist. Matching punishment to crime is an art, like the physician's art. Crimes are symptoms of an underlying disorder, and, in company with the symptoms of a physical disease, crimes can mislead as to their proper diagnosis. The same offense committed by different individuals may indicate different underlying conditions, each requiring a distinct punishment. Yet laws must be enunciated and applied to the populace as a whole according to a principle of proportionality that punishes equally all crimes falling into the same category. The resulting tension plagues the Athenian throughout his criminal legislation; and in most instances his prescribed penalties focus more on the symptoms, the crimes themselves, than on their various underlying conditions. Though Plato may never fully resolve this tension in practice, his curative theory indicates where one might begin. The starting point lies in examining how a just measure of pain effects its cure. This approach must, in turn, be referred to its own original—namely, the process of educating the soul to virtue.

Just as it is better for a body to have health always rather than to be returned to health by the painful interventions of a physician, Plato makes clear that the most blessed souls would never deviate from virtue and would never require correction. Far from being natural to human beings, however, the semblance of virtue to which most people are restricted results from a disciplined upbringing. In the *Republic* only the few superior souls capable of philosophy will ever achieve true virtue (via perception of the Forms), and their task thereafter will be to maintain order in the state by holding the other classes to the imitative virtue inculcated by discipline. By contrast, the doctrine of virtue in the *Laws* is less intellectualist, for virtue seems to lie simply in regulating the passions and appetites. In consequence, a large portion of Book I and the whole of Book II is devoted to the subject of drinking sessions. Under supervision of their elders, young people ought to be subjected to such parties, Plato counsels, so that they may learn to conquer appetite, achieving self-control. Temperance is a matter of discipline, and discipline is learned by habituation to the proper pattern.

In the *Gorgias*, Plato suggests that the pain of punishment cures by reimposing discipline on the disordered soul. Socrates points out to Callicles that the physician does not allow a sick man to satisfy his appetites without restraint, then applies the same principle more broadly:

> And is it not the same, my good friend, with the soul? So long as it is evil, senseless and undisciplined and unjust and impious, it should be restrained from its desires and suffered to do nothing but what will improve it. (505b)

A similar view is endorsed in the *Republic*, where Socrates maintains that only the wrongdoer who is detected and so pays the penalty will be restored to sobriety, righteousness, and wisdom. Through chastening, the soul's "brutish part is lulled and tamed and the gentle part liberated" (591b).

Restraint, then, is the key to discipline; and to the disordered soul, restraint is painful, for its appetitive element must be denied the pleasure it craves. Though pain and cure are indissoluble, Plato elsewhere makes clear that pain by itself fails to constitute punishment, even when it is the inevitable consequence of vice:

> You see, practically no one takes into account the greatest "judgement," as it is called, on wrongdoing. This is to grow to resemble men who are evil, and as the resemblance increases to shun good men and their wholesome conversation and to cut oneself off from them, while seeking to attach oneself to the other kind and keep their company. The inevitable result of consorting with such people is that what you do and have done to you is exactly what *they* naturally do and say to each other. Consequently, this condition is not really a "judgement" at all, because justice and judgement are fine things: it is mere punishment, suffering that follows a wrongdoing. (*Laws*, 728a–c)

What the preceding "mere punishment" lacks, at least in this world, is a duly constituted authority to give it force and direction. It is not enough for vicious souls to congregate or to be thrown together: They must, in addition, be *judged* to be vicious. The curative pain of punishment is, in part, the pain of moral obloquy. If a soul is incapable of this kind of suffering, it is beyond recovery. Other pains ranging from boredom to physical deprivation may well attend punishment, but these are without effect unless the wrongdoer internalizes the judgment that has condemned him.

Plato's theoretical retributivism is either overlooked or dismissed for two main reasons. The first connects to his view that pain and pleasure are not contradictories—that a state of body can be both painful and pleasurable at the same time. Plato uses this view in the *Gorgias* (495d–497e) to argue against philosophical hedonism—that is, that good and evil are contradictories while pain and pleasure are not; therefore, the good cannot be identical to the pleasant. Plato further argues that punishment is a blessing to him who suffers it: so much so that one ought to punish a friend but keep an enemy from suffering punishment (*Gorgias*, 480b–e). When these two arguments are brought together, it may appear as if the first is grounds for the second: Punishment is a blessing because it is a disguised pleasure, unrecognized by the agent until after his cure. But Plato makes no such argument, and if he did it would not be in the spirit of his insistence that pleasure and pain fail to be contradictories. This latter claim neither denies the reality of pain nor renames it as its contrary if a greater balance of pleasure happens to ensue from it. Instead, the claim asserts that the same experience can be both painful and pleasurable in the same respect at the same time. Hence, even if the pain of punishment is simultaneously a pleasure, it is no less a pain for all that.

The second reason Plato's theoretical retributivism may pass unrecognized is that it enters his thought, not as an instrument for morally justifying punishment, but as a presupposition about natural processes. For Plato, retribution is an unavoidable element both of proper physics (as in the eschatology) and of proper physic (as in restoring balance to the homeostatic soul). As such, the belief extends beyond that of "logical retributivism" [14]—the claim that punishment, to be punishment at all, must be painful to him who suffers it. Plato's theory is retributive, not solely because pain is essential to cure, but also because he is theoretically committed to prescribing a specific degree and quality of pain for each wrongdoer. In answering the question What is our aim in punishing others? Plato develops his curative view. The retributive dimension of curing answers a related question: What kind and extent of pain should we apply? The pain of a just punishment is measured, subject to limitation by the nature of a given soul's disorder.

To be beyond cure is, for Plato, to be beyond a moral limitation on the extent of pain inflicted. In his eschatology Plato accepts that some few exceptional wrongdoers are subject to *eternal* punishment, but offers no reason for this treatment save that their fates serve as a warning to others (*Gorgias*, 525c, quoted on page 97). Accordingly, their punishment—strange as it may sound—is nonretributive, an analog of the unrestricted blood feud, or of taking two eyes for an eye. In other settings, however, the idea of eternal punishment is made retributive by likening the severity of punishment, not with the degree of suffering caused by the offense or the amount necessary to effect a cure, but with the majesty of the person offended. As God is an eternal being, offenses against him can be thought to justify eternal punishment. Saint Thomas Aquinas presses this line of reasoning to the fullest. Before turning to his views, however, we first consider the retributive web of Islam, where the ideal of self-surrender—total yielding to the majesty of God—overwhelms concern with fixing a logically apportioned term of postmortem punishment.

SEVEN

Self-Surrender

Though in concert with his overall views on punishment, Plato's retributive eschatology is tentative and undogmatic. His stories of the afterlife fate of the soul are sprinkled with confessions of uncertainty: The interlocutors believe these tales to be true but cannot prove them. Thus Plato's main use of a retributive eschatology is illustrative. The afterlife ideal of Rhadamanthus, of suffering what one does, makes the point that justice is the supreme virtue. Where curing the offender is consistent with justice, well and good, but where the two are inconsistent, justice must prevail. Even in the *Laws*, where the specter of afterlife punishment is urged for the possible moral improvement of wrongdoers, Plato seeks more to persuade than to intimidate. Winning someone to virtue through fear is, he thinks, self-defeating. Only cowards can be so manipulated, and cowards are incapable of virtue.

The logic of Plato's view, however, is undermined once hell becomes a dogmatic revelation rather than a point of speculation. Hell is the retributivist's construction par excellence, and, with hell a certainty, no means of avoiding it is unworthy unless prohibited by one's revelation. The all-powerful gods of the Old Testament, the New Testament book of Revelation, and the Qurʾan have this much, at least, in common: None hesitates to command obedience through fear. In assessing the sea change of ideas marking the difference between Hellenism and the monotheism of the Near East, we must focus on the implications of God's omnipotence.

This chapter examines the Islamic doctrine of yielding to God. Etymologically the term "Muslim" means "self-surrenderer," and as a highest conceivable duty the obligation to open one's heart and mind to God is enmeshed in a retributive web with distinctive social and metaphysical underpinnings. In its Islamic conception, all of physical nature is *muslim,* a surrenderer to God.[1] Superficially the ideal is reminiscent of Stoicism, but Islam celebrates it with unprecedented spiritual and communal tenacity. So far as threats of punishment are concerned, Jew and Christian will recognize the story in outline, if not in detail, for much that can be said of retributivism in Islam holds also for its two Near Eastern predecessors. Islam was shaped in an environment where Jewish and Christian visions of the apocalypse were a predominant factor in transforming pagan Arab tribal loyalty into a potent force for world conquest. The movement from Arab tribal confederacy to a pan-Islamic community is inextricably tied to the radical asymmetry in power between God and man. Solace in this life, whether gained in retaliation against or forgiveness of one's foes, means little or nothing when compared to the overriding importance of a believer's relationship to God. Suffering becomes a hallmark of faith, a means of attaining communal and personal identity. The only solace that matters lies in complete surrender to God's unity and majesty. It is a story worthy of attention, both for its intrinsic interest and for the light that it sheds on late twentieth-century Islamic fundamentalism.

Pre-Islamic Arabia

Muhammad, messenger of Allah in the seventh century C.E., was raised in the prosperous trading town of Mecca.[2] Its settled, commercial society stood in stark contrast to the nomadic life predominant elsewhere in Arabia. The nomads were fierce, proud, and governed by the pagan virtue of *muruwwa*—"manliness," understood as loyalty to the tribe and all it entailed: protection of its members, hospitality to strangers, and adherence to the blood feud.[3] Even though these same duties governed in the minds of the Quraish, Muhammad's tribe in Mecca, the nomads regarded the city dwellers with contempt. To their way of thinking, commerce had made the Quraish all too willing to forgive a slight in the interest of turning a profit. *Muruwwa* was correspondingly devalued, for one thing Arab honor did not involve was offering the other cheek. As a pre-Islamic proverb put it, "Good for good, he who starts is the nobler of the two; bad for bad, he who started is the guilty one."[4] A boasting poem from the same era makes the point in a commercial metaphor: "I hold good and evil on loan: evil I repay to him that does me evil and good I give unto him that treats me well."[5] Another factor underlying the nomads' contempt for the Quraish was the relative luxury in which the latter lived. To the genuine nomad, accumulated wealth is a chain binding one in unfreedom. The wealthy become a pampered and stingy lot—too concerned with acquisition to be capable of the lavish hospitality favored in the desert, which might involve giving away all of one's possessions. This particular pinnacle of *muruwwa* was the nomad's assertion of supreme self-confidence: His powers of survival were such that, tomorrow, he would obtain new bounty to replace the old. Characteristically, such replacement came in the form of a raid against a rival tribe.

Despite their differences, however, the Quraish and the nomads depended on each other. The Quraish needed alliances with the nomads to guarantee the safety of their caravans, whereas the nomads needed the Quraish to supply goods that could not be wrested from the desert. The Quraish also controlled access to an important pagan shrine—the Kaaba, a black stone. Pilgrimage to the Kaaba was a supreme religious duty among the polytheistic or henotheistic Arabs, who managed, as pilgrims still do, to spend money while in Mecca. Fear that Muhammad's new religion would undermine the pilgrimage became a focus of vigorous Quraish opposition.

Yet however much they objected to Muhammad, he remained a member of the tribe. He was thus protected against bodily harm (though not against ridicule) by the institution of the blood feud. When Muhammad's message was finally deemed intolerable (in part because it taught that pagan ancestors of the Quraish were consigned to hell),[6] his detractors beseeched Muhammad's uncle, Abu Talif, to withdraw his protection. This action would have allowed the Prophet to be killed with impunity, for Muhammad's kin would have had neither the duty of revenge nor the protection against reprisal that this duty entailed. Abu Talif refused to withdraw his protection with the same obstinacy with which he refused to embrace his nephew's religion. Muhammad was a blood relation, and *muruwwa* dictated that Abu Talif was honor bound to guarantee his safety. It is one of the ironies of history that Islam may owe its survival to the embodiment of a pagan virtue that Muhammad was determined—and destined—to transform.

The early (Meccan) revelations of the Prophet, recorded in the latter part of the Qur'an, establish the axis along which Arab tribalism was reshaped. Two main themes of Muhammad's call to prophecy were to remain constant throughout his life. First is the theme of the absolute unity of God, used initially to inveigh against Arab poly- and henotheism, and later deployed against Judaism and Christianity, which Islam was likewise to accuse of polytheism. Second—and only marginally less important than the unity of God—are the twin themes of reward in paradise and damnation in hell. On the latter two points the Qur'an plays like a stuck record, with more than 90 percent of its surahs warning of impending judgment. Non-Muslims can perhaps be forgiven a further impression that the warnings against damnation are both more persistent and more graphic than the corresponding promises of reward. Even so, we need not account for this asymmetry by pointing to anything indigenous to Islam. For sheer imaginative vivacity, depictions of hell outstrip depictions of heaven in Judaism and Christianity also—evidence that human beings agree on the ultimate constituents of misery much more than on the ultimate constituents of happiness. One person's vision of hell, centering on terrible physical suffering, can be readily assimilated to any other such vision. Differences lie in the details of the various punishments rather than in the horror and repugnance they evoke. By contrast, one person's ecstatic vision of paradise may easily strike someone else, differences of detail aside, as tepid and uninspiring.

Non-Muslim scholars have been unable to agree on the exact Judaic or Christian apocalyptic literatures that may have been known to Muhammad.[7] (Most Muslim scholars, of course, regard the Qurʾan as the uncreated speech of God and the Prophet's sayings as divinely inspired, blocking any search for ancestral literatures.) From the internal evidence of the Qurʾan, we may say with certainty that the Prophet found no need for elaborate introduction of the doctrine of hell. His hearers are presumed to be as familiar with it. The difference between them and Muhammad is that he has heard and taken warning, conjoining the promise of paradise and the threat of hell with awe at the unity and majesty of God. Muhammad's fellow Meccans, at least in the beginning, have heard without listening, and so are willfully and culpably deaf. They have yet to learn the way of true *muslims—surrenderers* to God.

God's Punishment in Islam

Like the Old Testament God, the God of the Qurʾan both punishes human beings directly and lays down rules for human beings to punish each other. Each of these treatments has at its core the retributive ideal of making the wrongdoer suffer what he does. We now explore God's direct punishment of human beings, reserving discussion of man's punishment of his fellows for the following section.

Direct punishment of human beings by God is a class with three subclasses. First are stories of God's collective punishment of faithless peoples. Many of these are retellings from the Old Testament, where the point is the same. Through a messenger (Abraham, Jacob, Moses, and others), God commands obedience based on faith in himself alone. The people comply when in need but neglect their duties when all seems well; as a consequence, God sends chastisement, destroying the nation: "How many a town We destroyed while it was iniquitous, so it is fallen down upon its roofs; and (how many) a deserted well and palace raised high!" (22.45). As Kenneth Cragg says of such Qurʾanic verses, "archaeology is . . . a lesson in retribution."[8]

These stories of collective punishment need detain us only to observe that the Qurʾan is more single-minded about them than the Old Testament. The latter provides instances both of collective punishment imposed on the basis of collective liability and of related, but conceptually distinct, instances of what David Daube aptly calls "ruler punishment."[9] In ruler punishment, God penalizes an entire people to redress the transgressions of their ruler. Both collective punishment on the basis of collective liability and ruler punishment may offend against an individualistic sense of justice, but in different ways. In the first case worries arise about differing degrees of liability: All may be guilty, but not all should be punished in the same degree. In the second case, however, the worry is about the morality of vicarious punishment: Is it right to strike at an agent through those he loves or is pledged to protect?

In the Old Testament the lives of David and Solomon each provide occasion for ruler punishment, but both the Qur'an and later Muslim authority are zealous in denying that these leaders were the objects of God's wrath.[10] The reason for this Islamic denial of ruler punishment is instructive. Muslim insistence on total surrender to God requires that his unity and purpose be perfectly clear, so that blame for disbelief rests with the individual. God has sent Muhammad as his messenger, but Muhammad is not the first. The same signs have been pronounced by other messengers, who have been disregarded. Like Muhammad himself, these other messengers had faults, but each of their failings is comprehended within God's mercy. To imply that a messenger's faults are the object of punishment is to imply that God's message has been tainted, rendered less than clear. Surrender to God is an unequivocal requirement of an unequivocal prophecy. Neither becoming nor remaining a Muslim partakes of stages or degrees; one's person yields as a whole or it yields not at all. Protection of spiritual progenitors against the calumny of appearing to merit punishment is dictated by Islamic holism.

Holism likewise pervades the Islamic doctrine of the last judgment, the second of the three manners in which God punishes human beings directly. Various natural calamities will proclaim the day: Heaven will be cleft asunder (82.1), stars will darken (81.2) and disperse (82.2), mountains will pass away (81.3), and graves will be laid open (82.4). A trumpet will blow (23.101), a balance beam will find each person either heavy or light in some relevant respect (7.8, 18.105, 21.48, 23.104), and account books of everyone's deeds will be prepared (17.14). If the book is given into the right hand (69.19–24, 84.7–9), the person will go to the garden, a place of splendor. If the book is given into the left hand (69.25–31) or behind the back (84.10–12), the person is consigned to the fire, a place of torment. Details of the Qur'anic hell are graphic but incomplete: Inhabitants have their skins burned, replaced, and burned again (4.56), or are made to eat from the bitter tree of Zaqqum, followed by draughts of boiling water (56.52–54). There are suggestions, too, of levels in hell, for hypocrites (those who embrace Islam by word, but not by heart) are consigned to the lowest depths (4.145). Finally, there are traces of mirroring punishments corresponding to an unbeliever's sins. Those who "swallow the property of orphans" will swallow fire as their reward (4.10), whereas those who hoard gold and silver will have their foreheads, sides, and backs branded by heated coins (9.34–35).

If we ask why these various punishments are meted out, we must content ourselves with a contradictory answer. Unbelief, meaning either denial of God or associating other gods with him, is the overwhelming grounds for condemnation, but this emphasis on faith ill squares with an account book or with mirroring punishments, for here the emphasis is on works. The picture is further confused by a combination of predestinarian pronouncements about God leavened with passages suggesting that individuals are responsible for what they do. Again and again we are told that God chooses whom he pleases for mercy (2.105), guides whom he pleases to the right path (2.142), and so forth. God also seals the ears and the hearts of unbelievers (2.7, 7.101) so that his message is not heard. At the same time, however, we are told that God will not impose on any soul a duty beyond its scope (2.286), and that he has sealed the ears of unbelievers because he has, antecedently, found nothing good in them (8.23). Muhammad was no theologian, and we should not expect to make philosophical sense of his pronouncements. As in Greek tragedy, the Qurʾan presents us with an unsystematic overdetermination of acts: People are both predestined by God and deserving of their fates. The key lies in a believer's total surrender, for in surrender there can be no separation of goodness from belief, works from faith. Love is seldom mentioned in the Qurʾan—perhaps, as Daud Rahbar argues, because love is a reciprocal emotion, and reciprocity is out of the question between God and humans.[11] By contrast, fear—by far the overwhelming God-inspired sentiment of the Qurʾan—is nonreciprocal. Fear strikes only in the hearts of the powerless; and as against God humans are wholly in this condition. To submit to God out of fear is not, for the Muslim, an act of cowardice, but of glorification; it is the highest good of which a person is capable. The prime human virtue espoused in the Qurʾan is *taqwa,* variously translated as "fear of God" or "piety" and understood as guarding oneself against evil.[12] The essence of this virtue is graphically conveyed in the prostration of Muslim prayer: worshipper on his knees, forehead against the ground. Prayer is prescribed five times a day, a repetitious physical and spiritual act that combines with the Qurʾan's incessant warnings of hell to forge a powerful kinesthetic and verbal reminder to creatures whose weakness is less pride than forgetfulness. Correspondingly, the God of the self-surrendering Muslim is less jealous than stern, implacably dispensing mercy or condemnation as the case may warrant.

One interesting wrinkle on escaping the torments of hell is less concerned with faith or with works than with raw suffering. Though torment in Islam may have less to do with redemption than with reminding the faithful of God's omnipotence,[13] tradition records that, along with the guiltless and the indisputably evil, the class of sufferers will be exempt from the balance beam on the day of resurrection.[14] The idea here seems to be less that of suffering as purifying than as a special token from God, a sign of early payment in the currency ultimately due from all who believe.

Perhaps nowhere is the Islamic emphasis on retribution better illustrated than in the third of God's direct punishments of human beings, the punishment in the grave. Though not directly mentioned, certain Qur'anic passages have been interpreted as implying this doctrine. For instance, after mentioning the evils in store on the last day, the Qur'an says: "And surely for those who do wrong there is a chastisement besides that; but most of them know not" (52.47). In the *hadith* (traditions based on acts or sayings of the Prophet) this and other intimations of a second afterlife punishment give rise to the view that between death and resurrection individuals will be interrogated in the grave; those found wanting will be punished.

In part, the doctrine of punishment in the grave appears to be an extension of pre-Islamic Arab practice. Believing that corpses retained some of their powers so long as they remained in bodily form, the pre-Islamic Arabs dug graves with either a narrow trench along the bottom or a niche at the side. Both types of grave were fashioned to give the corpse added room, allowing for physical movement during arousal at an unavenged wrong. Preserving the pre-Islamic configuration of graves, Islam has interpreted the purpose of the trench or niche as space for the corpse to sit up while answering the questions posed to it by the angels Munkar and Nakir. According to some *hadith* accounts, those who lack ready answers to such questions as Who is your Prophet? or What is your prayer direction? are consigned to interim punishment prior to the resurrection.[15]

One view of the punishment of the grave is that orthodoxy has simply settled on a way of making the best of a few ambiguous passages of scripture. There is, however, a deeper motive implicit in the virtue of *taqwa* and explicit in the Muslim emphasis on a stern and unyielding God. Guarding oneself through fear of God becomes, in the Muslim mind, a precarious undertaking exactly to the extent that any path other than the path of righteousness presents itself. The immediacy of the punishment of the grave slams shut the gate to wishfulness, to hoping that if the final judgment is delayed a bit, it will perhaps not come at all. By this doctrine also, God's justice and power are manifest at all times; at no instant does his vigilance against unbelievers wane.

By these three means—collective punishment of wayward nations, the fire of the Last Judgment, and the interim punishment of the grave—the Muslim God invokes fear to mandate human self-surrender. Yet the story remains incomplete, for in the eyes of a believer Allah is preeminently a God of mercy. Each surah of the Qur'an (except for surah 9) begins with the *Bismillah,* an invocation usually translated "In the name of God, the Beneficent, the Merciful." In requiting evil, God measures with strictness, like for like; but in rewarding good, the Qur'an tells us that God suspends the law of equivalence, calculating at a ratio of ten to one: "Whoever brings a good deed will have tenfold like it, and whoever brings an evil deed, will be recompensed only with the like of it, and they shall not be wronged" (6.161). Far, then, from being an example of strict kindly retribution, paradise offers a bounty far beyond the measures of human desert. Such is God's beneficence—an unproblematic use of the concept.

God's mercy, by contrast, is highly problematic, for the two most obvious interpretations of it are fraught with difficulty when applied to Islam. Mercy might, in the first instance, be God's refusal to requite evil with evil in some instances; for these selected cases, he chooses to requite evil with good instead. The problem with this interpretation is that such mercy entails a suspension of God's justice, which is steadfastly retributive. Not a single surah supports a view that would make mercy a suspension of justice. In the second instance, mercy might have nothing to do with the requiting of evil, but be restricted to God's rewarding of good with good. The trouble with this interpretation is that it makes mercy indistinguishable from beneficence. What is worse, it removes the concept from the usual context in which individuals are said *to plead* for mercy. Insisting that good merits good may be a plea for something, but that something cannot be mercy, for the concept is empty if it fails to involve, at some level, suspension of an impending evil.

Whatever else a merciful Qur'anic God does, he must act consistently with retributive justice while suspending a threatened evil rather than merely rewarding good with good. To the extent that these aims are contradictory, we may be tempted to see the Muslim God as an arbitrary tyrant, embodying neither justice nor mercy. Possessing raw power and demanding of humans a sign of submission, the Qur'anic God appears to the non-Muslim to resemble the triumphant wolf in a fight, with the devout Muslim taking on the role of vanquished wolf, throat bared and utterly vulnerable, bidding for clemency with the sole option left to it. Not so, answers the Muslim: What appears to the eye of the unbeliever as tyranny is in point of fact the very justice he or she complains of missing. Among human beings, only the surrenderer knows how God's justice and mercy intertwine. What is more, he possesses this knowledge only through the surrender itself—*taqwa* is self-vindicating, its absence self-defeating.

This disagreement is at one level merely verbal, for the phenomenon is accepted by both parties: God is unyielding and infinitely powerful; humankind is fearful and without power. There can be no reciprocity between two such parties; all is command on one side, obedience on the other. The moment less neutral language is employed to describe the relationship, one person's "tyranny" becomes another's "justice," and the two words describe a difference between the unbeliever and the believer rather than anything in the object of belief. At the same time, however, this difference between unbeliever and believer is the precise point on which God's justice (or tyranny) is alleged to turn: He will punish the one and exalt the other. To the believer, then, the difference cannot be merely verbal. He is conscious of his own surrender in a way that makes any other option inconceivable. This consciousness in turn produces a bond with others who have made the same surrender. A community of belief is forged, cutting across tribal loyalties to harness the morality of the blood feud in service of a new ideal— jihad, usually too narrowly translated as "holy war." In fact, jihad properly designates striving on behalf of Islam.[16] Before turning to this story, however, we first examine Islamic criminal law, deriving concepts that are indispensable to a rounded understanding of jihad.

Legal Punishment in Islam

The heart of Islamic criminal justice is the *lex talionis,* already familiar from Chapter Four. The Qurʾan makes clear its debt to Mosaic law, as when the following passage refers to God's earlier revelation of the Torah:

> And We prescribed to them in it that life is for life, and eye for eye, and nose for nose, and ear for ear, and tooth for tooth, and for wounds retaliation. But whoso forgoes it, it shall be an expiation for him. And whosoever judges not by what Allah has revealed, those are the wrongdoers. (5.45)

In the administration of Islamic criminal justice, the *lex talionis* provides the basis for *qisas,* exact retaliation, or *diyah,* payment of blood money.[17] Which of these is imposed depends on the will of the victim (in the case of physical injury) or of the appropriate blood relatives (in the case of death). Accordingly, the Islamic law of homicide and physical injury remains intimately concerned with satisfaction of the aggrieved feelings of the victim or of the victim's family.

At the same time, however, the promise of expiation for whomever abjures exact retaliation provides scriptural basis for urging *diyah* as opposed to *qisas.* This inclination is reinforced by passages suggesting that, among humans, evil need not always be met with evil:

> And not alike are the good and the evil. Repel evil with what is best, when lo! he between whom and thee is enmity would be as if he were a warm friend. (41.34)

Though it remains in principle the right of the victim and his kin to demand *qisas,* Muslim tradition has developed such passages into strong moral and institutional pressure on individuals to forego retaliation. Indeed, the treatment of retaliatory punishments in the Muslim *hadith* bears many similarities to the gutting of the *lex talionis* in the Babylonian Talmud, with Islamic jurisprudence tending to ameliorate the harshness of the law as a literalist might frame it.

Examples of such amelioration are clearest in another set of Islamic criminal penalties, the *hadud.* Specified either in the Qurʾan or the most reliable *hadith,* these penalties are exceedingly difficult to mitigate, for they are considered offenses against God. There are seven *hadud*, [18] but we shall here consider only two. First is the *hadd* for theft, which is cutting off the hand in accordance with Qur'an 5.38. Second is the *hadd* for adultery, which in accordance with Qur'an 24.2 is flogging with a hundred lashes, but which *hadith* literature, possibly influenced by the letter of Jewish law, increased to death by stoning.

A digression into Muslim jurisprudence shows how the task of ameliorating a retaliatory aim in Islamic law is much more formidable than the corresponding task confronted by the Talmudic rabbis.[19] In addition, the digression underscores the extent to which Islamic law is grounded in the Muslim surrender to God through the person, acts, and pronouncements of his prophet, Muhammad.

Talmudic commentators, embarrassed by the literal application of the *lex talionis,* could argue that it had been intended to apply only metaphorically. Their arguments were aided by the paucity of historical evidence, aside from the Torah itself, concerning the Mosaic era. To understand Islamic law, in contrast to Jewish law, we must start from the vast disparity in facts available to us about the respective lawgivers, Moses and Muhammad. Both men are bearers of the revealed word of God to their people, but the implications of this status are very different in the two cases. Nonscriptural acts and pronouncements of Moses do not exist to supplement the Torah, but corresponding nonscriptural acts and pronouncements of Muhammad make up the bulk of laws canonized in the Islamic *shar'ia*.

The overwhelming objective of *shar'ia* is to reinforce *taqwa,* guarding the believer against perdition. How, though, is one to be sure that he is on the right path, especially on points where the Qur'an is silent, ambiguous, or contradictory? To answer this question, in the centuries after Muhammad's death, various *hadith* gradually became accepted as supplements to God's pronouncements in the Qur'an. The favored method of expansion was casuistical—ideally, one pronouncement for each particular situation. *Hadith* expanded exponentially: It is reported that al-Bukhari, compiler of the earliest and most widely accepted collection, sifted through six hundred thousand reported *hadith* in selecting approximately two hundred thousand for inclusion.[20] The validity of a given *hadith* is determined in large measure by its *isnad* (support), a chain of authority tracing the lineage of the saying back to the Prophet or to one of his companions. Much of Islamic jurisprudence consists of scrutinizing *isnads,* ascertaining that each person mentioned in the chain of authority held sound views, had a good memory, and was a contemporary of the person whom the *isnad* names as passing the *hadith* on to him.[21]

From the perspective of this study, the details of Muslim jurisprudence are less important than its ambition and comprehensiveness. Each rule of *shar'ia,* however trivial, is holy, for it derives from the rightly guided messenger of God. The Qur'an and *hadith* are overwhelmingly the sources of Islamic law, for the other formally acknowledged sources—community consensus and argument by analogy—are the last to be invoked. In addition, when they are cited, consensus and analogy are always pointed in profitable directions by pronouncements of the Qurʾan and *hadith* thought to be relevant, though inexact.

We are now in position to return to the *hadud* penalties for theft and adultery. Taking theft first, we find that Islamic law renders it impossible to argue, in the manner of the Talmudic rabbis, that the mirroring punishment of cutting off the hand was meant to apply metaphorically. First off, the Qurʾan leaves little room for such an interpretation: "And as for the man and the woman addicted to theft, cut off their hands as a punishment for what they have earned, an exemplary punishment from Allah" (5.38). As if the preceding were not enough, *hadith* literature preserves a story that Othman (later to be the third caliph) tried to mediate with the Prophet on behalf of a woman thief from Makhzum. Muhammad angrily rejected any such mediation in God's *hadud,* saying that if his own daughter Fatima were caught stealing he would have her hand cut off.[22] The story has legal force, not only to buttress the prescribed penalty for theft, but to deny any clemency for a *hadud* offense once it has been proven.

Yet even in the face of these stringent requirements, Islamic jurists have found paths of mitigation. One is to point to the practice of the second caliph, Omar, who suspended the *hadd* for theft during a famine. This precedent is interpreted as extending clemency to anyone who steals out of hunger. Interpreted liberally, the plea includes cases where there can be the slightest possibility of hunger as a motivation.[23] If a plea of hunger does not succeed, tradition records the Prophet's approval of ex post facto selling of a stolen mantle by the owner to the thief.[24] In practice, such an option can be removed from the discretion of the victim and extended as a general policy to the detected thief. In sum, such extenuation leads to the point where, in today's Saudi Arabia (one of the few countries where *sharʿia* has the force of law), the *hadd* for theft is rarely executed.[25] At the same time, it must be said that the penalty retains a high symbolic value, especially among fundamentalist Muslims. The effect of this symbolic importance can be compared to the emotive attachment of many people in the United States to the death penalty, despite its infrequent application.

The mitigation of the *hadd* for adultery consists of raising the standards of proof to nearly impossible levels. For death or flogging to be imposed for adultery, one of two conditions must be met. The offender must either confess four times (which confession may not be used as evidence against the other party), or the act must have been witnessed by four adult males. Such daunting levels of proof are rarely achieved, though here too the symbolic importance of the *hadd* deserves mention. As a kind of corollary to the promise that foregoing the right of retaliation will be an expiation, there is a *hadith* to the effect that bringing down a deserved retaliation on one's own head is likewise an expiation. According to this story, a self-confessed adulterer by the name of al-Ashamy was ridiculed by two of his fellow Muslims for disclosing a hidden offense that would result in his being stoned to death like a dog. Overhearing their mockery, Muhammad pointed to the carcass of a donkey and bade the men to eat of it. When they registered their disgust, the Prophet said that their glee in the misfortune of al-Ashamy was worse than eating putrid meat, whereas the adulterer would be purified by the stoning and reside in paradise.[26]

Reflecting on this *hadith* leads us to see that the retributive pattern of Islamic jurisprudence cannot be confined to what passes in nontheistic codes for "criminal law." We have already seen that the pervasiveness of the retributive *like for like* lies as much in suspending as in imposing a threatened punishment. The fate of al-Ashamy is a case in point: Temporal evil, the stoning, suspends the afterlife evil of the fire.

To complete our study of sanctioned retaliation in Muslim thought, we turn finally to the transformation of the tribal blood feud in a pan-Islamic context. Here as elsewhere, we discover that the ideal of total surrender based on faith in God's ultimate retributivism is the key ingredient. We find active in a political context the same like for like exchange between this-life and afterlife penalty or reward as demonstrated in the context of criminal punishment.

Political Retaliation: Jihad and Apostasy

It is a commonplace in the non-Muslim world to observe that Islam was spread by the sword. As often as not, one who endorses this remark has in mind the zeal of the Muslim warrior who, mindful of Muhammad's promise of instant ascension to paradise if he dies fighting for God's unity, marches ferociously into battle. This picture dominates the non-Muslim concept of jihad, sometimes misconceived as one of the five pillars of the faith. It is a view brought back to Europe during the Crusades, reinforced not only by battles between Christian and Muslim but also by bloodshed within the Muslim world itself. Three of the four caliphs following Muhammad fell to political murder, leading among other things to schism between Sunni and Shiʿite and to the order of *hashishiyyin*. For two centuries the *hashishiyyin* carried out a program of political terror motivated in part by zeal to maintain their vision of religious orthodoxy.[27] Favoring stealth, selectivity, and the dagger, the *hashishiyyin* provided both French and English with the word "assassin."

In the conventional Western view, then, Islam was not only spread by the sword, but employed the sword to consolidate its gains and to enforce orthodoxy. Jihad and the punishment of death for apostasy are perceived as two sides of a single coin. Non-Muslim captives condemned to death for battling against Islam were given the chance to save themselves by professing belief in the message of Muhammad. Many did so with alacrity, and once claimed by the faith were accorded full rights as Muslims. The sword showed its second edge, however, for they dared not lapse because of the penalty for apostasy.

As might be expected, the "sword view" of the triumph of Islam is too simple. It underestimates, for instance, the considerable force of Muhammad's personality in appealing to his fellow Quraish, particularly to the young. It underestimates the weakness of Arab paganism, a "religion" that its adherents were only too willing to give up as Islam began to vindicate itself with success.[28] It underestimates the weakness of the Persian and the Byzantine empires, which had fought each other to exhaustion, opening both east and west to seventh- and eighth-century Muslim conquest in a way that would have been impossible a century earlier. Finally, and most important for this study, the "sword view" construes the concept of jihad too narrowly, and in the process obscures the continuity between pre-Islamic Arab practice and the highly effective political ideology evolved by Muhammad. Not surprisingly, this ideology has its roots in the same retributivism as pervades Qur²anic views of God's punishment of man, and of man's punishment of his fellows.

Between Muhammad's flight to Medina and the subsequent capture of Mecca, rules for engaging a political enemy came to him, like all else in the Qur²an, in the guise of divine revelation. Some of these revelations are topical, speaking to the circumstances in which the exiled fledgling Muslims found themselves. In largely agricultural Medina, for instance, the Prophet's following of commercial Quraish had no means of making a living. They thus hit on the expedient of raiding caravans bound for Mecca. The first successful raid transpired on the last day of a sacred month during which the pagan Arabs were agreed that fighting was an impiety. Muhammad's own followers were shocked by this violation, and in response God sent the following message:

> They ask thee about fighting in the sacred month. Say: Fighting in it is a grave
> offence. And hindering men from Allah's way and denying Him and the Sacred
> Mosque and turning its people out of it, are still graver with Allah; and perse-
> cution is graver than slaughter. And they will not cease fighting you until they
> turn you back from your religion, if they can. And whoever of you turns back
> from his religion, then he dies while an unbeliever—these it is whose works go
> for nothing in this world and the Hereafter. And they are the companions of the
> Fire: therein they will abide. (2.217)

Here lies the genesis of jihad, striving for Islam. Though not restricted to combat, the doctrine embraces fighting against an enemy determined to eradicate the Muslim faith.

Fighting in God's way can in this manner be interpreted as defensive, and hence endorsed by the ancient prerogatives of the blood feud: "And there is life for you in retaliation, O men of understanding, that you may guard yourselves"

(2.179). Let no Muslim, however, be first to start: "And fight in the way of Allah against those who fight against you but be not aggressive. Surely Allah loves not the aggressors" (2.190). Solidarity based on an aggrieved sense of the enemy as an unjustified attacker is part and parcel of the psychology of war. It is a higher duty to protect oneself and, as a consequence, one's belief in the unity of God than to scruple over traditional religious obligation:

> The sacred month for the sacred month, and retaliation is allowed in sacred things. Whoever then acts aggressively against you, inflict injury on him according to the injury he has inflicted on you and keep your duty to Allah, and know that Allah is with those who keep their duty. (2.194)

Thus is *lex talionis* more than a precept for punishing crime; it is a precept, also, for contending with external enemies.

In the early stages of Muslim development, however, the political face of the doctrine of retaliation was opposed by the old feelings of kinship and tribal loyalty. Half of Muhammad's Medina following, the emigrants from Mecca, were members of the Quraish. At the first critical skirmish (the battle of Badr) against a Quraish war party, there was thus an unsettled feeling among the emigrant Muslims. What was to become of their personal security if kin were now to be fought rather than relied on as a guarantee of safety? (Recall how Muhammad's pagan uncle, Abu Talif, kept the Prophet secure in Mecca by refusing to withdraw his protection.) The answer lies in the founding of a more fundamental identity as a surrenderer to God. In effect, fellow Muslims become one's sole next of kin. A believer's protector, in a very real sense, is God:

> So you slew them not but Allah slew them, and thou smotest not when thou didst smite the enemy, but Allah smote him, and that He might confer upon the believers a benefit. (8.17)

In battle as elsewhere, God's retributive nature is paramount:

> O you who believe, when you meet those who disbelieve marching for war, turn not your backs to them. And whoso turns his back to them on that day—unless maneuvering for battle or turning to join a company—he, indeed, incurs Allah's wrath and his refuge is hell. And an evil destination it is. (8.15–16)

The corollary to this promise, of course, is reward in paradise to him who fights; and in recounting the battle of Badr, Ibn Ishaq, the Prophet's earliest extant biographer, puts exactly this promise into Muhammad's mouth:

> By God in whose hand is the soul of Muhammad, no man will be slain this day
> fighting against them with steadfast courage advancing not retreating but God
> will cause him to enter Paradise.[29]

Hearing these words, a young Muslim asked, "Is there nothing between me and
my entering Paradise save to be killed by these men," threw down the dates he
was eating, grabbed up his sword, and fought to his death.

Whether this story is factual or a retrospective embroidery on success (Ibn
Ishaq died a century and a half after the Prophet), it goes a long way toward
defining an important political stance within Islam. Fighting among Muslims is
prohibited exactly as the old blood feud prohibited fighting among kin. *Hadith*
records the following exchange:

> Abu Bakrah said, I heard the Messenger of Allah say: "When two Muslims
> meet each other with their swords, both of them are in the fire."
> I said, O Messenger of Allah! This is for the murderer, but what about the
> one who is murdered?
> He said: "He was desirous of murdering his companion." [30]

By stipulation, then, neither of two professing combatants can be a true Muslim.
In the same spirit, the Qur'an declares (4.92) that one believer would never kill
another except by mistake.

Against unbelievers, by contrast, the proper response is to guard oneself with
retaliation. The unbeliever who is a lapsed or faithless Muslim is especially re-
viled. Though the Qur'an promises no more than that God will punish the apostate
or hypocrite in the afterlife fire, many in the political upheavals of the first centuries of Islam were ill content to wait so long. Accordingly, *hadith* records the
following command of Muhammad: "Whosoever changes his religion from Islam
to anything else, bring end to his life." [31] Though lacking the unequivocal sanction of the Qur'an, the death penalty for apostasy nonetheless worked itself into
Islamic law to become a potent factor in maintaining Muslim solidarity.

Against other unbelievers—pagans, Jews, or Christians—the striving on behalf of Islam is more complex. Martyrs are created elsewhere than in war; anyone
who dies generally in the cause of Islam will be translated to paradise. In order
to claim for himself the status of martyr,[32] Muhammad held that his own death
was occasioned by poisoning at the hand of a Jewess. Nevertheless, jihad against
the other "Peoples of the Book" is no simple matter. If they have listened to their
own prophets with care, Jews and Christians will be rightly guided; believing
as much, Muslims have an incentive against hostility toward them. Finally and
most critically important in treating unbelievers is the Qur'anic injunction to be

aggressive only in response to aggression. In theory, a defensive campaign alone is warranted.

At this point a final parallel to the pre-Islamic blood feud proves instructive. Bound as it is to the virtue of *muruwwa,* the blood feud castigates as unmanly any killing not in reprisal for an earlier killing. But in a series of tit-for-tat slayings between tribes, who is to determine the right and wrong of it all? Certainly not the immediate blood relatives of any slain person, for they are duty bound to exact vengeance in return. It falls, then, to the tribal leader to negotiate a settlement, which might sometimes involve the banishment (hence, the withdrawal from protection) of a tribal member. If not exactly a system of retributive justice, the pre-Islamic blood feud was very much a system of retributive order, for it seems to have worked tolerably well. The blood feud's claim on stability rested on the savvy of the acknowledged tribal leader—a factor transferred from pagan Arabia into Islam. It is a matter for the leader, the Prophet or his successor, to determine with which unbelievers to conclude a peace and with which to go to battle, judging them aggressors against Islam. For every early battle the Prophet won to the glory of God, he concluded a dozen alliances to keep potential enemies at bay. Amongst these alliances, certainly during the Prophet's lifetime, jihad took the form of vigorous preaching and demonstration of a superior *muruwwa* in service to God's unassailable unity.

That the pre-Islamic Arab *muruwwa*—"manliness"—finds itself transformed in the unflinching ability to follow God's stringent path is suggested by the several *hadith* claiming that women comprise the chief population in hell.[33] Women face impediments to gaining the Islamic paradise on two counts. First, in keeping with similar prejudices in Judaism and Christianity, women are viewed as inconstant, changeable. Their surrender to God is thus always more suspect than the corresponding surrender of a man. Second, women face the disadvantage that they do not die in battle as often as men. A prime glory of jihad is thus denied them. If women are to be directly rewarded with paradise, their striving must be of a less emphatic sort, liable to be overlooked by the compilers of *hadith.*

Yet whichever sex predominates in hell, the devout Muslim is bent on guarding against its fires. This objective pervades his consciousness of God, his solidarity with fellow Muslims, and his ideas about relations with non-Muslims. Nonetheless, what should, on logical grounds at least, be the most frightening aspect of hell—its eternity—receives little attention. The pronouncements of the Qur'an on the eternity of hell are deeply ambiguous, and the following passage can even be interpreted as a sign of universal salvation: "Only those accept who listen. And as for the dead, Allah will raise them, then to Him they will be returned" (6.36). It seems likely that Muhammad himself had no fixed idea of the eternity of hell, concentrating instead on depicting its torments in such graphic terms that a believer would not want to undergo them for any period.

Only after Greek rationalism gained influence in Islam did the notion take hold that an eternal being offended might mandate eternal punishment. The orthodox position eventually espoused by al-Ashari held that only complete unbelievers were consigned to the fire forever; an atom of faith would be enough to take a believer, however sinful, eventually to paradise.[34] The Muslim hell thus serves as both a place of purification and of imposing a fitting punishment on the ultimate evil of disbelief. The scale of divergence from this orthodoxy, however, is quite remarkable, with many Muslims professing hell to be noneternal.[35] To explore the ramifications of eternal damnation more fully, we thus pass to the Christian views of Saint Thomas Aquinas and his sometime follower, Dante Alighieri.

EIGHT

Eternal Torment

Surah 17, verse 1, of the Qur'an mentions an enigmatic night journey of Muhammad from Mecca to Jerusalem. Embroidering on this passage, biographers and compilers of *hadith* offer numerous accounts of a vision of hell and an ascension to paradise experienced by the Prophet during this journey. Many of these stories bear striking resemblance to other such fanciful wanderings—particularly, as it happens, to Dante's travels in *The Divine Comedy*. Miguel Asin goes so far as to proclaim that the religious literature of Islam

> offers to investigators a more abundant harvest of ideas, images, symbols, and descriptions, similar to those of Dante, than all the other religious literatures together that have up to now been consulted by Dantists in their endeavors to explain the genesis of the Divine Comedy.[1]

This view has more detractors than adherents,[2] but, irrespective of the actual degree of Dante's borrowing from Islamic sources, the striking parallels documented by Asin reflect a preoccupation of the Middle Ages with supramundane existence. Seldom has belief in hell, purgatory, and paradise waxed stronger; seldom have the trappings of retributive thought—doers suffering what they do via an elaborate, ingenious, and sometimes revolting proliferation of mirroring punishments—been so prominent.

Despite many similarities, there are also important differences between Muslim and Christian conceptions of the afterlife. In Canto 20 of *The Inferno*, Dante is moved to tears by the lamentable fate of the sorcerers, who, having twisted nature by their spells, are literally twisted in return, their heads screwed around so that their tears spill onto their own buttocks. An angry Virgil admonishes Dante:

> Here pity, or here piety, must die
> If the other lives; who's wickeder than one
> That's agonized by God's high equity?[3]

A Muslim weeping at such a sight would be due similar chastisement, but it is doubtful that a Muslim guide in hell would have occasion to speak. Dante's tears are prompted by a sense that Christian love ought to extend even to the damned. The devout Muslim, by contrast, surrenders to God's majesty rather than to his love, leaving no space for questioning the divine judgment, whether by head or by heart.

The Christian heart, however, is educated to a belief in God's universal love. As a consequence the doctrine of hell presents a unique set of difficulties. As the retributivist creation par excellence, hell stands beyond the bounds of mercy, clemency, and forgiveness. How, then, is it to be what it is, a place of eternal torment, without also standing outside the purview of God's love? Only corrective punishment is reconcilable with love, yet hell is purely punitive, its inhabitants beyond change for good or ill. Islam knows no such dilemma, for its God commands with the ferocity and unassailable will of a desert patriarch. Hell may be but a purgatory, as some Muslims believe, yet its threat remains undiminished. Eternity is an abstraction, adding little to the terrors of Islamic eschatology. Muslims strive to imitate God's unity in the unity of mutual self-surrender, emphasizing the present and particular: prayer *now*, obedience *now*, punishment *now* serving as the main forces of Islamic reckoning. Forgetful human nature needs constant reminders of the judgment to come, and God's fearsome majesty is served by threatening a punishment so graphic that no believer would risk it whatever its duration.

Where eternal torment of the damned becomes a fixed article of faith, as in much of Christianity, apologists face a tall order. Not only must eternal punishment be reconciled with God's universal love, it must also be reconciled with his justice. The problem is as follows. Any mortal sin that a human being commits must transpire in time. Temporal offenses have a beginning and an end, and so would seem to warrant no more than a temporal punishment, making eternal punishment inherently excessive—analogous to the unrestricted vendetta rather than to the like for like limitation of the moralized blood feud.

Saint Thomas Aquinas's rationalization of the dogma of hell answers the preceding charge. He justifies eternal torment by insisting that it is essential to the orderly maintenance of creation. God's love is reconciled with everlasting punishment of the damned through the intervening theological virtue of charity, whereas

God's justice is vindicated by equating the gravity of the offense to the majesty of Him against whom the offense is committed. It is Aquinas more than Virgil who admonishes the sentimental Dante to dry his eyes at the suffering of the damned.[4] Sympathy is out of place, for, in addition to manifesting God's justice, the sufferings of the damned provide solace to the blessed:

> Now everything is known the more for being compared with its contrary, because when contraries are placed beside one another they become more conspicuous. Wherefore in order that the happiness of the saints may be more delightful to them and that they may render more copious thanks to God for it, they are allowed to see perfectly the sufferings of the damned. (*S.T.* Suppl., Q. 94, Art. 1)

This view is the result of astringent logic carried to compassionless extremes. Seldom has dogma been so ruthlessly served by the light of reason. By assimilating suffering to God's overall design, Aquinas attributes a dubious solace to one portion of humanity (the blessed) while altogether denying it to a second portion (the damned).

Fitting Punishment to Eternity

Rather than concern itself with the amount of suffering inflicted by the original offense, Aquinas's strategy for fitting eternal punishment to temporal wrong focuses on the dignity of the person offended. In this aspect his view is in concert with the class-conscious penalties meted out in the *Code of Hammurabi*. The Babylonian patrician, zealous to a fault in protecting honor against the smallest slight, has nothing on the Aquinian God when it comes to the prerogatives of status. Citing with approval Aristotle's insistence that punishment should be correlated with the authority of the person offended, Aquinas argues:

> Now, whoever sins mortally sins against God, Whose commandments he breaks, and Whose honor he gives another by placing his end in some other than God. But God's majesty is infinite. Therefore whoever sins mortally deserves infinite punishment; and consequently it seems just that for a mortal sin a man should be punished for ever. (*S.T.* Suppl., Q. 99, Art. 1)

In this passage Aquinas falls as much under the spell of the like for like formula as those who would match a temporal offense measure for measure with a temporal penalty. Indeed, looked at from the perspective of the dignity of the person offended, eternal punishment is merely a special case of a more general retributivism governing every kind and degree of penalty imaginable. For Aquinas this more general retributivism characterizes punishment of all sorts, comprehending earthly as well as divine justice in both hell and purgatory.[5]

Though committed to this more general retributivism, Aquinas is loathe to hang the justification of eternal punishment on one peg only. Moreover, the argument from the majesty of God is too strong, for every sin, mortal as well as venial, is an offense against God. Since only mortal sin relegates an offender to hell, there must be something intrinsic to it that underwrites eternal torment. The difference between mortal and venial sin must be such that it does not overwhelm Aquinas's more general retributivism. That is, the distinction must allow punishment both in hell and in purgatory to be imposed measure for measure with, and only for the sake of, the offense in question.

How, though, can one retributive punishment for offense against an infinite being be eternal and another not? To answer, we must find a way in which the concept of eternity applies differently to mortal as opposed to venial sin. The most obvious difference would be to assert that mortal sins, unlike venial ones, are inherently unforgivable. A corresponding retributive view of forgiveness would then underwrite the difference sought: "Inherently unforgivable" would equal "never-to-be-forgiven" would equal "eternally unforgiven." In this way an eternally unforgiven person would merit eternal punishment.

The problem with this suggestion is that it flies in the face of the Catholic doctrine by which any sin, mortal or venial, is forgiven if the conditions of confession, sincere contrition, and a subsequent penance are met. Far short of proclaiming mortal sins to be inherently unforgivable, Aquinas stresses the ease with which forgiveness, even of the most heinous act, may be obtained. The standing offer to remit all sins during life on earth is, Aquinas argues, a manifestation of God's love, but it is likewise a reason why those failing to avail themselves of his forgiveness have no cause for complaint when the fires of eternal torment envelop them (*S.T.* Suppl., Q. 99, Art. 1). The conclusion that an unforgiven person in mortal sin merits eternal punishment is one that Aquinas endorses, but for reasons having nothing to do with the inherent unforgivability of certain acts.

For Aquinas, mortal sin merits eternal punishment only when conjoined with an accompanying refusal of the sinner to make confession. These joint conditions are, at their heart, one and the same, for both involve "turning away from the immutable good" (*S.T.* I-II, Q. 87, Art. 4)—a phrase capturing the essence of mortal sin. A venial sin, by contrast, is merely "an inordinate turning toward a mutable good" (*S.T.* I-II, Q. 87, Art. 4). In each case the sinner incurs a "debt of punishment," but only in the case of the mortal sin is the debt eternal.

So far, however, introducing the concept of an immutable good only adds another form of words to the puzzle. The question remains, Why does a turning from the immutable good incur a debt of eternal punishment?

To answer, Aquinas follows Augustine in arguing that every element of God's creation is inherently good. Equally good is his ordering of the whole of creation. Sometimes, however—on a partial view—things fall into disorder. The result is evil, which is nothing positive in itself. Evil for Aquinas consists in elements positive in their own right standing in wrong relation to each other. Such disorder appears both in nature and in human affairs, but in each realm there is a larger and frequently unperceived order. In nature this larger order is tolerably straightforward:

> It belongs to God's goodness that he leaves nothing out of order: hence we may observe in natural things, that every evil is contained in the order of some good: thus corruption of the air is the generation of fire, and the slaying of the sheep is the meal of the wolf. (*S.C.G.* III, 140)

Thanks to free will, maintaining order in human affairs is more problematic than maintaining order in nature. God's goodness prohibits him from directly bending man's will to his own. Christian love, the basis of charity, must be unforced, voluntary. To uphold the order of goodness, God punishes for acts of will contrary to his ordinance:

> Since . . . human actions are subject to divine providence, even as natural things are: it follows that whatever evil occurs in human actions must be included in the order of some good. This is most fittingly done in the punishment of sins. For thus things that exceed in due quantity are included in the order of justice, which reduces them to equality. Now, man exceeds the mark of his right quantity, when he prefers his own will to God's, by gratifying it against the divine ordinance. And this inequality is removed when, against his will, man is compelled to suffer something according to divine ordinance. Therefore man's sins need to be punished by God: and for the same reason his good deeds should be rewarded. (*S.C.G.* III, 140)

Thus, in nature and in human affairs, evil is partial, privative, and disordered, whereas good is whole, positive, and harmonious.

To this Augustinian conception of the relation between good and evil Aquinas adds an Aristotelian teleology. Goods are ranked in a hierarchy, with each lower good chosen for the sake of some higher one until choice is directed toward the highest good of all. This, the "immutable good" of Aquinas's definition of mortal sin, is life eternal. By spurning it, a mortal sinner earns its opposite—death eternal, or punishment forever in hell:

> Natural equity would seem to demand that everyone be deprived of that good against which he has acted. . . . Therefore he that sins against his last end, and

against charity, which is the bond of the society of the Blessed, and of those
who are tending to beatitude, ought to be punished eternally, although his sins
may have occupied but a short time. (*S.C.G.* III, 144)

A fearsome symmetry thus binds eternal torment to eternal bliss. Hell is part of
God's plan, part of the eternal order of goodness—a view at home with predes-
tination, and thus with Aquinas's conception of grace descending only at God's
election. Without sinners to punish, God's justice would not be manifest. For a
determinist—a Jonathan Edwards, for instance—nothing more need be said. It
is God's glory that is vindicated in the punishment of the damned. The wills of
those who are punished, evil though they be, have been determined to be evil by
the withholding of grace. In rejecting the doctrine of free will, Edwards at least
renders his view consistent.[6]

Aquinas, however, upholds both the doctrine of grace and the doctrine of
human free will. According to the latter, human beings must in some sense merit
their punishment. In preferring their own wills to God's ordinance, people open
themselves, in justice, to suffering something contrary to their wills. The evil of
punishment is apposite because it rightly opposes an errant will. Accordingly,
Aquinas supplements the argument from the symmetry of God's plan with an
argument purporting to show that an eternity of suffering is prefigured in the very
act that gives it rise. In a conditional sense, a person in mortal sin "sins in his
own eternity" (*S.T.* I-II, Q. 87, Art. 3). Given his unrepentant will, the sinner
not only wills to sin, but wills to sin forever. Only natural death puts an end to
unremitted mortal sin—so, in concept, the sin is as eternal as the punishment
to follow. In another articulation of much the same point, Aquinas notes that a
mortal sinner places

> his end in a creature; and since the whole of life is directed to its end, it follows
> that for this very reason he directs the whole of his life to that sin, and is willing
> to remain in sin forever, if he could do so with impunity. (*S.T.* Suppl., Q. 99,
> Art. 1)

The sinner should thus be little surprised to find the whole of death given over to
opposing his will. His debt of punishment is eternal.

After accounting for its role in justifying eternal torment, the most interesting aspect of the Aquinian debt metaphor is its application to punishment in
purgatory. On the face of it, purgatorial punishment would seem to be nonretributive—aimed primarily at preparing the soul for bliss. For Aquinas, however,
this function is fortuitous, an advantage taken perhaps to good advantage but ultimately inessential. The debt of punishment owed by souls in purgatory is equally
as retributive as that owed by the damned in hell. Not surprisingly for a meta-

phor stretched beyond the breaking point, we find that the idea of a debt fails to illuminate when applied to such disparate realms.

Debt of Punishment in Purgatory and in Hell

In the first article devoted to explaining the debt of punishment, Aquinas again ties the ideas of penal debt and penal compensation to maintenance of the divine order:

> It has passed from natural things to human affairs that whenever one thing rises up against another, it suffers some detriment therefrom. For we observe in natural things that when one contrary supervenes the other acts with greater energy, for which reason *hot water freezes more rapidly,* as stated in *Meteor. i 12.* Wherefore we find that the natural inclination of man is to repress those who rise up against him. Now it is evident that all things contained in an order, are, in a manner, one, in relation to the principle of that order. Consequently, whatever rises up against an order, is put down by that order or by the principle thereof. And because sin is an inordinate act, it is evident that whoever sins, commits an offense against an order: wherefore he is put down, in consequence, by that same order, which repression is punishment. (*S.T.* I-II, Q. 87, Art. 1)

Aquinas begins with the idea of a thing rising up against and suffering reaction from something else. The example of hot water freezing faster suggests the contending of opposites, whereas the reference to "the natural inclination of man to repress those who rise up against him" suggests a more general drive toward self-preservation. In neither case, however, is maintenance of the more general order an essential feature of the process described. That is to say, amidst the greatest general disorder, we can well imagine the same contending between opposites and the same (though perhaps futile) efforts at self-preservation as Aquinas envisions. Indeed, disorder might consist in exactly this—the perpetual strife of opposites and mindless contending of each existing entity against every other.

Clearly, however, Aquinas believes just the opposite. He holds the reactive tendency of one thing to rise against another to be inconsistent with a general disorder, for he speaks in the latter part of the passage of rising up against an order as if it were on a par with rising up against a person or a thing. Just as it is natural for a thing or a person to repress anything that rises up against it, so also is it natural for the principle of an order (or the order itself) to repress anything that commits offense against it. The two processes, in fact, fit hand in glove: The bipolar process of a thing resisting invasion from its opposite is part and parcel of maintaining a larger order.

In essence, then, Aquinas makes a sustained effort to reduce a homeostatic metaphysics of retribution to a narrower hydraulic metaphysics. His concern, ultimately, is with the overall order of divine justice, but he rejects the homeo-static implication that order can be restored by any number of adjustments among elements. Instead, each discrete instance of disorder is attributable to a spe-cific cause—each sin belongs to some discrete, identifiable sinner. By a properly gauged, hydraulic reaction against the distinct cause of a particular disorder, order is restored. Metaphysically, the simplest way to envision such a reduction is to turn the cosmos from a dynamic system with any number of equilibria among elements to a system with only one ideal—and hence privileged—point of equi-librium. The pursuit of justice, then, requires restoration to this one privileged balance among elements.

There is evidence that Aquinas in fact conceives of divine justice as involv-ing only one ideal point of equilibrium. In explaining how a debt of punishment remains after a sinner has ceased to sin, Aquinas says:

> Now it is evident that in all actual sins, when the act of sin has ceased, the guilt remains; because the act of sin makes man deserving of punishment, in so far as he transgresses the order of Divine justice, to which he cannot return except he pay some sort of penal compensation, which restores him to the equality of justice. (*S.T.* I-II, Q. 87, Art. 6)

A return to the single equilibrium point of God's orderly creation requires meeting sin with the equal but opposite reaction of penal compensation. Despite Aqui-nas's closing invocation of equality (which suggests a balance beam made level when the amount of penal compensation weighs exactly the same as the sin), we may be forgiven for wondering how the metaphor of debt bears any connection to the restoring of an order. Other metaphors better capture the idea of restoration: for instance, that of patching a hole in fabric, or of removing grime from a paint-ing without altering the underlying image. From Aquinas's perspective, however, the advantage of the debt metaphor is that it fixes responsibility on a particular individual. The debtor must either pay or fall upon the charity of another. Further, when the sum owed reaches zero, it makes some sense to speak of the attainment of "equality." Former debtor and former creditor achieve an identical status in relation to each other, as if leveled on the balance beam. By contrast, there is no such role for the concept of equality in the ideas of repairing fabric or restoring a painting.

For Aquinas debt serves as a flexible concept that, if not examined too closely, seems ideal for explaining the punishment of offenders against an order. A debt is typically owed by someone to someone else, thereby capturing the bipolar ele-ment of one thing or person pitted against another. A debt may also be owed to a collective entity (as in fines levied by the state), thereby capturing the idea of offending against an order or principle. A debt may be voluntary or not, bridging the divide between a voluntary sin and an inherited, original sin. A debt may be paid by someone else, thus reflecting the redemption, through Christ, of mortal sins that humans, unaided, can never redeem. Finally, a debt may be paid in kind or in currency. Either is a ready analog to punishment, for payment in kind (an ox for an ox) directly exemplifies like for like, whereas payment in a currency divisible into discrete units may serve as the prototype for "payment" in pain, conceived of as similarly divisible. A negative felicific calculus is sometimes as much at home in retributive as in utilitarian thought.

Quantified suffering finds ready application in the Aquinian conception of both purgatory and hell. In purgatory, the venial sins to be expiated differ in degree. Hence it is in keeping with justice to proportion severity independently from length of suffering:

> Severity of punishment corresponds properly speaking to the amount of guilt: whereas the length corresponds to the firmness with which sin has taken root in its subject. Hence it may happen that one may be delayed longer who is tormented less, and *vice versa*. (*S.T.* Appendix 1, Q. 2, Art. 6)

Since a currency reduces diverse values to a single unit, we may well ask how the idea of a debt of punishment accommodates these two aspects of purgatorial suffering, intensity and duration. The most obvious answer lies in the practice of repaying large debts in fixed installments over time. The magnitude paid in each period corresponds to severity, whereas the number of installments corresponds to length of purgatorial suffering.

It might be objected that this suggestion takes the debt metaphor more literally than Aquinas intends it. In reply, we may cite his own persistent and consistent literal use of the idea:

> Whosoever is another's debtor, is freed from his indebtedness by paying the debt. And, since the obligation incurred by guilt is nothing else than the debt of punishment, a person is freed from that obligation by undergoing the punishment which he owed. Accordingly the punishment of Purgatory cleanses from the debt of punishment. (*S.T.* Appendix 1, Q. 2, Art. 5)

Here the debtor (a venial sinner) is obligated to a debt holder (God) and is freed on satisfying the debt. The metaphor is more than sufficiently literal to warrant its extension to payment over time, for in the case of purgatory the extension illuminates Aquinas's retributivism: A fixed, fair sum is owed and a schedule of repayment, consonant with the gravity of the offense and the stubbornness of the offender's will, is devised. Reference to other supposed benefits of purgatorial suffering (e.g., preparation of the soul to receive bliss) is, strictly speaking, a happy but nonessential bonus.

When it comes to extending the fixed-installment proposal to hell, the process seems tolerably straightforward. The intensity of suffering bears the same relation to gravity of sin as in purgatory, and the duration of suffering bears the same relation to the offender's will. Since in mortal sin the offender's will is eternally perverse, it simply happens that the debt of punishment is eternal.

At this point, however, the debt metaphor comes under tremendous strain. What kind of monetary debt could require an individual to pay forever? One answer is a debt on which interest is charged and for which the debtor can never produce a sufficient sum to reduce the principal. In this way of explicating the metaphor, God stands to the damned in hell as a usurer stands to the helplessly impoverished. Punishment in hell covers, at best, the interest, leaving the principal untouched throughout an eternity of payments.

Aquinas would naturally object to this modest proposal, for it demeans God by comparing him to a usurer. A more appropriate alternative is to think of the debt as permanent but without interest, unpayable because the damned lack means of paying. The problem is that the damned in hell "pay" an enormous amount. Their suffering is infinite in duration, and, as for intensity, Aquinas asserts that suffering in hell is worse than the greatest suffering on earth, surpassing even that of Christ on the cross (*S.T.* III, Q. 46, Art. 6). To hold that the damned lack means of paying is thus to assert that their suffering has nothing to do with a debt of punishment. The metaphor becomes gratuitous.

A third and final alternative is to think of the debt as infinite. Doubtless this is what Aquinas has in mind, for the proposal allows suffering to divide into payments while explaining why such payments never end. At this point, however, the metaphor loses all reference to actual monetary transactions, voluntary or otherwise. Disallowing interest, no monetary debt is infinite.

Pursuing this disanalogy underscores a point about the use of retributive metaphors. What one naturally wants to say is that Aquinas has not conceived of a monetary or commercial debt at all. Instead, he thinks of such "debts" as are "owed" when, for instance, someone saves another person's life. The beneficiary commonly says in such cases "I can never repay you" or "I am eternally in your debt." Each human being stands to God in exactly this relation, Aquinas might wish to say—we are eternally indebted to him for our very lives.

This way of preserving the metaphor will not work, however, for what it conveys is actually a repudiation of the idea of a debt. Its main point is to stress, not the degree of analogy with a monetary transaction, but the degree of disanalogy. By saying "I can never repay you" one wishes to underscore that the "debt" is extraordinary—in effect, not a debt at all. Owing one's life to someone else creates an obligation beyond price.

Such considerations point to a grave incoherence in the Aquinian architecture of hell. Suffering is a currency owed to God because of the eternal debt created by unforgiven mortal sin, yet it is owed in a transaction beyond price, for one cannot recompense God. Unlike other economic transactions, there is no reciprocal exchange conducive to the mutual benefit of relative equals. Instead, the debt of punishment in hell is like a fine imposed by a state that refuses to accept the normal kind of payment, then rejects all proposed alternatives as well. A fine that cannot be paid, however, is pointless—one might as well proceed directly to the penal sanction for which it is but poor camouflage. Perhaps the state will execute anyone unable to pay—which is the same as saying it will execute everyone who is "fined." Or perhaps the state will impose life imprisonment. Whatever the alternative, all talk of a "debt" or a "fine" is dispensable; it does no analytical work, it clarifies nothing.

We are left, then, with the conclusion that either pain is a gratuitous addition to the suffering of the damned in hell, or it is imposed for some other reason than because the damned continue to owe a debt of punishment.

In fact, Aquinas admits two nonretributive reasons for the eternal torment of the damned. The first we have already mentioned—namely, that in witnessing the suffering of the damned, those who are saved will find their beatitude perfected. The second nonretributive use of the suffering of the damned is that they serve as a warning to those who, still alive, may yet be induced to repent of their mortal sins (*S.C.G.* III, 145). In each of these cases, however, Aquinas cautions that we must not rejoice "directly" in the suffering of the damned, but only "indirectly" insofar as such torment is necessary to uphold divine order (*S.T.* Suppl., Q. 94, Art. 3).

But if Aquinas pulls his punches on this point, it is only to deliver blows with greater ferocity when it comes to depicting the suffering of the damned. Throughout its architecture, the Aquinian hell consistently follows a principle of never mitigating an agony. Even if there were solace to be had (say, in remembering delights from their former existence), the damned are given no surcease of pain in which to enjoy it.

Privation, Pain, and Plenitude

At the gates of hell Dante encounters a sign proclaiming "Lay down all hope, you that go in by me." [7] In Aquinian theology, the sign is significant in that hope, along with grace and charity, is a theological virtue that, transcending all natural virtue, is a necessary condition of salvation. Those without hope are equally without grace and charity. They are therefore lost, cut off, liable to the severest punishment imaginable.

Yet by Aquinas's own admission the worst torment of hell is a privation—one's knowledge of exclusion from eternal bliss (*S.C.G.* III, 141). Given the doctrine of evil as nothing positive in its own right, why is not awareness of such momentous loss the sole torment suffered by the damned in hell? Why is physical pain added?

Part of the answer is that the machinery of hell embodies like for like not only in duration of punishment (eternal torment for the eternal willingness to remain in sin) but also in intensity of punishment. Mortal sins differ in their gravity; hence lesser mortal sins must receive less punishment than greater mortal sins. What is more, sinners differ in the number of mortal sins that they have committed. This difference in number cannot be comprehended by lengthening an already eternal torment; it must therefore be comprehended by the severity of punishment administered. We thus find that privation of bliss, great as it is, serves as the baseline penalty to which other penalties, different in degree according to a difference in gravity or number of sins, are added. In keeping with this scheme, Aquinas reserves the mildest punishment (which is still greater than the greatest punishment suffered on earth) for infants who die without baptism. Still stained by original sin, these infants cannot merit salvation, but they at least do not suffer physical pain. Having never acted, they suffer only privation in the momentous loss of salvation (*S.T.* Appendix 1, Q. 1, Art. 1).

For sinners who have acted, by contrast, simple privation is insufficient. The Aquinian hell relies on intensity of pain to reflect the different orders of demerit. Physiologically, pain has the twin advantages of lasting for longer or shorter periods and of coming in bundles ranging from less to more intense. God's justice is impeccable: No sinner guilty of fewer offenses or a lesser offense than his neighbor in hell can complain that all are punished alike—that is, eternally. His guiltier neighbors suffer an appropriate amount more intensely throughout eternity than does anyone whose offenses are less. Cold solace to those of lesser culpability, but perhaps a solace all the same.

We soon discover, however, the resolve with which Aquinas stamps out any possible mitigation of pain in hell. Whatever intensity is its just measure for the given individual, the suffering of the damned is unremitting. Aquinas's insistence on this doctrine shows itself in three distinct contexts, each of which derives from a particularly strong interpretation of the reactive component of retribution. The generalized intuition that we should return evil for evil says nothing about a possible admixture of good. Accordingly, a wise parent's censure of a child might justly combine with a reassuring hug. Evil in this case is met with an evil conjoined with a restorative good. In this weaker version, the reactive principle implies, *some* evil for an evil. The conjunct good may be added or not as circumstances dictate. By contrast, the stronger interpretation of the principle implies, *only* evil for an evil. This version is adopted in the Aquinian hell, meaning that the evil returned to mortal sinners contains not the slightest admixture of anything save suffering.

One appearance of Aquinas's insistence on unmitigated pain occurs in his dis-

cussion of the punishment of the damned after death but before the resurrection
and the final judgment. During this interim, mortal sinners await restoration to
their bodies, yet their status as disembodied souls does not for an instant stand in
the way of their suffering. The sole question for Aquinas is how, not whether, a
disembodied soul can experience physical pain. He finds his answer by analogy
to necromancy:

> For a spirit can be coupled with a body either as its form;—thus the soul is
> coupled with the body to give it life:—or without being its form; thus necro-
> mancers, by power of the demons, couple spirits with apparitions and the like.
> *A fortiori*, therefore, can the divine power bind the souls of the damned to a
> material fire: and thus it is painful to them to know themselves to be united to
> the lowest things as a punishment. (*S.C.G.* IV, 90)

Though its solution is perhaps a bit abstruse, the puzzle is resolved: The damned
prior to the resurrection do not escape pain despite lack of a physical body. Just
as there are no gaps in the goodness of the created order, so also are there no gaps
in the retributive order erected by God to punish deviations. Plenitude prevails on
both sides in the fearsome Aquinian symmetry of heaven and hell.

Plenitude also governs in the second appearance of the doctrine that the
damned never experience surcease of pain. In answer to the question "Whether
in Hell the Damned Are Tormented by the Sole Punishment of Fire," Aquinas
concludes that it befits God's justice to punish in a variety of ways. After all, as
mortal sinners "placed their end in material things which are many and various,
so should they be tormented in many ways and from many sources" (*S.T.* Suppl.,
Q. 97, Art. 1). Harsh as it sounds, this conclusion gives rise to the worry that
mitigation may sneak in through the back door: Perhaps in passing from one torment to another, the damned will have a moment's respite. If physiologically they
resemble human beings on earth,.their passing from painful cold to painful heat
would involve an intermediate period of nonpain, if not actually of pleasure. So
strong is this presumption that Aquinas offers it as an objection to the view that
hell's torments are numerous—and thus in support of the contrary view that fire
is its sole torment. (The advantage of fire as a single torment is that it can feast
eternally at a body without giving surcease of suffering.)

It turns out, though, that the damned in hell—once reunited with their
bodies—suffer by a spiritual action much like that of the souls tormented prior
to their resurrection. Pain is placed safely beyond mitigation, allowing Aquinas
to answer the objection with confidence: "The damned will pass from the most
intense heat to the most intense cold without this giving them any respite" (*S.T.*
Suppl., Q. 97, Art. 7).

The third appearance of the doctrine that the damned suffer no release from
pain is the most explicit. It arises in conjunction with Aquinas's wondering

"Whether the Damned Are in Material Darkness." After considering the views both that the darkness is and is not material, he says:

> The disposition of hell will be such as to be adapted to the utmost unhappiness of the damned. Wherefore accordingly both light and darkness are there, in so far as they are most conducive to the unhappiness of the damned. Now seeing is in itself pleasant. . . . Yet it happens accidentally that seeing is painful, when we see things that are hurtful to us, or displeasing to our will. Consequently in hell the place must be so disposed for seeing as regards light and darkness, that nothing be seen clearly, and that only such things be dimly seen as are able to bring anguish to the heart. (*S.T.* Suppl., Q. 97, Art. 4)

Bifurcation of heaven and hell is complete. All pleasure, including rejoicing at the punishment of the damned, is reserved for the blessed in heaven. The damned have only pain—the pain of multiple physical torments, the mental anguish of envying the blessed, and, surprisingly, the pangs of conscience.

Coda on Conscience

Aquinas adds the pangs of conscience to hell in interpreting two passages from the Apocrypha referring to "worms" in the torment of the damned. He concludes that their mention is

> not of a corporeal but of a spiritual nature: and this is the remorse of conscience, which is called a worm because it originates from the corruption of sin, and torments the soul, as a corporeal worm born of corruption torments by gnawing. (*S.T.* Suppl., Q. 97, Art. 4)

The surprise in this assertion is that Aquinas equally represents the damned in hell as unrepentant. Conscience would seem to characterize a being only to deter or to reform, but the damned are past deterrence and incapable of reformation. Logically speaking, therefore, aside from the subjective experience of a bad conscience as painful, there seems a far more plausible role for conscience in purgatory, where fire is refining and where acceptance of fault prepares the way for ascent into heaven.

Here is a point on which the pupil, Dante, surpasses the master, Aquinas. In Dante's hell, where the damned are just as unrepentant as in the pages of the *Summa*, there is no mention of conscience in respect to torments suffered. In Dante's purgatory, by contrast, release from the dictates of conscience speeds the penitents to the next level in their ascent to God. The inhabitants of Mount Purgatory in *The Divine Comedy* actively seek the suffering ordained for them. Their pains are no less real for their relishing of them, but the inward turn is crucial.

Nothing external binds an inhabitant of Dante's purgatory to the level to which she has progressed. Each person is bound solely by an inner sense that pain must act where voluntary contrition has failed. The release of a soul to a loftier stage causes the entire mountain to shake as all inhabitants celebrate with a shout. The triumph lies not in overcoming an external obstacle imposed by God, but rather in a self-willed hurdling of a self-imposed limit:

> The will itself attests its own purgation;
>> Amazed, the soul that's free to change its inn
>> Finds its mere will suffices for liberation;
>
> True, it wills always, but can nothing win
>> So long as heavenly justice keeps desire
>> Set toward the pain as once 'twas toward the sin.[8]

In sum, Dante's penitents on Mount Purgatory have to stop desiring pain before they can will their own release. They are bound internally by a consciousness of fault, which must be appeased by suffering if they are to take themselves to a higher level. Conscience for Aquinas is a faculty that merely inflicts a retributive pain. For Dante, by contrast, conscience does not inflict, but rather cries out for, suffering in order that the soul may free itself.

Conscience takes on the role of penalizer as the result of Aquinas's linking of justice to order. Human beings, he writes, are properly subject to a threefold order—that of their own reason, of the state, and of the divine.

> Now each of these orders is disturbed by sin, for the sinner acts against his reason, and against human and Divine law. Wherefore he incurs a threefold punishment; one, inflicted by himself, viz. remorse of conscience; another inflicted by man; and a third, inflicted by God. (*S.T.* I-II, Q. 87, Art. 1)

Eternal rebels against order, the Aquinian damned in hell thus punish themselves—but not for any purpose, as they stand outside the hierarchy of ends that gives an action its meaning. As it happens, however, their mindless self-torment coincides with the doctrine that they must never have surcease of pain.

The fully retributive conscience met with in Dostoevsky combines the two roles assigned to it singly by Aquinas and Dante. That is to say, the fully retributive conscience both metes out suffering and is a repository for suffering believed to be due. As we shall see, Dostoevsky "naturalizes" conscience in a way inconceivable during the Middle Ages—namely, by positing it as an unconscious retributive process struggling toward the light.

Yet we must delay an examination of the fully retributive conscience in Dostoevsky. We prepare the ground for it by looking, first, at the revenge tragedy in

the theatre of the English Renaissance and, second, at the purely juridical conscience of Immanuel Kant. The first is a retributive web with implications for the
solace of self-control. The imitative art of the stage has been alleged both to stir
up and to quell an observer's passion for revenge. How to deal with that passion
is a great preoccupation of Renaissance drama. Kant's juridical conscience, by
contrast, seeks a retributivism devoid of passion, vengeful or otherwise—a web
of belief bearing stern implications for the solace of duty.

NINE

Theatre of Judgment

The Spanish Tragedy of Thomas Kyd—the most popular and widely imitated revenge tragedy of the English Renaissance [1]—begins with the ghost of Don Andrea
and the allegorical character of Revenge sitting down to watch the drama unfold.
Later the play's revenger, Don Hieronomo, uses the guise of a tragic performance
to strike down Lorenzo and Balthazar, the killers of Hieronomo's son, Horatio.
Kyd thus uses the play-within-a-play in two different but equally intriguing ways.
In the first instance Don Andrea and Revenge occupy a seat of judgment akin to
that of the audience. They do not influence the action, having only shadow bodies
to animate their craving for vengeance. Their sole power is that of sympathetic
imagination, gorging on the passions of those who enact "real" vengeance on the
stage.

In the second use of the play-within-a-play, Don Hieronomo assumes the
much more active role of playwright. As author, his vengeance is parasitic upon
the stage's power to create a veil of illusion. The victims of Hieronomo's de-
ception anticipate pretended stabs, but the stabs prove genuine. Lorenzo and
Balthazar likewise anticipate pretended pain (and this to strike not in their own
breasts but in those of their onlooking fathers, audience to the tragedy) but the
pain too proves genuine. Illusion achieves ironic perfection, with death lurking
behind the mask of death.

Whenever stage violence—including the violence of revenge—comes under
scrutiny, reactions may be framed by these disparate uses of the play-within-a-
play from *The Spanish Tragedy*. The first use embodies the idea of theatre as
cathartic—revenge tragedy serving the civic order via productive channeling of

retributive passion. The illusion of the drama is encouraged to work its magic, indulging an audience's desire for vengeance while simultaneously unmasking the threat of this passion to the administration of justice. The second use embodies the idea of theatre as accomplice to crime. It suggests that the shadow play of impulses encouraged by revenge tragedy is a genie best left in the bottle for fear that witnessing theatrical violence serves as prelude to enacting it.

In a popular image supplementing the hope for catharsis, theatre is a court of poetic justice:

> If we present a Tragedy, we include the fatall and abortiue ends of such as com-
> mit notorious murders, which is aggrauated and acted with all the Art that may
> be, to terrifie men from the like abhorred pratises.[2]

And in a fourth image, supplementing the idea of the stage as criminal accomplice, theatre is the devil's dwelling:

> In the times of the primatiue Church, a Christian woman went in to the Theatre to
> behold the plaies. She entred in well and sound, but she returned and came forth
> possessed of the Diuell. Wherevpon certine Godly brethren demanded Sathan
> how he durst be so bould, as to enter into her a Christian. Whereto he answered,
> that *hee found her in his owne house,* and therefore tooke possession of her as
> his owne. A fearefull example this indeede, able to afrighten and deter any from
> entring into Theaters, least they incur the like danger as this woman did.[3]

Satan, as is well known according to this author, works by deceit and pleasing disguise—the exact tools of dramatic art.

But if theatre can be variously a relief valve for dangerous passions, an author of despicable violence, a court of poetic justice, or the devil's dwelling, we may ask whether each of these things might also be theatre. One answer of the Renaissance was that, yes, each is part of the grandest theatre of all, *The Theatre of God's Jvdgements*. Via a selection from both secular and ecclesiastical sources, the treatise bearing this title depicts "the admirable justice of God against all notorious sinners, both great and small, but especially against the most eminent persons of the world."[4] Compilation of such moral exempla enjoyed enormous popularity coincident with the heyday of revenge tragedy. For instance, John Reynolds's *Triumph of God's Revenge against the crying and execrable Sinne of Murther* (1621) ran to five volumes and was reprinted four times before its condensation in 1661 into a single volume titled *Blood for Blood or Murthers Revenged*.[5] So attractive was the theme of God's inevitable vengeance that a Royalist abridger of *Blood for Blood* could not resist adding a sixth set of exempla vindicating Charles I and detailing the punishments meted out by God to those responsible for his execution.[6] History, too, becomes a theatre of judgment.

But if the Christian God is playwright, he is equally critic and (in the person of Christ) leading actor. These multiple roles lead to anomalies, if not downright contradictions, in the conception of the world as a theatre of judgment. If God has scripted the parts for which he condemns human beings, where is his justice? If instead he is merely an impartial critic, what becomes of the assured beauty and splendor of a creation left in irresolute human hands?

Though a curse in the rational theology of Aquinas, such dilemmas are a blessing to the playwright. By deliberately courting ambiguity, theatre exploits the diverse biases and contending impulses brought to a performance by members of the audience. Thriving on the contradictions that philosophy and rational theology eschew, the stage holds its audience intensely or not at all. A playwright's aim is to induce impassioned self-scrutiny, touching the inner springs of judgment.

Strong effects require strong medicine. For theatre to touch the inner springs of judgment, it must converse with the preoccupations of its age. This chapter explores three scraps of dialogue between Renaissance theatre and popular moral sentiment. The first, already adumbrated, is the debate between partisans of the *Theatre of God's Jvdgements* and theatre *simpliciter*. The second is between *The Atheist's Tragedy*, by Cyril Tourneur, and popular reviling of atheists and epicures for their presumed lack of a Christian conscience. The third dialogue is between partisans and critics of dueling, a dispute presupposed in and illuminated by *A Fair Quarrel*, by Thomas Middleton and William Rowley. If the charge against the atheist is that he lacks all conscience, the charge against the duelist is that his conscience, based on a rigorous code of honor, is too keen.

Parallels abound between the English Renaissance and our own age in respect to theatrical violence (the bounds of modern theatre being expanded to encompass cinema and television). The question implicit in Kyd's two uses of the play-within-a-play in *The Spanish Tragedy* is shared between our two eras: Does imitation of violence induce, or does it provide a safe outlet for, the impulse to violence in real life? Partisans of an unambiguous answer either way seem to read from a script denied the rest of us. The sword of vengeance cuts both ways, with art imitating life and life imitating art. As is evident in the following section, those claiming either a uniformly productive or a uniformly pernicious role for revenge tragedy in the order of justice can as easily find as unwittingly manufacture examples suited to their case.

Vengeance Is Whose?

The primary Christian text inspiring God's theatre of judgments is Romans 12.19: "Beloved, never avenge yourselves, but leave it to the wrath of God; for it is written, 'Vengeance is mine, I will repay, says the Lord.' "[7] The passage serves clear warning against private revenge, for Paul goes on (Romans 13) to identify the power of God with the power of rulers ordained to punish evil.

In many instances, however, God's justice is a long time coming. Perhaps the prince expected to enforce God's ordinance grows corrupt, becoming the very individual against whom a just vengeance is wanted. Whose hand is to strike him down? Or perhaps the just prince is murdered in his sleep by a usurper. How is the usurper's claim to be overthrown? Or perhaps the just prince fails to discern the identity of a criminal. What human ruler, possessed of the best intentions in the world, can punish an offense whose author remains unknown?

A first concession of moralizing treatises depicting the inevitability of God's justice is "yet let us understand that Heaven is just though slow." [8] Other emendations follow, each stressing that the observer's time frame must be adjusted to the right dimension. The unjust prince is eventually killed or vanquished in a trial of strength against a virtuous rival. The usurper is driven mad. Undiscovered crimes are unexpectedly disclosed, sometimes years after the event. [9]

Space permits a look at only this last solution to the vindication of divine justice. *The Theatre of God's Jvdgements* offers examples of the unexpected detection of murder in three main categories: murders disclosed by animals (five by dogs, and one each by cranes, crows, and swallows); odd coincidences that induce confession from guilty minds; and lurid miracles pointing to an otherwise unsuspected person.

Sometimes the stories are told in ways that unwittingly contradict the desiderata of divine justice, as in one example of a dog's disclosure of murder. Lothebroke, a Danish favorite of King Edmund, was vilely slain by Berike, the king's falconer. As the corpse lies in the woods, Lothebroke's dog runs between it and the hand of the king, who is prompted to investigate. Berike is apprehended and, for a fitting punishment, set adrift in Lothebroke's boat, presumably to die; the winds, however, take it to Denmark:

> Here the boat of *Lothebroke* being well knowne, hands were laid vpon him, and
> by torments he was enqu'rd into: but hee, to saue himselfe, vuttered an vntrvth
> of King *Edmund,* saying that the king had put him [i.e., Lothebroke] to death
> in Northfolk. Whereupon reuenge was deuised, and to that end an armie of men
> prepared & sent ouer: which was the first occasion of the Danes arriuall in this
> land. [10]

Ostensibly told to emphasize God's justice, the story becomes one of an evildoer's escape by compounding murder with lying. This consideration, however, passes unnoticed as the next sentence exhumes the original point, by now as deeply buried as Lothebroke's unavenged corpse: "Thus was this murder wonderfully discouered by meanes of a dog." [11]

To any but the eye of faith, the examples in the second category are equally problematic. Bad conscience leads to confessions of murder in the following two circumstances: A man admits to an earlier slaying when apprehended in the course of a second murder, and a miller confesses to murder when, years after he has sold his property to a second miller, a body is discovered under the floor.[12] It is difficult to see anything especially remarkable in either confession. The first man was bound to hang for the subsequent murder, so why not confess the first? As for the miller, suspicion would naturally have fallen on him—perhaps on no one else.

Two further examples of guilty conscience raise doubts of another kind. In one case a murderer undergoing examination is betrayed by his uncontrollable sighing; in another, by the trembling of his heart when a Spanish magistrate orders all suspects to bare their chests.[13] Given the ready disposition of the age to use torture in judicial inquiries, we can well understand why even the innocent might sigh or tremble under official scrutiny.

To illustrate guilt signified by miraculous events, Beard's treatise tells of a magistrate who cut off the hand of a murdered traveler and hung it above the prison door:

> About tenne yeares after the murderer comming vpon some ocasion into the prison, the hand which had beene a long time drie began to drop bloud on the table that stoud vnderneath it: vvhich the gaoler beholding, stayed the fellow, and aduertised the magistrates of it, vvho examining him, the murderer giving glorie to God, confessed his fact, and submitted himselfe to the rigour of the law, vvhich was inflicted on him as hee well deserued.[14]

Even more miraculous is the case of a German thief and murderer brought to justice through his purchase of three calves' heads. When he put them into his wallet, they

> seemed to the standers by to be mens heads; vvhereupon being attached and searched by the officers, and he examined how he came by them, answered and proued by witnesses, that he bought Calves heads, and how they were trans-formed he knew not: vvhereupon the Senat amazed, not supposing this miracle to arise of naught, cast the partie into prison, and tortured him to make him con-fesse what villanie he had committed, vvho confessed indeed at last his horrible murders, and was worthily punished for the same, and then the heads recouered their old shapes.[15]

Beard admits to scruples at including this story among his examples

> lest I should seeme to insert fables into this serious Treatise of God's judge-ments: but seeing the Lord doth often vvorke miraculously for the disclosing of this foule sinne, I thought that it would not seem altogether incredible.[16]

One could scarcely ask for a better example of circular argument: The story must be accepted as an instance of the miraculous hand of God in disclosing murders because it is well known that God works in such a way.

The conclusion of *The Theatre of God's Jvdgements* follows readily from its overriding faith in God's active supplementing of human justice:

> By all these examples we see, how hard it is for a murderer to escape without his reward: vvhen the justice of man is either too blunt, that it doth not strike with seueritie the man appointed vnto death, then the justice of God riseth vp, and with his owne arme he discouereth and punisheth the murderer; yea, rather than he shall goe unpunished, senceless creatures and his owne heart and tongue riseth to giue sentence against him.[17]

So appealing is this idea of the hidden hand of God in meting out justice that Thomas Heywood unwisely produces his own examples in defending the theatre. At least twice, we are told, wives have confessed to murdering their husbands after watching stage productions of similar homicides. The first case involves a woman in "Nolfolk" who, after watching a stage ghost torment a character guilty of homicide, cries out "oh my husband, my husband: I see the ghost of my husband fiercely threatening & menacing me." [18] She turns out to have poisoned him. Another example, from Amsterdam, concerns a woman who watches the stage murder of one good Renaldo, killed when jealous fellow workers nail a spike into his head. The woman is overcome, raving and calling her husband's name. When later, quite by accident, the local sexton discovers a twelve-year-old skull with a nail in it, she likewise confesses to murder.

In a theatre of judgment, however, the meaning of such confessions is open to interpretation, as Heywood's critics are anxious to demonstrate. Short of indicating God's use of the stage to unite divine and poetic justice, the confessions may be seen as a judgment against theatre. God, angered at the women's lack of confession,

> tooke them napping in the Diuells Sanctuary: that where they thought to conceive much mirth from vanity, there they might bee prickt in conscience, and receiue the beginning of their sorrow, at last to bring them to repentance, that God might saue their soules, though in his justice hee brought their bodies to destruction.[19]

By counting equally for either side, moral exempla fail to resolve debate over theatre's influence on conscience and self-control. At one extreme the machinery of divine justice devalues conscience, turning it into a base calculator of expected utility, as when belief in hell induces a confession solely for avoidance of damnation. At the other extreme conscience becomes (as for Aquinas) a mere instrument of torment, prefiguring or even supplementing the eternal torment to come.

But if the Renaissance could not agree on the positive workings of a good conscience, it came near consensus on the pernicious effects of a lack of conscience. This void was widely believed to stem from atheism, which the age was as zealous to persecute by law as to condemn on stage.

"The Honest Man's Revenge"

One possible implication of believing in God's ultimate retributive standard is quietism in the face of personal insult or injury. Not only will the injurer receive his just deserts, but patience and resignation become means of earning one's own reward. In Tourneur's *Atheist's Tragedy* (subtitled *The Honest Man's Revenge*) the wisdom of leaving vengeance wholly to God is juxtaposed against the folly and dangers of atheism. The play is unrivaled for sheer didacticism and listless drama, but when viewed as a scrap of dialogue in the theatre of judgment it yields unsuspected depth.

Let us begin with the play's social context, describing the unsavory reputation of the theatre for harboring such atheists and libertines as Robert Greene, Christopher Marlowe, and Thomas Kyd. Greene's dying admonition to fellow reprobate playwrights to mend their ways is delightedly seized upon by partisans of God's judgment.[20] Equally heaven-sent is Marlowe's violent death—killed by his own knife in a barroom brawl. In recounting this tale as evidence of God's justice working invisibly against atheists, *The Theatre of God's Jvdgements* embellishes the story so that Marlowe's hand is on the knife as it stabs into his brain.[21] Divine justice sometimes benefits from poetic license.

A more telling side of the ill fate awaiting the presumed atheist involves active persecution by public sentiment. During a search for unrelated items, the authorities found in Kyd's room certain documents containing "vile hereticall conceiptes denyinge the deity of Jhesus Christe o[r] Savio[r]."[22] Though Kyd protested that the papers belonged to Marlowe, who died shortly after Kyd's arrest, the association with atheism was enough to cost him his patron, dealing his career a blow from which it never recovered.

If we ask what the age so feared from atheism, part of the answer hinges on wide acceptance of the doctrine of hell. Because the atheist possesses the seductive ability to lead others to hell alongside him, he is more dangerous even than a murderer. Unafraid for his mortal soul, he is without conscience, though he cleverly appeals to conscience in others to gain his ends. Like the witch, his near kin, the atheist has extensive power—not the supernatural power manifest in spells and curses, but rather the devil's limitless power of disguise and deceit.

Unmasking the atheist is a difficult and dangerous task, one in which God may be expected to render every aid. So we read of Hermanus Biswick, who in 1502 was struck down, not by a miracle or the pangs of his own conscience, but by judicial decree. After sentencing he was "together with his bookes burnt in Holland."[23] This example reveals the self-vindication of the theatre of judgment. If among the means God uses to punish atheists is the hand of his fellow citizens, there can be no mistakes when it comes to putting atheists to death. From the mere fact that the accused was burnt we may infer (God permitting it to happen) that the victim was indeed a threat to others.

Against this backdrop of revulsion toward unbelievers, *The Atheist's Tragedy* offers its pleasing spectacle.[24] At one level, the play exonerates theatre, tidying up the revenge genre to preclude all possibility of the audience's sympathizing with a private revenger. The play turns traditional elements of Senecan revenge tragedy on their head, none more so than when the ghost of Montferrers reveals that he has been murdered by his brother, D'Amville. Appearing before Montferrers's soldier son, Charlemont, the ghost says:

> Return to France, for thy old father's dead
> And thou by murder disinherited
> Attend with patience the success of things
> But leave revenge unto the King of kings.
>   (II,vi,20–24)

The Senecan ghost is typically counsel to revenge (or at least its approving admirer, as in *The Spanish Tragedy*),[25] but the ghost of Montferrers will not abide his son's striking a death blow even in a fair quarrel. After Charlemont subdues the attack of D'Amville's youngest son, Sebastian, he is on the verge of delivering a fatal thrust when the ghost intervenes:

> Hold, Charlemont!
> Let him revenge my murder and thy wrongs
> To whom the justice of revenge belongs.
>   (III,ii,31–34)

Though complaining that the advice is torture, Charlemont obeys, only to be arrested for debt and for causing a riot.

Opposing Charlemont is the force of his uncle's atheism. The taint of atheism cut such a wide swath in Renaissance England that it included many unorthodox Christians, especially Puritans.[26] Tourneur satirizes Puritanism in the comic figure of Languebeau Snuffe. Though willing enough to abandon his conscience at the hint of self-advancement, Snuffe lacks the strength of will to be anything but an accessory to crime. D'Amville, by contrast, has no such weakness. He is a full-blooded and willful atheist, believing only in the force of nature and so discerning no difference between man and beast. Nature dictates self-advancement in order to secure wealth for his sons, whom D'Amville claims are "as near to me / As branches to the tree whereon they grow" (I, i, 53–54). This paternal sentiment, however, has no redeeming touch of compassion or tender feeling. D'Amville's sole aim in life is to

> have all my sense feasted in
> Th' abundant fulness of delight at once,
> And with a sweet insensible increase
> Of pleasing surfeit melt into my dust.
>   (I,i,18–21)

This aspect of D'Amville's character echoes a more general association between atheism and hedonism, as for instance when one contemporary guide to manners declares, "Take this for a foundation, *Euery Atheist is a Epicure*."[27]

By this formula, inside every atheist lurks an unscrupulous sensualist who will stop at nothing to satisfy his desires. D'Amville cleverly perverts the language of morality to achieve his ends, claiming that true charity requires serving oneself first (I,i,34–40). After wresting Castabella away from Charlemont and forcing her to marry Rousard, his elder son (conveniently ill unto impotence so that Castabella's chastity lies untouched), D'Amville plots to have her for himself. Once again he perverts the language of morality, saying

> By my
> Persuasion thou wert forc'd to marry one
> Unable to perform the office of
> A husband. I was author of the wrong.
> My conscience suffers under 't, and I would
> Disburden it by satisfaction.
>   (IV, iii, 90–94)

Charitably (by his definition), the father prepares to fill in for his son, siring for Castabella the children she must, like D'Amville, so naturally crave. When Castabella objects that such a union would be incest, D'Amville points to nature: Why should humans be less free than other creatures, who enjoy a license to copulate as they choose (IV, iii, 128–30)?

To one without conscience who uses nature as his precedent, all is permitted. If nature were the sum of all existence, there would be no stopping such men; but fortunately for the patient Charlemont and Castabella, an invisible world, a supernatural world, intervenes to protect them: D'Amville is destined for the extramundane damnation presaged in his name.

The invisible world of ultimate retributive justice shows its hand in a variety of ways. Rousard's impotence, for instance, is no mere accident of nature:

> Sick indeed.
> A gen'ral weakness did surprise my health
> The very day I marry'd Castabella,
> As if my sickness were a punishment

That did arrest me for some injury
I then committed.

(III, iv, 62–67)

Charlemont is preserved from murder at the hands of D'Amville's henchman, Borachio, when the pistol misfires—again, no accident, but rather divine protection of an honest man. Eventually, even D'Amville experiences the clammy touch of the invisible world. His mind begins to trouble him. He imagines, for instance, that a distant cloud is the ghost of Montferrers mounting to heaven to accuse him in a celestial court. Though he quickly reinterprets the apparition in naturalistic terms, the seed of doubt has been sown. He begins to suspect a power above nature, but the suspicion is misshapen, constantly misunderstood. When both his sons die, D'Amville urges the doctor to restore them to life with gold, the nearest thing to a divine element that his naturalism can envisage. He mistakes the power of his own greed for the power miraculously to heal.

The theme of conscience achieves its highest pitch as the play reaches its climax. D'Amville becomes obsessed with his lack of ease, stumbling onto a death's head that induces chills he cannot comprehend:

Why dost thou stare upon me? Thou are not
The skull of him I murder'd. What has thou
To do to vex my conscience?

(IV, iii, 211–13)

Shortly afterward he encounters the chaste figures of Charlemont and Castabella sleeping together in the midst of slaughter and mayhem, their heads pillowed together on a death's head, which image troubles them not at all. "Sure," cries D'Amville, "there is some other happiness within the freedom / of the conscience than my knowledge e'er attaint to" (IV, iii, 286–88).

But D'Amville's knowledge remains defective to the bitter end. With Charlemont bravely mounting the scaffold to die for killing Borachio, D'Amville requests an "anatomy" to disclose the configuration of Charlemont's body that has issued in such fortitude and ease of mind. He persists in thinking bad conscience a disease of body rather than of soul, yet the details elude him: "For all my learning I am still to seek / From whence the peace of conscience should proceed" (V, ii, 158–59).

Out of respect for his nephew's repose in the face of death, D'Amville dismisses the executioner:

Down, you shag-hair'd cur.
The instrument that strikes my nephew's blood

> Shall be as noble as his blood. I'll be
> Thy executioner myself.
>
> (V, ii, 226–29)

Entranced by the spell of like for like, D'Amville feels honor bound to give Charlemont the kind and quality of death appropriate to his social station. But a snare has been set within the invisible world. As D'Amville raises the axe, its blade miraculously crashes onto his own head. More literally than D'Amville had intended, the victim's blood is equally noble as the executioner's. Awkward stagecraft included, the scene is reminiscent of the assertion from *The Theatre of God's Jvdgements* that Christopher Marlowe's knife penetrated his skull by the power of his own hand.

D'Amville's fate hinges on the Renaissance code of honor. He believes it wrong for his nephew's noble blood to be spilled by a commoner. Under other circumstances, this insistence that nobility be granted its prerogatives might as easily issue in a challenge as in a pledge to serve as executioner. *The Atheist's Tragedy* sums itself up with the moralizing piety that "patience is the honest man's revenge" (V, ii, 278). In the contemporary parlance of dueling etiquette, an honest gentleman's patience could abide anything save to be "given the lie." This language introduces our last scrap of dialogue between Renaissance theatre and the retributive obsessions of its day. In the honor-bound ideals explored by Middleton and Rowley's *Fair Quarrel*, we reencounter the ethics of the blood feud. Its garb has changed, however, for it is dressed as courtier rather than as desert nomad.

The Bewitching Duel

In 1613 King James I issued an *Edict and Severe Censure Against Private Combats and Combatants*. Among other sanctions, it threatened prosecution for murder of anyone slaying another in a duel (p. 70).[28] If both parties left the field alive, the combatants were to be imprisoned until repentant (p. 87), banished from court for seven years, and suffered never to apply to the crown for grants and favors (p. 88). That such penalties had to be published explicitly under the king's name reflects the degree to which public sentiment favored allowing a "fair quarrel" to escape the eye of the law. In fact, James's edict is as interesting for what it presupposes about the mind of its public as for its formal sanctions against dueling. Coroner's juries, for instance, are cautioned against returning charges of involuntary manslaughter in dueling prosecutions (p. 188)—a concession that this verdict had found favor in the past.

In addition to issuing the edict, James spurred his attorney general, Sir Francis Bacon, into immediate prosecution. During the most famous of these trials, Bacon calls to mind his sovereign's words:

The King, in his last Proclamation, doth most aptly and excellently call them, *bewitching* Duells. For, if one judge of it truely, it is noe better than a sorcery that enchanteth the spirits of young men, that leave great myndes, with a false shew, *species falla;* and a kind of satanicall illusion and apparition of honour.[29]

Bacon's allusion to sorcery is more apt than perhaps he or King James realized: Staving off dishonor by fighting a duel against one who impugns your reputation shares in many features of the ancient superstitious belief in pollution.

As with pollution, the stain of dishonor is invisible. If not removed, it provokes horror in others, causing one to be ostracized. Dishonor is likewise contagious; if not repulsed, it can infect one's fellows and, especially, one's lineal descendants. Finally, if an imputation of dishonor falls on one too old or too infirm, the obligation of defense passes to a near male relative, much as in the pollution-haunted context of the blood feud. Taken together, these attributes constitute a tidy, self-reinforcing web. The incentive to remove dishonor, like the incentive to be absolved of pollution through ritual, is both personal and social. If a dishonored person wavers in his resolve to remove the stain, he will be urged to the mark by family and friends who fear dishonor by association or contagion.

All of which signifies, of course, that dishonor is more a matter of perception in others' eyes than a discernible quality of the individual. As a consequence, duels tend to escalate beyond the scope of an original grievance. Whether truly or falsely imputed, the stain of dishonor must be eradicated, appearances must be saved. Failure to appear when challenged becomes itself a mark of dishonor, a cowardice sufficient to blot one's reputation. Conversely, death in a duel capably fought is a magical vindication of both parties. The victor proves the truth of his allegation (or his refutation of an allegation), whereas the loser proves himself no coward.

The bewitchment of the duel was all the more potent thanks to historical ties to chivalry, soldiership, and aristocracy. Cowardice could be tolerated, even expected, among the lower classes, but not in those called to arms or nobly born. Though the letter of the law under both Elizabeth and James prohibited dueling, these laws were administered by gentlemen, many of whom tacitly supported the code of honor. Even so enlightened a figure as Chief Justice Sir Edward Coke believed that a properly conducted trial by combat was a means of ascertaining truth, with providence guiding the victor's hand.[30] How could mere human law presume to interfere in the affairs of providence?

Those in sympathy with the duel as a trial by combat could choose from any number of handbooks on the etiquette of dueling. A sampling of titles suggests the riches from which a well-nurtured soldier or gentleman could draw: *The Booke of Honor and Armes* (1590), *A Treatise of True Fortitude* (1594), *The Mirror of Honor* (1597), *The Courtiers Academie* (1598), and *The Dvello, or Single Combat* (1610). Most of these treatises adhere to the letter of the law, professing

mere theoretical or historical interest in the topic of honor and stressing the rarity
with which, in civilized society, a gentleman has to resort to extralegal means in
defense of honor. At the same time, under the unstated assumption that the law
would look the other way, the handbooks also instructed on the proper conduct
of a duel.

Despite certain differences in detail, these treatises espouse what may conveniently be considered a single code of honor. Two basic suppositions underlie this
code. The first is that honor is more valuable than life.[31] Accordingly, a soldier
or a gentleman ought not scruple to put his life at risk in defense of his reputation. The second supposition, based on a Christian fear of damnation in dying
for a false cause, is that a duel ought only to be fought in defense of truth.[32] This
supposition puts the professed code of honor on a collision course with the social
fiction of the stain of dishonor. One who allows a dishonorable but true aspersion
to go unchallenged is condemned to a life without reputation, but if he fights and
dies, he risks eternal torment. What is more, if he tries to articulate his grounds
for refusing the duel, he subjects himself to a taunt of making "his conscience a
cloak of cowardliness."[33] Which should prevail, rational scruple or the desire to
maintain one's reputation in the eyes of others?

Exactly this dilemma provides the meat of Middleton and Rowley's *Fair Quarrel*, probably first produced in 1616, three years after promulgation of James I's
edict.[34] The play feigns to depict its central action, a duel between Captain Ager
and the Colonel, as "fair" in the sense of "just," but, thanks to its comic ending
and a play on words (a "fair" outcome, as in a "fair" day), the play satisfies
sentiment against dueling by reversing the code of honor to affirm the value of
life above that of honor.

The action begins with Russell lamenting that his daughter, Jane, has formed
a romantic alliance with Fitzallen, a penniless relative of the Colonel's. Russell
vows to foil the match and to see to it that Jane marries a wealthy man instead.
In the meantime, friends of Captain Ager greet friends of the Colonel, daring to
equate the valor of the two men. The Colonel's friends take umbrage, wondering
how a mere captain presumes to compare himself to a colonel. When the two
principals arrive, the hotheaded Colonel rouses himself to the point of issuing a
challenge, but is mollified by Ager. Russell, anxious to prevent a battle on his
property, confiscates all swords. When, later, the Colonel becomes enraged with
Russell, he vents his spleen against Ager—an apt substitute, for, given Russell's
advanced age, the nephew would be deputized to take the field in case of a
challenge. The Colonel short-circuits this formality by addressing Ager directly,
proceeding from foul words to the most grievous of insults: "Thou'rt the son of a
whore" (I, i, 342).

By the code of honor this slander could be cause for one thing only—a challenge. To cast suspicion on Ager's paternity is to question his "natural honor,"
his birthright as a gentleman. All honor he has acquired by valor and fortitude as

a soldier (and the play makes clear that it is considerable) is forfeited if he loses his natural honor. He thus has no choice but to meet the Colonel on the field.[35]

Middleton and Rowley thicken their plot by soon throwing Ager into a fit of tender conscience. What, he wonders, if there is truth in his antagonist's words? Dare he take the field without being absolutely certain of his mother's fidelity?

> I am too full of conscience,
> Knowledge, and patience, to give justice to't;
> So careful of my eternity, which consists
> Of upright actions, that unless I knew
> It were a truth I stood for, any coward
> Might make my breast his foot-pace.
>
> (II, i, 9–14)

Pretending that the allegation has come from some "foul-mouth'd villain" whom the Colonel has offered to fight, Ager asks his mother for the truth. He assures her that he would not broach the delicate subject of his own paternity were it not that the Colonel risks perdition if the charge is true. Lady Ager strikes her son, indignant that he should doubt her. Calling it "the joyful'st blow that e'er flesh felt" (II, i, 94), Ager reveals the ruse to her, declaring himself free to fight with a clear conscience—a man not simply of honor, but of *Christian* honor. Fretful for her son's safety, Lady Ager cobbles together a ruse of her own, telling him that, alas, the allegation is true: She was once betrayed from chastity by a corrupted kinswoman.

Ager now faces the prospect of fighting against what he believes to be the truth. The irony is palpable, for his mother's lie prevents him from giving the lie to the Colonel. Moreover, he deserves his fate, for his mother has simply matched one falsehood with another. If anything, her lie is the less culpable, based as it is on a valuation exactly opposite that of the code of honor. She acts instinctively on the view that her son's life is more valuable than any degree of honor, natural or acquired.

Made scrupulous by his mother's falsehood, Ager refuses to press the quarrel. When he and the Colonel meet again in Act III, Ager tries to negotiate peace. He is in an awkward situation, neither wanting his mother's "infidelity" to be known nor daring explicitly to deny the Colonel's words. He thus shifts attention to his opponent's rashness, offering pardon if the Colonel will show repentance. This proposal infuriates the Colonel: "By fame's honor, I am wrong'd! / Do you seek for peace, and draw the quarrel larger" (III, i, 98–99)? When Ager refuses again to fight, the Colonel speaks to his sword:

> But as I put thee up, I must proclaim
> This captain here, both to his friends and mine,

> That only came to see fair valor righted,
> A base submissive coward; so I leave him.
>   (III, i, 107–10)

At this point Ager has an imputation against which he can fight in good conscience. To the surprise of everyone, he draws his sword to press a new quarrel. Technically, he should give the lie and await formal challenge, leaving the parties to retire and fight another time in a temper fit for gentlemen. Ager's friends, however, are keen to press matters. They are amazed that "coward" has stirred Ager's blood where the far worse "son of a whore" has failed, and they no doubt fear that a second respite will produce the same inexplicable change in Ager as the first. In any case, when Captain Ager and the Colonel clash swords, the Colonel receives a wound that both men interpret as a providential sign. Thus Ager: "Truth never fails her servant, sir, nor leaves him / With the day's shame upon him" (III, i, 165–66). And the Colonel:

> Oh, just heaven has found me,
> And turn'd the stings of my too hasty injuries
> Into my own blood.
>   (III, i, 174–76)

It is now the Colonel who is pricked by tender conscience, yielding up his most precious possession, the hand of his dear sister, to Captain Ager.

But before this comic epithalamion rings down the curtain on a happy ending, the code of honor comes in for one last jibe. Ager returns in triumph to his mother, only to learn of her futile deceit, which has brought about the very end (endangering her son's life) that she intended it to prevent. His reaction is two-fold. First, he is relieved at escaping a base bastard's life, devoid of natural honor. Second, he prays for the Colonel's recovery so that they can fight another duel. After all, the Colonel's injury has only disproven the charge of cowardice; the imputation of bastardy has been neither given the lie nor put to trial by combat.

Both Fredson Bowers and George Price interpret *A Fair Quarrel* as a partial vindication of the code of honor.[36] These critics support their view with a favorable appraisal of Ager's character in contrast to the Colonel's. Their point is the same as the apologists' in offering their treatises on dueling: If every gentleman were as scrupulous about truth and honor as Ager, few duels would be fought. Neither the code nor the practice of single combat is at fault. Rather, dueling gets its bad reputation from such foolish men as the Colonel, who, in the words of one contemporary, "fall out for feathers."[37] Middleton and Rowley could not, Bowers argues, have satisfied the partisans of honor among their audience with an unambiguous play along the lines of King James's edict.

The problem with this interpretation is that it blinks at the absurdity of Ager's relish to have the Colonel restored to health. If left unchecked by an appreciation that life and honor are indeed incommensurate, not in honor's but in life's favor, hewing to the code of honor produces an individual (Ager) as reckless in one way as the Colonel is in another. Only Ager's mother, who has embodied the proper valuation of life over honor throughout the play, stirs him to bury the thought of a further duel.

This reading puts honor in proper perspective without reducing it to a phantom. It also avoids viewing Middleton and Rowley as slavish adherents to the king's edict. After all, King James himself does not attempt a wholesale overthrow of the code of honor. Rather, as is often a tactic of reforming movements, the king manipulates the code to his own ends: "Wee hold the partie that prouokes him to the perill of his Honour, fortune, conscience & life, to be timourous, and base."[38] Short of being, as he fancies himself, a man of honor, the challenger proves exactly the opposite. So emphatic is this judgment that, in detailing sanctions against combatants, the king finds the charge worth repeating: "And which is heauiest of all, wee doe protest for our owne part, we shal neuer account of them but as *Cowards*."[39]

As with other concepts invoked within any given retributive web, honor awaits our interpretation. We may think that it requires us to meet in single combat; or we may, with James, think it requires us at all cost to refuse such combat. In both cases, the dictum that honor must have satisfaction drives the retributive search for a fitting evil. The important difference is that it hurts far less for the sovereign to call you a coward than to take a sword thrust to the belly.

As watchers at the theatre, of course, we have the luxury of embracing, or of ridiculing, both sides at once. Theatre allows for an unending duel of wits. Hieronomo's play-within-a-play aside, stage thrusts do not prove fatal: A dead or dishonored player is ready to repeat his performance the next day. Only an audience's lack of interest brings the curtain down for good. If either the Renaissance or our own age is anything by which to judge, themes of revenge, conscience, and honor will continue—barring another Puritan Revolt—to play before packed houses.

TEN

Punishment and Duty

In the theatre of the English Renaissance, passion and vengeance are inextricable. Whether his cause is endorsed, condemned, or consigned to an inconclusive moral limbo, the private revenger is never an object for remote, disinterested contemplation. He suffers and seeks vindication; when he finally strikes, we in the audience sympathize or feel repelled—or share in both reactions simultaneously. If we feel nothing, the dramatist has failed, for vengeance is a slender reed for challenging the intellect.

By viewing retaliation as a rogue passion underlying the quest for vindictive solace, Renaissance theatre parallels many of the retributive webs so far examined. The main problem becomes that of providing acceptable channels for expressing this fervor. In ancient Near Eastern law the channeling of revenge entails gradual state assumption of the private prerogatives of the injured party's blood relations. In Aeschylus the process requires taming the Erinyes. In Plato it is helped along by heuristic tales of ultimate justice in the afterlife. In Islam, similar tales are preached as dogmatic fact rather than speculative heuristic. Aquinas places vengeance among God's special virtues, making eternal suffering a logical corollary of blessedness. For all these cases, as for generating tension in the revenge tragedy, there is an assumption that vengeance is a primitive moral right of human beings (or of God, as the context warrants).

The philosophy of Immanuel Kant rejects this idea of retribution as the proper channeling of a primitive moral right of vengeance.[1] While Kant is the philosophical defender par excellence of a classically retributive view of legal punishment, there is for him no resemblance whatsoever between seeking revenge and achieving retributive justice. The passion for vengeance is, like any passion, the basis for a hypothetical rather than a categorical imperative. Whereas hypothetical imperatives command from inclination, from the physical desire for a certain end, categorical imperatives command absolutely, in accordance with duty. To seek revenge is to seek satisfaction for a perceived wrong; as a motive, therefore, revenge is always for Kant a violation of moral duty.

There is a second reason for Kant's utter divorce of retribution from revenge. He holds the very idea of a primitive moral right of revenge to be incoherent, for rights exist only within a civil society based on the rule of law. A primitive moral right of revenge must either precede or follow the establishing of civil society. If it precedes such founding, it is by definition something other than a right. If, on the other hand, it arises after the founding of civil society, the alleged right of revenge disrupts the universal rule of law. Revenge is always of someone against someone else for the sake of satisfaction (i.e., Kantian inclination); as such, there is nothing to block an antagonist's desire for a countersatisfaction. Kantian retribution, by contrast, is always of *the state* against someone—namely, against a violator of the criminal law. The state alone possesses both a right and, more important, a duty of retribution; and as the state is impersonal, devoid of passion, its acts cannot be described as the "channeling" of vengeance. In punishing offenders, the will of the state is holy; that is, in acting only according to duty, the state blocks all claim to satisfaction or countersatisfaction on the part of offender and victim alike.

Given its dispassionate perspective, Kantian moral philosophy seems at first blush to contradict the thesis that retributive thought is best understood as providing solace for suffering. Because Kant holds that the state, whatever the sentiments of its individual citizens, has a stern duty to punish legal offenses, it is too weak to say that the state *may* punish legal offenders; instead, it *must* punish them. Legal punishment of criminals, Kant argues, is a categorical imperative, rationally universalizable. As such, it does not share in the merely hypothetical aims of relieving the distress of victims inflamed by the desire for vengeance. Still less does it share in the aims of humiliating the offender or of communicating love via forgiveness once the debt of punishment is paid. When understood as comfort for distress of any sort, solace derives from humankind's passional nature and is for Kant as morally irrelevant as the desire for happiness or success.

This strict Kantian dichotomy between reason and passion creates a puzzle in assessing the motivational roots of morality. We know that reason commands moral action, but why we should obey its dictates is a distinct question—one that may *not* be answered by positing a desire or an inclination to do so. Reason for Kant is intrinsically self-commanding, relying on neither fear nor hope of satisfaction. The result when it comes to motivation is that human emotions have rational Kantian analogs. Kant stipulates that reason may take "practical interest" in an action without thereby declaring itself to have "pathological interest" in the outcome.[2] Thus love, for instance, can assume either a "practical" or a "pathological" guise. The former is rational in character, the latter passional. If one comforts a friend because of a prior emotional bond, the action stems from pathological love and is, strictly speaking, without moral worth. If, on the other hand, one acts from respect for the universalizability of comforting those in need, the action stems from practical love and has a moral worth beyond all price.

The thought that pathological love has a Kantian moral analog suggests that the same may be true of retributive solace; it too may have a corresponding form that is both moral and rational. Solace as relief from distress lies beyond Kantian moral bounds, but solace as imperviousness to distress does not. Kant's retributive web is woven from familiar strands of duty, conscience, honor, and respect for persons. Each of these good things, however, is to be cognized rather than relished or enjoyed. So too for the duty of legal punishment. For Kant, judicially imposed suffering is a fit object neither for relish nor revulsion. A proper comprehension of duty will disengage promptings of sympathy and antipathy so that retributive solace becomes a kind of *apatheia*—a rational sense of satisfying one's moral obligations.

Freedom and Duty

Kant minces no words in articulating his conviction that the state possesses an inflexible duty to punish criminal offenders:

> Even if a civil society were to dissolve itself by common agreement of all its members (for example, if the people inhabiting an island decided to separate and disperse themselves around the world), the last murderer remaining in prison must first be executed, so that everyone will duly receive what his actions are worth and so that the blood-guilt thereof will not be fixed on the people because they failed to insist on carrying out the punishment; for if they fail to do so, they may be regarded as accomplices in this public violation of legal justice. (*The Metaphysical Elements of Justice*, p. 102 [333])

Let us postpone scrutiny of Kant's insistence that the only appropriate legal penalty for murder is death, concentrating for the time on his view that civil society has an obligation to punish even when such generally utilitarian ends as deterrence, protection of the innocent, and the like cannot be achieved.

We begin with Kant's mention of blood guilt—a concept associated with nonrational beliefs in pollution and ritual purification. Blood guilt seems the last concept that Kant, an ethical rationalist above all else, should wish to invoke in arguing that retribution bears no relationship to revenge. We must bear in mind, however, that his objective is to express "woe to him who rummages around in the winding paths of a theory of happiness looking for some advantage to be gained by releasing the criminal from punishment or reducing the amount of it" (*Justice*, p. 100 [332]). Kant's colored language thus reflects polemical engagement with a detested rival, and need bear little argumentative weight.

This allowance made, it remains incumbent on Kant to provide a positive account of the duty to punish all legal offenders irrespective of the consequences, good or bad, in particular cases. The burden is a heavy one, for it seems to exclude humane considerations that might extend mercy or clemency to selected individuals—say, to those who express contrition for their crimes. Kant would seem to treat criminal offenders with the same merciless refusal to ameliorate suffering as Aquinas displays in tormenting the damned in hell.

Kant nevertheless insists that an axiomatic connection between crime and punishment is, despite first appearances, the only humane position available. It is the only view recognizing the inherent dignity of the individual, founded on freedom. Any alternative to axiomatic connection between crime and punishment is bound to violate the categorical imperative, especially that formulation which enjoins us to treat humanity, whether in our own person or in the person of another, as an end in itself and never solely as a means.[3] To discharge a criminal offender from a due punishment is to treat her under some category other than that of a free being, equal to the rest of humanity. The goal of freedom, though not demonstrable in itself, is deduced by Kant as a regulative idea of pure reason, the supposition of which is necessary to the very possibility of morality.[4] To suspend a due punishment thus involves civil authority in the deep inconsistency of willing a morality the essential condition of which it refuses to accept.

But why must civil authority will a morality of freedom rather than of some other ultimate human end—happiness, for instance? The Kantian answer is that a morality of some end other than freedom is a logical impossibility. Whatever other objective one prescribes as higher than freedom must by default yield to freedom whenever rational creatures struggle with the issue of how to treat one another. The only logical course, valid even for a society of devils wishing to inflict misery on each other, is to embrace equal freedom for all. Any departure from equal freedom would necessitate that some individuals could not realize the ends their freedom is intended to serve. Accordingly, any will that tries to make departure from equal freedom into a universal law of nature will defeat itself. Nature could not subsist under such an arrangement any more than it could subsist under a law that caused some particles to interact with like particles by an equal and opposite reaction, while causing other such particles to interact with an unequal but opposite reaction. What happens when wills (or particles) engage each other under such conditions? The Kantian answer is, nothing—for nature could not (logically could not) exist under such conditions.

For Kant, then, a will is not a will unless it is free for the same reason that a natural law is not a law unless there are no inexplicable (by another natural law) deviations from it. The connection is analytic. Human freedom, Kant believes, is regulated by two different sorts of law—those that command internally and those that command externally.[5] Internal law is prescribed by each agent to herself. To provide for full human freedom, the maxim of an agent's action must not only accord with duty but be undertaken *because of* duty. Motive is decisive; without stemming from the command of a proper maxim, no action, however praiseworthy in its consequences, is morally good. The second sort of law, by contrast, commands only externally—the agent's motive is irrelevant. All the state can ask is that its citizens act in conformity with positive law. Some citizens will conform for morally sound reasons (e.g., because inner duty commands it); others for morally unsound reasons (e.g., because they fear legal punishment); but the state cannot commit to detecting differences in motivation. No external observer can determine if someone else acts because of the moral law. The best such an observer can do is to determine that someone has (or has not) acted according to the law of the state.

Whether for laws that command internally or externally, Kantian freedom bears an interesting relationship to coercion. On the face of it, coercion appears to be the contradictory of freedom—where coercion exists, freedom is banished, and vice versa. But things are not so simple. A will internally "coerced" (i.e., commanded) by duty is the only one capable of positive freedom—a freedom destroyed when the will is commanded by inclination. Similarly, a will externally coerced by the rule of law possesses the maximum freedom available to it. Only when a will is commanded by a source lacking the proper moral standing is its external freedom destroyed. This latter sort of coercion is typical of crime, and is exactly the sort of coercion against which the legitimate moral coercion of the state must direct itself.[6]

For Kant there is only one kind of punishment, namely, legal punishment. The state possesses a moral monopoly on the legitimate use of coercion, and punishment is a variety of coercion directed against the errant will of the offender. Any nonlegal coercion, even if in redress of a serious breach of law and otherwise identical to the coercion that the state would impose if given the chance, is illegitimate. What distinguishes legal punishment from other uses of external coercion is that the state possesses the authority of a categorical will—one that never posits for itself hypothetical ends. The legitimacy of legal punishment is for Kant a matter of the state's maintaining proper moral standing by protecting the equal freedom of each of its citizens.

The state discharges its duty to protect freedom in two ways—positively, by promulgating the criminal law; negatively, by the retributive legal punishment of offenders against that law. The duty in question is one of *perfect* obligation. Such duties are those whose nonperformance violates someone else's right. They are, Kant maintains, logically distinct from *imperfect* duties, nonperformance of which does not violate someone else's right.[7] Both kinds of duties pass muster in according with universal law, and both are further divisible into duties to oneself and duties to others.

We shall have occasion in the concluding section to discuss duties to oneself, but for now let us concentrate on duties to others. Kant's favored example of a perfect duty to others is the obligation to keep a promise.[8] A promise (and, by extension, a legal contract) creates a right in the strongest possible way, for it can validly come into being only via the exercise of an agent's freedom. Action that violates a valid promise is action that violates a valid right. Kant's favored example of an imperfect duty to others is that of charity.[9] By failing to provide for others, even a wealthy person violates no rights. The failure to be charitable is morally reprehensible, but not in the especially deep way that the violation of a right is morally reprehensible. The major difference lies in the end served by the two cases. In that of promising, the end served is freedom, for in honoring a pledge one honors the freedom to have chosen the particular bondage that the promise represents. In the case of charity, however, the end served is happiness, which can only bind the will hypothetically. A Kantian right thus has freedom as its sole end, whereas a Kantian duty may have either freedom or happiness as its goal.

The main external condition for preserving freedom is that of human beings uniting in civil society under the rule of law. It is an individual's duty, if he happens to find himself in a state of nature, to join civil society. Others have a duty to force him to join if he refuses.[10] The duty to punish is analogous to this duty of forcing others to join civil society. Both are justified uses of coercion for the only reason that coercion can be justified—namely, as a necessary condition for maintaining freedom. The refusal to join civil society and the commission of crime are, for Kant, both manifestations of an irrational urge to destroy freedom, the very end that gives human life its intrinsic dignity.

Thus, in addition to whatever else it is, a person's crime is against himself— an attack on his own intrinsic dignity:

> Accordingly, any undeserved evil that you inflict on someone else among the people is one that you do to yourself. If you vilify him, you vilify yourself; if you steal from him, you steal from yourself; if you kill him, you kill yourself. Only the Law of retribution (*jus talionis*) can determine exactly the kind and degree of punishment. . . . All other standards fluctuate back and forth and, because extraneous considerations are mixed with them, they cannot be compatible with the principle of pure and strict legal justice. (*Justice*, p. 101 [332])

Kant's idea that unlawful activity is an attack on the intrinsic dignity of the criminal is easily overlooked, in part because this passage is followed by a gloss on a different sense in which crimes are self-inflicted. To the extent a person steals, Kant tells us, he subtracts from the security of ownership in general, including his own security of ownership. If his errant will were universalized, possession would be impossible. The only fitting punishment is to replicate for the thief exactly these conditions. He is to have nothing and, by his own powers, be able to acquire nothing. Yet he wants to live, so

> he must let the state have his labor at any kind of work it may wish to use him for (convict labor), and so he becomes a slave, either for a certain period of time or indefinitely, as the case may be. (*Justice*, p. 102 [333])

The preceding view of what it means to say that the thief steals from himself all but eclipses the complementary view that crime is an attack on the criminal's intrinsic dignity. The argument from security of possession is based on reciprocal relations among members of civil society. As such, it is strong enough to ground the duty of punishment so long as civil society persists, but it is insufficient to ground Kant's more rigorous claim that punishment is due the last convicted criminal even if civil society were to disband in the next moment. By disbanding, civil society abolishes the reciprocal equality that the criminal's errant will has threatened. Only a view that the duty of punishment is owed by the criminal to himself will justify the more rigorous claim that he must be punished under any circumstances. As we shall see in the next section, Kant provides the elements of such a view in the second part of the *Metaphysics of Morals*. In so doing, he connects human dignity to a concept of honor that exerts a tremendous, but too little appreciated, influence on his theory of punishment.

Death versus Honor

After arguing that the thief steals from himself (i.e., that he makes property, including his own, less secure), Kant infers that the murderer kills himself. Here the argument cannot be, by analogy to theft, that the murderer makes life less secure. In that case anyone (e.g., a dynamite manufacturer) who contributes to an increased risk of death might be said to deserve death. Kant must adduce other grounds for claiming capital punishment as the sole fitting penalty for deliberate homicide.

He begins by insisting on the incommensurability of the death penalty for homicide with any punishment short of death:

> There is no sameness of kind between death and remaining alive even under the most miserable conditions, and consequently there is also no equality between the crime and the retribution unless the criminal is judicially condemned and

put to death. But the death of the criminal must be kept entirely free of any
maltreatment that would make an abomination of the humanity residing in the
person suffering it. (*Justice*, p. 103 [333])

For many people, the assertion that we must respect the humanity of criminals is
the first stage in an argument against the death penalty. Why does Kant believe
that respect for humanity attaches to the mode and manner of execution rather
than to the fact of execution itself? Why is not the will of the state kept holy if, out
of reverence for life, it refuses categorically to take life? After all, Kant himself
insists on the duty to preserve life, employing it when arguing against suicide.[11]

The answer to these questions lies in expanding on Kant's assertion that there
is no sameness between the death of the victim and the continued life of the murderer. The retributive principle of like for like, Kant believes, requires a duty of
execution that the state may not shirk if its will is to remain holy. At the same
time, if this duty to preserve life were a perfect duty, then any taking of life,
even by the state, would be a violation of a right and hence, according to Kant,
immoral. Preserving life must therefore be an imperfect duty—one that is not
violated in the state's just execution of one of its citizens. Kant occupies the curi-
ous position of asserting that preserving life is an imperfect duty connected with
the hypothetical end of happiness, whereas taking life in the service of criminal
justice is a perfect duty connected with the categorical end of human freedom.
How is this position to be maintained against the thought that death is the termi-
nation of an individual's freedom no less than of her happiness? What is more, if
freedom is so important, why is not life imprisonment, rather than execution, the
retributively fitting penalty for murder? Why cannot the state fix the retributive
penalty of taking freedom (but not life) from one who commits homicide?

In pursuing these questions, we disclose a Kantian commitment to the value of
honor—a commitment nearly as emphatic as his commitment to freedom. Honor
combined with conscience is, in effect, the moral person's solace, the source of
imperviousness to desire and inclination. Kant's legal philosophy often invokes
the value of honor, but his remarks on the subject are baffling unless read in light
of his more systematic investigation of it in *The Doctrine of Virtue*. After concluding this section by pondering instances from *The Metaphysical Elements of
Justice* where Kant claims that death is less evil than dishonor, we shall follow, in
the next section, with a look at how honor is bound to conscience in the Kantian
ideal of moral personality.

Kant tells us that death is due crimes in respect of their "inner viciousness,"
a condition of will varying in degree from criminal to criminal.[12] Deliberate
homicide, for instance, is more vicious than manslaughter, and thus retributively
deserves a greater penalty. But deliberate homicide is far from the sole offense
that merits death according to Kant. Treason likewise deserves capital punish-

ment, for it pits the will of the individual against the holy will of the state, seeking to undermine the reciprocal legal rights and duties that exist only under the rule of law. In this respect treason and homicide are on a par, both constituting especially grave attacks on civil society's attempt to maintain equal freedom for all.

To support the death penalty for treason, Kant offers a reductio ad absurdum of any penalty less than death.

> Suppose that the highest court were to pronounce as follows: Each person shall have the freedom to choose between death and penal servitude. I say that a man of honor would choose death and that the knave would choose servitude. . . . The first is without doubt less deserving of punishment than the other, and so, if they are both condemned to die, they will be punished exactly in proportion (to their inner viciousness); the first will be punished mildly in terms of his kind of sensibility, and the second will be punished severely in terms of his kind of sensibility. On the other hand, if both were condemned to penal servitude, the first would be punished too severely and the second too mildly for their baseness. (*Justice*, pp. 103–4 [334])

In view of the preceding passage, I suggest that "inner viciousness" means for Kant "degree of (dis)honor." This degree is determined by the extent to which a person tolerates others' using him as a means only. "Juridical honor," Kant writes "consists in asserting one's own worth as a human being in relation to others" (*Justice*, p. 42 [236]). Usually juridical honor stands on the side of law, dictating death in cases of deliberate homicide. On occasion, however, the demands of juridical honor conflict with the categorical rules of law. Kant cites two such cases, both creating a dilemma for the rational legislator.

The first example is infanticide committed by the mother of an illegitimate child. The second is the killing of a fellow soldier in a duel. Both pose problems for Kant because the disgrace of an unwed mother or of a soldier refusing to defend his honor cannot be addressed by legislation. Further, there is a respect in which murdering an illegitimate infant or killing a soldier in a duel are acts outside the bounds of civil society. Kant says of the infant that "it has crept surreptitiously into the commonwealth (much like prohibited wares), so that its existence as well as its destruction can be ignored" (*Justice*, p. 106 [336]). As for the duel, Kant thinks that a challenge brought forward and accepted by both parties creates a miniature state of nature in which deliberate slaying falls short of homicide (*Justice*, p. 107 [336]).

The dilemma Kant sees in these two cases is as follows. Either the penal law must

> declare that the concept of honor (which is no delusion in these cases) is null and void in the eyes of the law and that these acts should be punished by death or it

must abstain from imposing the death penalty for these crimes, which merit it;
thus it must be either too cruel or too lenient. (*Justice*, p. 107 [336])

To resolve the dilemma, he embraces the horn of too much cruelty, insisting
that "the categorical imperative involved in the legal justice of punishment remains valid (that is, the unlawful killing of another person must be punished by
death)" (*Justice*, p. 107 [337]). At the same time, however, he suggests that law-
makers are to blame for promulgating bad laws. So long as it is "barbaric and
undeveloped," legislation itself

> is responsible for the fact that incentives of honor among the people do not
> accord (subjectively) with the standards that are (objectively) appropriate to their
> purpose, with the result that public legal justice as administered by the state is
> injustice from the point of view of the people. (*Justice*, p. 107 [337])

The idea that a people's subjective incentives of honor can be out of line suggests
a standard by which the degree of misalignment can be measured. A mother's
murder of an illegitimate infant and a soldier's defense of reputation in a duel
are both, *ex hypothesis,* cases where incentives of honor clash with appropriate
moral standards. For the sake of contrast, we require Kantian examples where the
subjective incentives of honor are in harmony with justice.

Such instances are not far to seek. Kant provides them in the course of discussing how to address class bias in the rule of law. Every just punishment, he
explains, rightfully hurts the sense of honor of the accused. As a one-way use
of coercion, punishment is a deliberate attack on an offender's juridical honor,
which demands that coercion be reciprocal. It is only because he has dishonored
himself that the criminal offender may have his juridical honor attacked. The
depth of Kant's concern for juridical honor shows in his insistence upon special
modes of punishment when members of a higher class offend against their social
inferiors. Contrary to the class biases of ancient Near Eastern law, Kant believes
that offenses of a superior against an inferior are properly subject to greater rather
than to lesser penalties in comparison to the commission of similar crimes against
members of one's own class. In part, this belief stems from a worry that cus-
tomary penalties do not bear sufficiently hard on the higher classes. For instance,
the nobility is untroubled by a fine that would bear hard on the lower classes.
In answer to this problem, Kant recommends punishments for the nobility (e.g.,
apology coupled with "solitary and painful confinement") that especially humble
the pride of the offender. Only thus do we ensure that "his humiliation will
compensate for the offense as like for like" (*Justice*, p. 102 [333]).

But what is likened to what in this argument? It cannot be that the dishonor
imputed to the member of the lower class is likened to the dishonor suffered by
the offender in committing the offense. If this were the case, the existence of class

distinctions would favor the interpretation of the like for like formula embodied in the *Code of Hammurabi*. A commoner possesses less honor than a patrician; hence an affront to a commoner demands a lesser punishment (a lesser hurt to the offender's sense of honor) than an affront to a patrician. Kant, though, concludes exactly the opposite: He requires a greater hurt to the offender if a member of a higher class offends against a member of a lower. So the question persists: What is likened to what in Kant's retributive prescription?

The best answer is that the degree of dishonor imputed to the offender rather than to the victim controls in such cases. The pain of punishment must be especially humiliating because a nobleman does *himself* an especially grave dishonor when he offends against his social inferior. (For the same reason, the pain of punishment is too great in prescribing imprisonment to the treasonable noble whose sense of honor compels him to prefer death. He, at least, does not compound the dishonor of treason with the dishonor of cowardice.) We thus again encounter the protean nature of the retributive like for like, for in matching punishment to the degree of (dis)honor we confront the question, Whose dishonor—that of the victim or offender? Less sophisticated applications of the formula (i.e., those focusing on degree of suffering) are not, whatever other faults they possess, subject to similar ambiguity. In matching the pain of the punishment to the pain of the crime, it is clearly the degree of the victim's suffering that fixes one end of the balance beam.

To explore in greater depth Kant's claim that the offender's degree of dishonor controls the just meting out of punishment, we must turn from *Rechtslehre* to *Tugendlehre*, from justice to virtue. We must, that is, make sense of the notion of doing a dishonor to oneself, which is in turn explicable only in light of Kant's conception of owing a perfect duty to oneself. In the process we examine Kant's view of conscience, a faculty that combines with honor to provide individuals with the solace of dutiful action.

Honor and the Juridical Conscience

Initially the concept of a perfect duty to oneself seems contradictory. Perfect duties are those whose nonperformance violates a right. In the most obvious cases (e.g., promising) the moral right violated by the nonperformance of a duty is held by someone other than the agent whose behavior is open to judgment. Rights arise within civil society to govern the external relations of one person to another. There is thus an important strain of Kantianism militating against the idea of owing a perfect duty to oneself, for in such a case the right violated by the duty's nonperformance must be held by the agent herself. But what sense can be made of an agent's violating her own right? And what kind of right is subject to disregard by the person possessing it?

To answer these questions we return to the Kantian concept of freedom. Whatever else may be true of a right that one can violate in her own person, it cannot be a legal right. It must instead be an innate (i.e., prelegal) right independent of one's entry into civil society, and the only such innate right that Kant allows is that of freedom. Since only other people can violate an agent's outer freedom, the sense at issue must be that of inner freedom. Accordingly, we may conclude that the right violated when an agent fails in performing a perfect duty to herself is the right of inner freedom.

This conclusion fits the various examples Kant gives of violations of duties to oneself. Suicide and self-mutilation, for instance, each violate the imperative of self-preservation, which is in turn founded on the idea of inner freedom. In criticizing the Stoic for believing in the permissibility of suicide, Kant writes:

> But in this very courage and strength of soul, by which he scorned death and knew of something that man can value still higher than his life, he must have found a still stronger reason not to destroy a being with so much power and authority over the strongest sensuous motives and so not to deprive himself of life. (*The Doctrine of Virtue*, p. 85 [421])

The Stoic's self-sufficiency, which he values so highly, is one of the manifestations of inner freedom. As reason is the foundation of freedom, to entertain the option of suicide is to have the inner freedom either to do it or not. Yet if one does commit suicide, one subverts the very condition that made it an option in the first place. Only by perceiving the option and refraining from it do we persist in honoring our unique rational natures.

A similar point goes for truth telling. Kant holds lying to be "the greatest violation of man's duty to himself . . . as a moral being" (*Virtue*, p. 92 [428]). Lying to others is a violation of an external perfect duty in that its maxim cannot be universalized. At the same time, telling a lie either to others or to oneself violates a perfect duty to oneself: "For dishonour (being an object of moral scorn), which accompanies it, also accompanies the liar like his shadow" (*Virtue*, p. 92 [428]). Truth telling, by contrast, honors the person in her own humanity. Fundamental to Kant's moral system is a concept of personal integrity such that, from an extreme vantage, moral harm to others is beside the point, a "mere consequence" having nothing to do with the principle of one's action. The most serious moral harm connected with any piece of wrongdoing is suffered by the offender in her own person—a doctrine that helps us fathom the stern principle of honor underlying Kant's otherwise perplexing reluctance to punish the woman who commits infanticide against her illegitimate child.

If dishonor accompanies a lie as a shadow accompanies a person, it follows that dishonor can be obscured by keeping away from the light. In essence, the person who evades her own conscience (another violation of a perfect duty to oneself) is guilty of hanging about in the shade. Kant understands conscience as a purely juridical faculty, restricted to judging and then either acquitting or condemning oneself for particular actions. Every rational agent, insists Kant, possesses an infallible conscience such that one cannot err in acquitting or condemning oneself. At best (really, at worst), one keeps to the shadows: "*Unconscientiousness* is not a lack of conscience but rather a tendency to pay no attention to its judgment" (*Virtue*, p. 61 [400]). According to this view, unconscientiousness is a variety of dishonesty—the pretense that judgment has not been rendered when in fact it has. Whatever aspect of personal integrity is violated by lying is also violated by the evasion of one's judgments against oneself.

In Kant's view self-judgment and self-condemnation, even when recognized, do not issue in self-punishment. The juridical model presumed in Kant's analysis of conscience is at home in the courtroom, not in the prison yard or atop the gallows. The accused in conscience is her own defense attorney, prosecutor, and judge. Acquittal presents no special problem, for a judgment in one's favor will likely be heeded. Self-condemnation, on the other hand, may fall on deaf ears; and it is here that personal integrity comes to the fore. Conscience is the faculty of making authoritative pronouncements based on the moral law, and to evade these pronouncements is to dishonor one's person. When issuing a negative verdict, the Kantian conscience deems one *deserving of* punishment, but—in contrast to the Aquinian conscience—imposes no penalties of its own.

There are two main reasons for Kant's adopting a purely juridical view of conscience and dispensing with the idea of an internally punitive faculty. The first (but least interesting) reason follows from his definition of punishment: "A self-chosen and self-inflicted punishment is a contradiction (because punishment must always be inflicted by another person)" (*Virtue*, p. 159 [484]). According to this definition the idea of a self-punishing conscience is incoherent. But how about a conscience that simply imposes pain, like the "worm" gnawing at the damned in the Aquinian hell? Why should not the faculty of conscience both pronounce sentence and, when the judgment is condemnatory, mete out some sort of internal hard treatment? After all, a negative judgment of conscience proclaims us to deserve suffering. Why are we not duty bound to give life to the pronouncement even if we call the pain suffered something other than a "punishment"?

At this point we may invoke Kant's second (and more interesting) reason for insisting on a purely juridical conscience. To act for the sake of pleasure or for the avoidance of pain is to act from inclination rather than from duty. If conscience worked by imposing its own pains, its pronouncements would be merely hypothetical: Do such and such or else you will suffer for it. Worse, any agent who followed such pronouncements for the sake of avoiding pain would be inherently servile, demeaning of her own person. The Kantian injunctions "Be no man's lackey.—Do not let others tread with impunity on your right" (*Virtue*, p. 99

[435]) apply as much to our inner selves as to our external relations with others. A conscience that threatened and imposed penalties would rob each person of her right to obey the moral law out of respect for it. Obedience would not be chosen for its own sake, but commanded out of a servile fear of living in reduced circumstances.

Like other key concepts in Kant's moral philosophy, the integrity of conscience is, at bottom, a rational integrity. To the extent that actions are motivated by such nonrational factors as passions and inclinations, they are either nonmoral or immoral. Thus, no person may morally punish herself; she can at best declare herself deserving of punishment at the hands of others. Even if self-punishment were not a contradictory notion, Kant offers us grounds for rejecting it. Reason commands us to honor ourselves—a charge we violate if we deliberately mete out pain to ourselves in a misguided effort to control our inclinations. Self-punishment becomes indistinguishable from self-abasement.

Honor and conscience together lead Kant's ideally rational personality toward the imperturbable solace of duty. Perfect freedom is realized in an ultimate realm of ends, rational, eternal, and unchanging.[13] Ironically, a radically different conception of freedom—the irrationalist freedom of Dostoevsky—also links self-punishment with self-abasement. Kant views self-abasement as a denial of freedom, whereas Dostoevsky views it as the ultimate expression of freedom. In Dostoevsky, the will to self-punishment is driven underground, where it lurks amidst dank webs spun from a retributive unconscious.

ELEVEN

The Retributive Unconscious

When Raskolnikov, the murderer in Dostoevsky's *Crime and Punishment*, meets his double, Svidrigaylov—the immoralist—Raskolnikov expresses disbelief in a future life. Their conversation continues:

> "And what," [Svidrigaylov] said suddenly, "if there are only spiders there, or something of the sort?"
>
> "He's mad," thought Raskolnikov.
>
> "We're always thinking of eternity as an idea that cannot be understood, something immense. But why must it be? What if, instead of all this, you suddenly find just a little room there, something like a village bath-house, grimy, and spiders in every corner, and that's all eternity is. Sometimes, you know, I can't help feeling that that's probably what it is."
>
> "But don't you ever imagine anything more comforting and more just than that?" Raskolnikov cried, unable to suppress a painful feeling.
>
> "More just?" Svidrigaylov retorted with a vague smile. "But how can you tell that that is not just? I, you know, would certainly have made it so deliberately!" [1]

Though it would be pretentious to claim that the sprawling vision of *Crime and Punishment* is summed up in a single passage, we are warranted in the more modest assertion that Svidrigaylov's version of eternity expresses a key Dostoevskian insight into human consciousness. Discontent at the injustices of life, our consciousness seeks transcendental grounds for the resolution of suffering. Belief in the conventional heaven and hell promises an end to the problem of suffering.

Anxieties over merit and desert no longer arise: There is no pleasure where there should be pain, no pain in the place of pleasure. Though the condemned in hell are miserable, visited with excruciating torments, they are not plagued by the consciousness of deserving a good thing but receiving its opposite.

In contrast to the conventional hell, Svidrigaylov's vision of eternity is a bit of cynical posing. His immoralist's contempt for humanity comes through loud and clear: Such vermin as we do not deserve a grandiose theatre of judgment. Hell is too dramatic, too spectacular. A gloomy, confined space, fetid as Raskolnikov's "coffin" of a room, is our proper destiny.[2] In Svidrigaylov's eternity, nothing is resolved—no rewards, no punishments. The vision seems on a par with Raskolnikov's skepticism about the conventional Christian afterlife, yet Raskolnikov finds Svidrigaylov's vision infinitely more abhorrent than the prospect of personal annihilation. Why?

We must not forget the spiders. Raskolnikov recoils at their inclusion in the image. Spiders! spinning out sticky, speculative webs in a vain attempt to define and configure human destiny. The fundamental horror in Svidrigaylov's vision of eternity is that consciousness persists—and with it the deepest source of human suffering. Eternal consciousness offers no prospect of escape, no hopeful distractions from our self-inflicted misery. Bodily pain is transitory, but the wounds of the mind endure.

One description of Raskolnikov by the novel's authorial voice says that "he was a skeptic, he was young, fond of abstract reasoning and, therefore, cruel" (IV, 4). This idea of abstract reasoning as a source of cruelty pervades the novel. Human consciousness too readily divorces itself from life, seeking to address injustice via abstract formulas. It is a disease, a madness, affecting us all to greater or lesser extent. Like a spider toiling away in the dark recesses of his room, Raskolnikov has spun out two abstract theories in justification of his crime. Both repudiate the retributive conscience, but by the time he confronts Svidrigaylov's vision Raskolnikov's life repudiates his theories. He is in the grips of his own fully retributive conscience, which combines the two aspects treated separately by Aquinas and Kant. As with the damned in the Aquinian hell, Raskolnikov's conscience is a source of punishment; but, as with Kant's juridical conscience, it is likewise a source of judgment. Though both processes are unconscious and unacknowledged, Raskolnikov's experience of them is sufficient to underwrite his revulsion at an eternity riddled with spiders.

Crime and Punishment is first and foremost a novel of detection, but, with the murderer known from the outset, we are left to seek a motive. The quest occupies us all: Dostoevsky, his readers, Porfiry (the examining magistrate), and—most important—Raskolnikov himself. In searching for his motive, the novel sets us simultaneously on a second quest—one outlined by a soldier as he idly contemplates murdering the despicable money-lending hag Raskolnikov himself intends for his victim: "People talk of duty and conscience. Well, I have nothing against duty or conscience, but are you quite sure we know what those words mean?" (I, 6).

The question is a good one. Raskolnikov's fondness for abstract thinking leads him to twist the concept of duty so that he fancies it an obligation, a service to humanity, to kill the useless old woman. In addition, both of his primary motives for murder rest on unsustainable theories of conscience and self-control. According to the final vision of the novel, we must look to life rather than to theory, and in life we are all (a few freaks of nature excepted) prey to the fully retributive conscience. Punitive as well as judgmental, this conscience lies beyond the reach of deliberate will.

For Dostoevsky, solace for suffering can be achieved only by capitulating to forces beyond our understanding. In exalting reason and seeking imperviousness to ordinary human emotion, Raskolnikov intensifies rather than escapes the torments of his conscience. Only by opening himself to Sonia's unconditional love does he eventually achieve a measure of repose. As in the Muslim quest for self-surrender, Dostoevskian retributive solace partakes in an impassioned yielding that is the exact opposite of Kantian consciousness of duty.

Raskolnikov's Two Motives and the Theme of Conscience

Dostoevsky's notebooks for *Crime and Punishment*, discovered in 1921, provide an illuminating glimpse into the author's struggle to reconcile Raskolnikov's motives for killing the greedy "parasite." Both novel and notebooks contain persistent references to two different motives, each spun from the cruelty inherent in Raskolnikov's fondness for abstraction. The first is derived from utilitarianism, already well known in the rest of Europe but sweeping across Russia as a new, exciting, and ameliorative social doctrine. In seeking "the happiness of all," the happiness of some selected few may justifiably be trampled in the dirt. Thus, on one plane, Raskolnikov kills the old woman because she is an impediment to the general happiness and because he, Raskolnikov, can better use her money in service to humanity.

More dramatically, however, Raskolnikov is enticed by a second motive—the prospect of proving himself a superior being. Forget happiness and the crusade to spread its blessings to all humanity. Forget the needs and wants of others—dare, like Napoleon or Muhammad, and if successful be exempt from the piddling morality of the masses. If Dostoevsky follows Jeremy Bentham in disclosing the first incentive, he anticipates Friedrich Nietzsche in disclosing the second.[3]

Only an author of genius could integrate the two motives into a single character, for their implications are radically at odds. The tension is nowhere more evident than in the different ideas of conscience associated with them. In sanctioning sacrifice of one miserable life to benefit the happiness of all, the first motive substitutes one kind of conscience for another. A murderer with a utilitarian bent does not put himself beyond conscience; rather, he redefines it. Declaring a retributive conscience irrational, he looks to a guiltless life guided by an alternative sense of right and wrong. He has done the best thing; why punish himself for something that has produced a greater balance of happiness? By contrast, the murderer who seeks to be a Napoleon or a Muhammad places himself beyond conscience. His desire is to cross an important line, seeking freedom and power in place of a few miserable scraps of contentment.

In the notebooks the duality of Raskolnikov's motivation is more pronounced than in the novel. Despairing at the vacillations in his conception of Raskolnikov's reasons for the murder, Dostoevsky reminds himself:

> After the illness, etc. It is absolutely necessary to establish the course of things firmly and clearly and to eliminate what is vague, that is, explain the whole murder one way or another, and make its character and relations clear. Only then start the second part of the novel: Clash with reality and the logical outcome in the law of nature and duty.[4]

Fortunately, the novelist proves untrue to his words. The murder is never explained in one way only. Instead, the two motives become foils clashing in Raskolnikov's consciousness. He despises himself for weakness in ever entertaining the insubstantial fantasy of using the old woman's riches to benefit others. He has no idea how much he has stolen, for in horror and revulsion, spiked by the fear of detection, he buries the loot under a stone. Such irresolution becomes a proof in Raskolnikov's eyes that he is *not* a Napoleon. He is a louse, a vermin like the vermin he sought to extinguish in the person of the old woman. He is—in his own cruel, abstract judgment—suited to eternity in a gloomy room with spiders, for he can neither steel his will nor even fix his own motives with clarity, as would the extraordinary man beyond the bounds of conscience.

Biography tells us something of Dostoevsky's personal assessment of the two abstract motives clashing in Raskolnikov's perfervid brain.[5] Following a youthful flirtation with socialism, Dostoevsky developed a passionate hatred for utilitarian thought in all its forms—moral, social, and economic. To excise our native retributive conscience and to replace it with a mental felicific calculator is, he believed, to debase and demean human nature in the worst way. Even the spiteful narrator of *Notes from Underground* is a better specimen than this, for his degradation is at least self-willed and self-inflicted. The utilitarian conscience, in Dostoevsky's judgment, sacrifices everything to externals, counseling us to forfeit our freedom in the mistaken belief that justice can be rationally calculated.

When it comes to placing oneself permanently outside the bounds of conscience, however, Dostoevsky's attitude is more equivocal. His own experience

of prison convinced him that certain "extraordinary" individuals exist. Easily the
most compelling portraits from *The House of the Dead* are those of men—for
example, Gazin and Orlov—who in truth feel no remorse for the vilest of crimes.[6]
Faced with the reality of such people, Dostoevsky ponders the mystery of their
existence. They are, he concludes, accidents of nature. They have not created
themselves by gargantuan acts of will and self-definition. Rather, they plain and
simply *are*. It is a mistake to postulate for them a hidden pattern of repentance
and self-punishment. Equally, however, it is a mistake self-consciously to imitate
them.

In keeping with his disparate attitudes toward the utilitarian man as against
the extraordinary man beyond the bounds of conscience, Dostoevsky introduces,
in the finished novel, Raskolnikov's two ostensible motives in tellingly different
ways. The utilitarian motive is one that Raskolnikov chances upon, hearing it
from the lips of others. To the extent he snatches at it, the protagonist repudiates
his other desire willfully to cross the line of morality, proving himself a Napoleon.
This second motive has deep roots in Raskolnikov's character, for it is revealed
in his own words from an article written months before the murder and published
without his knowledge. Raskolnikov's error is the dual one of thinking himself an
extraordinary man because he mistakenly believes such a person to be a product
of self-conscious striving.

Given that extraordinary individuals simply *are*, Raskolnikov's experiment
in murder constitutes a gamble. Killing the old woman cannot, as he fancies,
make him a Napoleon; it can at best only prove that he already is a Napoleon.
In the event, of course, the murder proves just the opposite—namely, that he
is a "louse," trapped in the web of his own retributive conscience. Even so,
Dostoevsky deliberately underscores the extent to which chance plays a role in
Raskolnikov's fate. Following a horrible dream of a horse beaten to death by its
cruel owner, he disavows all thought of carrying out the murder, only to stumble
upon knowledge of an exact time when the contemptible hag will be alone.

This first bit of serendipity is reinforced by a second—Raskolnikov's chance
eavesdropping as two soldiers discuss the moneylender's odious treatment of her
half-sister, Lisaveta. The soldiers toy with the idea of murdering the old woman
for the sake of the rest of suffering humanity: "Kill her, take her money, and
with its help devote yourself to the service of humanity and the good of all. . . .
One death in exchange for a hundred lives—why, it's a simple sum in arith-
metic!" (I, 6) Here is the first appeal, from outside, of the utilitarian motive to
Raskolnikov's diseased consciousness. He is struck less by the content of what
the soldiers say than by the coincidence that they should discuss the same topic
which has obsessed him for weeks: "This idle talk at a restaurant was to exert
a very great influence on him as the whole thing grew and developed. It was

as though there had really been something pre-ordained here, a kind of a *sign*" (I, 6).

Raskolnikov allows the utilitarian motive to reinforce his determination. He does not, of course, perceive the irony that the extraordinary individual would be contemptuous of any such need of reinforcement. Such a man lets his deeds suffice for their own vindication and, even if subdued by a will more powerful than his own, will never fall prey to the disease of scrutinizing his motives. He acts, literally, with animal cunning and with animal instinct: There is no dual vision, no weak, conditional "could have been" to undermine either his failure or his success. The superior man is blessed (or cursed) with an inhuman consciousness.

Yet when Raskolnikov seeks to imitate the superior man, his efforts, paltry as they may be, are self-prescribed. He does not chance upon this particular motive in a scrap of conversation. On the contrary, he is author of its ideals, giving painful birth to them during long hours of solitary brooding in his oppressive garret. Even so, when he strikes—when he actually commits the crime—he for the most part forgets the theory. All Raskolnikov remembers is a small part pertaining, not to the extraordinary, but to the merely ordinary man. He believes that the ordinary man who commits a crime will fall apart, suffering a critical breakdown of his faculties that will lead to self-betrayal. Thanks to his theoretical bent, Raskolnikov concludes that mere awareness of this danger will transform him into an extraordinary man who remains calm during the execution of deeds forbidden to others. Events, of course, prove the protagonist wrong; he completely loses control, forgetting to shut the door to the old woman's apartment, botching the robbery, and having to kill the half-sister, Lisaveta, in the course of an escape that succeeds purely by accident.

When his theory of the extraordinary man is recalled during his first meeting with Porfiry, Raskolnikov defends his ideas with the vanity of an acutely sensitive author. Porfiry misrepresents the article's thesis by generalizing it into an unqualified permission "to wade through blood" (III, 5). Raskolnikov argues that the extraordinary man may have to wade through blood, but he denies him the license to commit random murder. Rather, such a man must focus his cruelty on those who stand in his way. A Kepler or a Newton would be justified in slaying a hundred men for blocking dissemination of his discovery, though it is not progress or the welfare of others that the extraordinary man protects in thus stepping beyond the bounds of morality. He simply acts to demonstrate greatness of soul.

In the course of discussing this theory, Raskolnikov's friend, Razumikhin, is troubled by it:

> But what is really *original* about it all, and what, to my horror, does seem to be your own idea, is that you permit the shedding of blood *in accordance with the*

dictates of one's conscience and, I'm sorry to say, with such fanaticism even. . . .
But this permission to shed blood *according to the dictates of one's conscience*
is—well, I think it is more awful than any official, legal sanction to shed blood.
(III, 5)

Here is an illustration of how the ordinary language of morality fails to capture
the action of the extraordinary man. Razumikhin portrays such an individual
as refashioning his conscience to sanction what he does. In truth, however, the
extraordinary man is beyond conscience, as Raskolnikov soon makes clear:

> "Whoever has a conscience will no doubt suffer, if he realizes his mistake.
> That's his punishment—on top of penal servitude."
> "Well, and the real geniuses," Razumikhin asked, frowning, "those who
> have the right to kill, should they not suffer at all for the blood they have spilt?"
> "Why *should*? There's no question here of any permission or prohibition.
> Let him suffer, if he is sorry for his victim. Suffering and pain are always neces-
> sary for men of great sensibility and deep feeling. Really great men, it seems to
> me, must feel great sorrow on earth," he suddenly added wistfully, not in tone
> with the conversation. (III, 5)

Raskolnikov's theory separates guilt from suffering in a vain attempt to deny his
own retributive conscience—that native faculty to which only ordinary men are
slaves. The extraordinary man suffers because he is highly strung, because he can
sympathize with his victims, because suffering is unavoidable—for any and all
reasons except that he feels guilty for what he has done.

Killing a Principle and Killing Oneself

During one of his compulsive mental reviews of the murder, Raskolnikov
cries out to himself, "I didn't kill a human being—I killed a principle" (III, 6).
Given his dual thread of motivation, we may ask which principle he killed. The
answer consistent with Raskolnikov's experience of the retributive unconscious is
that he kills both the principle of murdering to benefit others and the principle of
murdering to prove himself an extraordinary being. Neither of these principles,
however, dies like the old woman—quickly, bludgeoned with a hatchet. Rather,
each dies a lingering death, a death protracted by Raskolnikov's agonized taste
for reviewing and reliving his crime.

The novel's second mention of the utilitarian motive is equally as external to
Raskolnikov as the first. In the aftermath of the murder, he listens to Luzhin—
the disagreeable suitor of his sister, Dunya—expound an economic theory of
bettering the lot of all by encouraging each person to pursue his or her own self-
interest. Growing more and more sullen, Raskolnikov at last bursts out, "Well, if

the principles you've just been advocating are pushed to their logical conclusion, you'll soon be justifying murder" (II, 5). To the other characters, the accusation is wildly excessive, a product of illness and malnourishment. Both to the reader and to himself, however, Raskolnikov's outburst contains a chilling kernel of truth. In his quest for a new meaning of duty and conscience, the utilitarian deludes himself by believing that his theory absolves him from the pangs of conscience whenever it becomes necessary to impose suffering on one who impedes the greatest happiness. This delusion overlooks the retributive conscience native to human beings (excepting, of course, nature's few extraordinary accidents). Though we cannot cognitively fix its meaning, we must act according to the dictates of the retributive conscience. The arrogance of abstract principle, of aspiring to remake or to dismiss conscience, cannot be borne by one like Raskolnikov, in whom judgment and self-punishment achieve a terrifying pitch.

The moment Raskolnikov hears the language of utilitarianism parroted back to him in the self-serving words of Luzhin, he recognizes that the principle of sacrificing the happiness of the few for the sake of the many is, and deserves to be, dead. He sees his snatching at the principle for what it is—a contemptible means of reinforcing his tremulous will. His diatribe against Luzhin is simultaneously a piece of self-accusation and a despairing loss of faith in the powers of abstraction.

If the utilitarian principle is killed when Raskolnikov hears it from the lips of Luzhin, the second principle dies in the course of Raskolnikov's confrontation with Svidrigaylov. Throughout his theorizing, Raskolnikov links the idea of the man beyond conscience to all manner of historically grand figures—to Napoleon, Newton, Kepler, Muhammad, and Solon. In misjudging his own capacities, Raskolnikov aims high. The very grandeur of his reach prolongs the death of his second principle, that of killing to prove himself an extraordinary man. On his own—ill in his room, wandering the streets in despair, or contemplating suicide—Raskolnikov is a "louse," a miserable weakling. But when he meets resistance, his pride rises, gathering strength. Twice he goes to Porfiry to confess, both times ending in a duel of wits in which parrying the magistrate's suspicion becomes a test of his extraordinary nature.

It is Svidrigaylov who ultimately undermines Raskolnikov's worship of the individual beyond conscience. There is nothing grand or imposing in Svidrigaylov, nothing of the deep suffering Raskolnikov believes that the extraordinary man must feel. Aside from his lack of conscience, Svidrigaylov is in every respect pedestrian, a drab embodiment of Hannah Arendt's idea of the banality of evil.[7] Restricted to the bounds of a narrow egotism, Svidrigaylov's "great achievements" include driving two helpless people to suicide (one is a fourteen-year-old girl whom he has violated). He escapes punishment for poisoning his wife, yet he is far from a daring Napoleon to whom "everything is permitted." Raskolnikov comes to see that his vision of the extraordinary man includes too much. Exemption from the bounds of conscience is an insufficient distinguishing mark, for otherwise ordinary souls like Svidrigaylov may achieve this dubious status while playing out an inexplicable string of luck. Superstitious in the extreme, Svidrigaylov relies on omens in place of the strong will that Raskolnikov has conceived as essential to the extraordinary man.

With the death of his two principles, we may ask what is left of Raskolnikov. His fondness for abstract reasoning has led him to unimaginable cruelty, and the question arises whether he has invested enough in his theories to die with them. "Was it the old hag I killed?" he cries to Sonia, to whom he finally confesses—"No, I killed myself, and not the old hag" (V, 4). This burst of self-pity misses the mark, for, though the notebooks show that Dostoevsky seriously considered having Raskolnikov end his own life,[8] it is left in the novel for Svidrigaylov alone to kill himself. Svidrigaylov serves as a double only to a point; some parts of Raskolnikov are thoroughly alien to him. Raskolnikov contemplates doing away with himself, but backs away at the last moment. Partly he is foiled because another desperate soul, a woman, preempts him by jumping first from the Voznessensky bridge into the black waters of the canal (II, 6). More important, however, is an unconscious sense that death is too light a punishment for what he has done. An abiding impulse toward self-punishment ultimately distinguishes Raskolnikov from Svidrigaylov. The immoralist kills himself, but not out of despair or self-hatred. Dunya's successful resistance of him exhausts Svidrigaylov's string of luck, so that suicide sets seal on a plain fact—life is void of interest. His death is neither self-punishment nor an escape from it. Were Raskolnikov to commit suicide, however, his act would be both of these, both self-punishment and escape. Such are the convolutions of the fully retributive conscience.

The Will toward Self-Punishment

On waking after his murder of the old woman and Lisaveta, Raskolnikov worries about disposing of the evidence linking him to the crime. He cuts off the cuffs of his trousers to remove bloodstains. He deposits the stolen articles into a hole under the wallpaper. Then, overcome by delirium, he curls up on his bed and falls asleep. Five minutes later he snaps awake, remembering that he has not removed from his overcoat the sling used to conceal and carry the hatchet. As he rips the sling to shreds, a thought occurs to him—"What if it is already beginning, if my punishment is already beginning?" (II, 1) The idea is confirmed when he gazes in horror at the floor to see, plainly visible, the frayed scraps of bloodstained cuff. He has not even bothered to conceal them.

In a letter to his publisher, Mikhail Katkov, outlining preliminary thoughts on *Crime and Punishment*, Dostoevsky says of his protagonist:

The feeling that he is separated and cut off from mankind, which he experienced immediately upon the completion of the crime, has tortured him. The law of justice and human nature have taken their hold. . . . The criminal himself decides to accept suffering in order to atone for his deed. . . . In my story there is, moreover, a hint of the idea that the criminal is much less daunted by the established legal punishment for a crime than lawgivers think, partly because *he himself experiences a moral need for it.*[9]

Though already a recluse, Raskolnikov finds that there is no solitude like the solitude of an unacknowledged guilty conscience.

Long before he commits murder, Raskolnikov suffers terribly. He is indeed "separated and cut off from mankind," scorning aid from those, like Razumikhin, who offer it. Raw pride leads him to starve rather than abandon his illusion of self-sufficiency. But if he is prideful, he is likewise instinctively charitable. On both occasions when he receives a bit of money, Raskolnikov gives most of it away to the pathetic Marmeladovs. Though acutely sensitive to suffering in others, he refuses to credit himself for this quality. The moment he has a chance to reflect, his abstract reason declares himself a fool for giving away his money. He conceives of needing it badly himself—true enough, but he is scornful of himself for a deeper reason. His thoughts, as opposed to his instinctive compassion, are dominated by infatuation with the extraordinary man. From the vantage of a Napoleon of the spirit, sensitivity to the suffering of others threatens to become a weakness. Raskolnikov cuts himself off from reciprocal relations because gratitude is a potential source of backsliding. If he is grateful for the assistance of others, he falls from the heights of self-sufficiency. Better to scorn aid and be done with obligation. If he accepts gratitude for aiding others, their affection becomes a trap. Better to leave money surreptitiously on the windowsill, where it will be found after he is gone. Better to upbraid and chastise himself as a fool for practicing charity in a world where suffering cannot be diminished. This intellectual repudiation of kindly reciprocity parallels his rejection of the retributive conscience. Ultimately, though, life proves stronger than intellect.

As in most of Dostoevsky's fiction, the will to suffer is a dominant motif of *Crime and Punishment*. Power and freedom are so precious to human beings that they will take on suffering as an act of radical self-assertion rather than let themselves be defined by and for the convenience of others. In the "unhealthy" or "sick" consciousness of Raskolnikov and of the narrator of *Notes from Underground*, the impulse toward suffering takes the form of self-abasement. "Generally speaking," says Svidrigaylov, "people rather enjoy being humiliated" (IV, 1). In humiliating themselves, people can only conceive that they act freely: What other motive could they have when they cannot possibly be accused of seeking gain by toadying to others? Better still, if people are humiliated by others, their suffering resounds with a cleansing cry for justice.

In perhaps the most profound and disturbing manner of any writer, Dostoevsky focuses on the problem of rendering suffering intelligible. The conscious mind struggles fruitlessly to make sense of its burden of torment, shame, and guilt. Theories spring up but prove inadequate. Insensitive souls like Luzhin abandon the unequal struggle, settling for hazy half-answers and a middling sensual life of conventional morality. Ordinary "extraordinary" souls like Svidrigaylov pass untroubled by living outside the bounds of morality, acquiescent to the gloomy belief that justice does not exist. For a sensitive soul like Raskolnikov, however, the lack of an answer is, literally, insufferable. His intellectual theories must be tested—an answer, even a negative one, must be had. Miraculously enough, through crime, an answer is given. Raskolnikov's hitherto unintelligible suffering makes sense, at least to his retributive unconscious. His crime clarifies all: Every act, every tormented thought and bit of carelessness, is a self-punishment. He is odious, a louse, he deserves to suffer. And if consciously he continues to insist that murdering the old woman was not a crime, the denial gives more punch, more vivacity, to the blows and condemnation administered by his conscience. For this reason alone, Raskolnikov's killing of the two principles must be a protracted affair. His rationalizations must live on, else redemption might come too soon—before he has suffered enough.

Sealed off from Raskolnikov's conscious mind, the fully retributive conscience works via nonrational anticipation and surprise. He constantly expects Porfiry to seal his cat-and-mouse interrogation with a clinching piece of evidence. In revisiting the scene of the crime, Raskolnikov is astonished to find that the blood has been wiped up—unacknowledged guilt leading him to anticipate that the crime will prove as indelible in the real world as in his memory. Slowly, the cumulative buffeting of anticipation and surprise masses into a need to confess. Who better for confessor than his other double, Sonia, the downtrodden daughter of the drunkard Marmeladov?

Sonia and Redemption through Suffering

During one of his meetings with Sonia, Raskolnikov says, "You, too, stepped over—you had the strength to step over—you've laid hands on yourself—destroyed a life—your own life (it's the same thing)" (IV, 4). This point of identification between the two characters is reinforced by other similarities. Sonia, too, possesses an impulsively charitable nature, selling herself into prostitution and penury for the sake of her stepmother's starving children. She is sensitive to a fault, punishing herself in conscience for acts that others would readily forgive. (She believes, for instance, that she is incorrigibly wicked for refusing to give an embroidered collar to Marmeladova [IV, 4].) Last but not least, Sonia, like Raskolnikov, is a mass of suffering.

As with Svidrigaylov to Raskolnikov, however, Sonia is a double only in certain respects. She is similar enough to Raskolnikov for attraction to grow between them, but different enough for that attraction to contain ominous dark spots. Sonia holds no theories about what she ought to do or how to reduce injustice in the world. Her reactions to suffering are instinctive; she accepts it for herself and strives to reduce it for others. She believes, also without theorizing, in a childlike and redemptive Christianity. Prostitution has degraded her body but left her soul without blemish, for she has no doubt that God will accept a plea of sin by virtue of necessity.

Redemption through suffering is articulated in many passages of *Crime and Punishment*, with both Sonia (V, 4) and Porfiry (VI, 2) urging it on and predicting it of Raskolnikov, whose embracing of redemption is postponed to the second chapter of the epilogue, where it is mentioned as "another story" rather than incorporated into the narrative. Critics dispute Dostoevsky's artistry in muddying the details of Raskolnikov's redemption.[10] Konstantin Mochulsky goes so far as to see Raskolnikov, despite the author's report to the contrary, as evidencing an entire lack of contrition—ironic proof that he really is an extraordinary man beyond all conscience.[11] This view, however, does not stand scrutiny, for it flies in the face of the final unmasking of Raskolnikov's theoretical principles during his confession to Sonia.

The stage is set for this confession by an earlier scene (IV, 4) in which Raskolnikov promises, if he visits the next day, to let Sonia know who killed Lisaveta. (The promise is conditional because Raskolnikov still wrestles against the temptation of suicide.) Immediately prior to the promise, Raskolnikov coerces Sonia into reading aloud the story of Lazarus. The scene sets up two conventional and mutually reinforcing expectations. The first is that the story of Lazarus parallels Raskolnikov's plight; he, too, is a dead man awaiting resurrection. The second is that the story of a miracle will work a miracle in Raskolnikov's heart, disposing him to accept suffering and to be redeemed by it. Dostoevsky, however, sees life far too roundly to endorse either of these expectations. In the first place, Raskolnikov does not die as a man, only as a thinker. The retributive unconscious is part and parcel of his natural life force; otherwise, like Svidrigaylov, he would kill himself. In the second place, Raskolnikov craves hearing the story of Lazarus predominantly for what its impassioned reading reveals about Sonia. He cannot believe what a child she is—that she actually believes in the miracle and hopes for a similar miracle in him. The reading of the story of Lazarus serves as prelude to Raskolnikov's confession less because it foreshadows his acceptance of redemption through suffering than because it foreshadows his conscious struggle against that possibility. Just as Raskolnikov cannot know, save in odd and unsustained moments of insight, that he is punishing himself, he cannot know that his redemption has begun.

Raskolnikov's confession consists in part of an unmasking of his two theoretical motives. He tells Sonia that he knew all along he was not a Napoleon and that he had no notion of committing murder to benefit humanity. Instead, he cries:

> I just did it; I did it for myself alone, and at that moment I did not care a damn whether I would become the benefactor of someone, or would spend the rest of my life like a spider catching them all in my web and sucking the living juices out of them. (V, 4)

The image of a spider sucking juices from its victims recalls Svidrigaylov's gloomy image of eternity. In at last disavowing the theories he has so proudly defended before Porfiry, Raskolnikov confronts the raw edge of his own egoism. Sonia instinctively follows his confession with the injunction "accept suffering and be redeemed by it—that's what you must do" (V, 4). The words have a double meaning, for if Raskolnikov had been able to accept his own suffering from the outset, he would never have murdered the old woman and Lisaveta. His consciousness struggles incessantly against an implacable, double-edged law of nature. By believing himself exempt from a retributive conscience, Raskolnikov commits the very act that opens the way for it.

Though the fully retributive conscience both punishes and judges, bringing its judgments to consciousness is far from easy. Only after much inward struggle and continuing denial can Raskolnikov bring himself to kiss the earth at a crossroads, as Sonia urges. He then goes to the police station to make public his confession. Still he vacillates. He cannot bring himself to say anything, and in the course of conversation with the assistant superintendent learns of Svidrigaylov's death. The news depresses him. The option of suicide beckons once more. Again he confronts the gloomy eternity of his consciousness, for only nature's extraordinary man has the will to foreclose or to embrace this option with clarity and resolution. Raskolnikov mutters something about having to go.

He stumbles out onto the steps of the police station and goes into the yard.

> There, close to the entrance stood Sonia, pale as death, and she looked wildly at him. He stopped before her. An agonizing expression of despair appeared on her face. She clasped her hands, too shocked to say anything. A forlorn, ghastly smile hovered over Raskolnikov's lips. He stood still for a moment, grinned, and went back to the police-station. (VI, 8)

At this crucial turning, Raskolnikov has no will of his own. He is driven in one direction by his double Svidrigaylov, in the other by his double Sonia. The living member of this pair wins out: He chooses life, and with it a public and institutional punishment that he views as irrelevant. It *must* be irrelevant, given the terrible suffering he has endured already.

Unknowingly, however, Raskolnikov takes a step toward conceding that justice is a social virtue, a matter of repairing relations rather than ensuring an abstract balance of suffering. How will he know when he has suffered enough, when his punishment matches his crime by the magic of like for like? The answer is that he will not know. The retributive conscience does not divulge its point of balance to the intellect. It is this insight that bridges the points of apparent inconsistency in the epilogue. Raskolnikov still cannot bring to light the judgment his unconscious has imposed:

> Oh, how happy he would have been if he really could have regarded himself as guilty of a crime! He would have put up with everything then, even with his shame and disgrace. But he judged himself severely, and his obdurate conscience could find no specially terrible fault in his past, except perhaps the fault of committing a simple *blunder* which could have happened to anyone. (Epilogue, 2)

This special pleading, this refusal to internalize the crime, is more than a vestige of the old Raskolnikov: It *is* the old Raskolnikov. Why, after all, should his theoretical consciousness draw any better conclusions after the fact than before it? In suffering toward redemption, the pain must be lived rather than conceptualized. The suffering must also be mediated by love—for it is love, connection to another human being, that differentiates the new Raskolnikov from the old.

Sonia comes to live near him during his prison term. He takes her for granted until she falls ill and cannot visit for a time. In missing her (and in seeing that the other prisoners miss her), Raskolnikov is able to reconcile her horror at his crime with her unconditional love for him. Reunited, they embrace in a way that adumbrates the untold story of redemption:

> They were both pale and thin; but in those sick and pale faces the dawn of a new future, of a full resurrection to a new life, was already shining. It was love that brought them back to life: the heart of one held inexhaustible sources of life for the heart of the other. (Epilogue, 2)

Those bereft of love have only justice to console them. That is the tragedy of the Raskolnikov who willfully cuts himself off from others to brood on the abstractions of suffering. Sonia, by contrast, has no illusion that justice alone is sufficient; though she speaks to Raskolnikov about her stepmother, the words apply equally to him:

> She believes there ought to be justice in everything, and she demands justice. And even if you tortured her, she wouldn't do anything that wasn't just. She

doesn't realize that it's impossible for people to be just, and she gets annoyed. Just like a child. Like a child. Oh, she is very just! (IV, 4)

Crime and Punishment is a counsel to believe in justice, but not in justice alone. If we look too passionately, too exclusively, for justice (especially for the retributive justice of doers suffering what they do), we follow Raskolnikov in becoming mesmerized by an ideal that seems right but cannot be lived.

III

Breaking the Spell

TWELVE

Retribution and Moral Theory

Part I showed that the retributive impulse has both reactive and epistemic components. Each is deeply embedded in our emotional and cognitive natures. The reactive tendency to meet hostility with hostility, aggression with aggression, lies at the root of the moralized emotions of resentment and indignation, both of which have a cognitive dimension. Neither resentment nor indignation is appropriate unless the evil to which they are directed is deliberate. Events outside the control of human agency, then, should neither be resented nor provoke indignation. They may be cause for anger or lamentation, but that is all. Further, when an evil does derive from human agency, it may be excused if accidental, involuntary, or innocently intended. All these considerations demonstrate that the correct object of resentment or indignation is the deliberate will of other human agents.[1]

In such creatures as ourselves, with long memories and powerful cognitive faculties, resentment and indignation can become long-lived states rather than mere affective flashes—particularly when the reactive tendency is reinforced by cultural beliefs that sustain a sense of grievance. Lost honor must be regained, a slight to kin is a slight to oneself, the son inherits wrongs done by or to the father—these and other such beliefs may keep resentment and indignation alive from youth into old age, from one generation into the next. Though cultural norms and institutions speak with mixed voices, many either approve the demand for vindictive satisfaction or view it as inevitable. Our metaphors suggest ties to natural phenomena: Resentment is said to simmer and boil over, to build pressure and explode.

So the reactive tendency requires limitation. The doer must suffer, but only to the extent he has caused suffering in the first place. Anything more will evoke further resentment and indignation. History is littered with examples of avengers who took more than their measure only to be set upon in their turn. The convenient idea—the epistemic component of retribution—is that excess would not give way to excess if only each response were measured in a particular way. If like could be returned for like in every case of evil deliberately inflicted on another, all would be well.

We are powerfully disposed toward the preceding ideal, both biologically and culturally. Vague and protean, the like for like formula underlies our ideas both of moralized retaliation and of causal connection. Despite withering under serious analytic scrutiny, the formula persists. In seeking solace for suffering, the more we are besieged by complexities and exceptions, the more we long for simple solutions. Demands for plain justice have much in common with demands that nature conform to the outlines of sympathetic magic. To ask why raw retributivism appeals in an age of complex, rule-laden institutional punishment is illuminated by asking why healing crystals and astrology appeal in an age of scientific explanations outstripping the capacities of the average citizen. Both responses are cries of frustration, pleas to order things according to a familiar, solacing pattern.

Part II provides ample reason to be skeptical of the quest for retributive solace. Whether we seek patient resignation in metaphysical belief, vindictive solace in the suffering of those who have harmed us, conscientious repose in the security of our own morality, or the solace of duty as we deliberately impose suffering on criminal offenders, we must guard against becoming too comfortable, too self-assured. The lessons of Part II are like stages in the education of Henry Adams: failures, but failures useful in overcoming the pretensions of reason. In the end, we must dispense with the idea that there is some fixed measure, some exact quantum of pain, for requiting every evil. The spell of like for like must be broken.

Demonstrating this thesis begins with analytic recapitulation of Part II, which suggests that no single retributive web is suited to all conditions and circumstances of humanity. Whatever our beliefs about the just requiting of moral fault, our practices are based on specific cultural influences. Each of us is born into a society in which institutions of punishment are hedged with ritual and nonrational commitment.[2] Some of our deepest intuitions about justice have historically contingent explanations. The search for a painless means of imposing the death penalty, for instance, reflects a sensitivity rooted in the successful banishment of physical pain from much of modern life, especially the practice of medicine.[3]

Yet we are discontent at the thought of contingent motives for our support of penal practice. Philosophical reason beckons with the idea that somewhere, deep down, lies the bedrock of just requital. If only we think long and hard enough, we will impose upon the diversity of retributive webs a timeless standard derived from timeless moral precept. From a rational point of view, retributive webs are messy and dissatisfying, replete with undefended assumptions and ad hoc exceptions. Misunderstanding the failures of Part II may tempt us to reimpose the standard of like for like on the one hand, or to concede everything to a purely utilitarian view of punishment on the other. The burden of Part III is to argue for a middle way—for a permissive retributivism free from the spell of like for like yet superior to utilitarianism.[4]

The present chapter follows its review of the lessons of Part II by examining what is meant by justifying legal punishment. One particular and widespread conception of justification is that derived from Kant—namely, that we are justified in legally punishing another only if we have a moral duty to do so. The duty in question is first order, that is, a duty derived from a moral theory conceived to be complete, consistent, and determinate. According to this conception, all moral dilemmas are in principle resolvable; the morally problematic has no place in reflective moral judgment. The chapter concludes by rejecting this conception of moral theory in favor of one that takes moral dilemmas to be ineradicable, as much a part of reflective moral judgment as of conflicting gut-level moral intuitions. Adopting this alternative view of moral theory places legal punishment in a different category of response than a duty-bound justification allows. As authorized response to wrongdoing, legal punishment is at best morally permitted rather than morally justified.

Chapter Thirteen—"Permitting Legal Punishment"—pursues instructive differences between the logics of permission and of justification in answering questions about morally authorized response to moral wrong. Every punishment is, in part, a vindictive reaction, and, if our question is, What morally authorizes vindictive reaction? we can answer by pondering the need for integrity in reciprocal human relations. As a vindictive reaction, punishment is permissible for the same reason that the retributive practices of censure and criticism are permissible. Reforming punishment by getting rid of blame and stigma would simultaneously undermine the meaning of praise and reward.

This said, the most important aspect of legal punishment remains to be considered. Insofar as the qualification means anything, legal punishment involves deliberate infliction of suffering (i.e., "hard treatment") beyond the suffering occasioned by stigma and censure. If stigma and censure were somehow sufficient, there would be no case for fining offenders, imprisoning them, or putting them to death. When we modify our original question to ask, What morally authorizes vindictive reaction beyond the suffering of censure and stigma? we enter a realm where classically retributive answers—those remaining under the spell of like for like—are insufficient. So too are classically utilitarian answers. At the same time, however, this lack of an "answer" proves bothersome only if what we seek is a duty-bound justification of legal punishment. If our aim, as it should be, is the more modest goal of demonstrating that legal punishment is morally permissible, we are required only to refute the charge that suffering beyond the suffering of censure and stigma is morally impermissible. We do so by arguing that legal punishment is permitted, first, out of considerations of fairness based on desert and, second, because it is a unique and irreplaceable means of communicating the seriousness of certain categories of moral offense.

The view that emerges in Chapter Fourteen—"Legal Punishment and Moral Standing"—locates legal punishment in relation to other permissible kinds of hard treatment, both deserved and nondeserved. The emphasis on permissibility underscores that, though the state may legitimately inflict suffering beyond that of censure and stigma, it must be ever mindful of its own moral standing. The state's authority can be undermined by punishing either too harshly or too leniently according to the plurality of nonretributive moral values embodied in whatever retributive web commands the assent of its citizens. Though moral theory has a useful place in reforming penal practice, it cannot provide a timeless measure of duty to solace us in superintending and administering institutional punishment. We will always be plagued by uncertainty about the proper kind and degree of legal punishment. The exercise of likening offense to punishment is to justice as the exercise of playing scales is to performing a fully fledged work of musical art. We cannot improve musically without mastery of such routine elements as scales, but we must not mistake these elements for the final product. Similarly, calls to liken offense to punishment (which will always be calls to liken it in one certain respect at the expense of others) may sharpen our thinking or point to abuses, but the final product—the proportion a given social order mandates between crimes and their requital—will never coincide with even the bravest of ex post facto rational reconstructions.

In thinking about retributive justice, then, impartiality must not be mistaken for proportionality: We treat like cases alike in criminal justice because we have a second-order duty to administer fairly—the same duty that constrains administration of every government program from welfare to criminal justice. Only by observing ethical constraints on their behavior can government officials maintain the moral standing requisite for discharging their responsibilities. Far from being determined by the rational "fit" between offense and punishment, the constraints—the canons of permissible hard treatment—binding prison officials are cultural products that overwhelm analysis. In deference to its symbolic, communicative, and expressive force, we may well continue to use the rhetoric of like for like in discussing "just deserts," but we should, following the lessons of the historical portion of this book, guard against its multiple seductions.

Doubts about the Quest for Solace

The diverse retributive webs of Part II underwrite a tragic thesis: We are condemned, like Sisyphus, to a perpetual, self-defeating labor. In pursuing solace for deliberate suffering, we end in disappointment. Retributive patterns of thought maintain their characteristic shape and disposition as much by a tension of opposites as by a logical interconnection of elements. Whatever else we might expect, we must not expect simple answers when pondering what justice demands. Our lessons come in the guise of various challenges to the quest for solace—challenges that we must heed in any final account of the relationship between moral deliberation and institutionalized criminal punishment.

Take first the quest for metaphysical solace. Though the patient resignation of awaiting retributive vindication, whether within a self-regulating cosmos or by edict of a personal God, is innocent enough, problems lie less in the desire for such solace than in the multiplicity of recommendations for achieving it. We have ample reason for skepticism in contemplating the contending leaps of faith required to embrace one set of metaphysical assumptions rather than another. Do we accept the retributivism of the Torah, of its apologetic Talmudic commentators, of the Christian God, or of Islam? Even if such questions do not arise for persons born and raised within a single tradition, we need only observe that debates within each such tradition may be as fierce and as far beyond resolution as debates between traditions. Is the Christian hell a portion of divine revelation or a poetic embellishment of commonsense warning and admonition? If the former, is it a place of mere privation, purgatorial suffering, or eternal torment? If the latter, may we not dispense with the poetic in favor of the commonsensical?

Details blur even further when we scrutinize the metaphors in which metaphysical solace is couched. Compensation is due, the debt of punishment is owed, the Lord will repay . . . but as we have seen the economic metaphor is ambiguous. Does restitution (e.g., slave for slave) satisfy, or must suffering serve as the sole acceptable currency? If the latter, is suffering a currency paid to the sufferer or one owed to a creditor? And how can any debt be infinite in extent without exploding the metaphor beyond all usefulness?

Finally, do we embrace a hydraulic or a homeostatic metaphysics—or do we subsume the first under the second? Is our picture that of requiting a discrete wrong (erasing it, perhaps, or knocking it back into place by an equal but opposite reaction), of repairing a hole in fabric, or of achieving a new and pleasing balance among elements?

History shows that human beings may derive metaphysical solace from any of these diverse metaphors and conceptions of impending vindication. At the same time, analysis calls them into question, reinforcing the conclusion of Part I that such patterns are appealing, not because they depict anything about nature or the cosmos writ large, but because they are projections from our biological makeup. Interpreted according to one or another of the moral equivalents supposed to give it content, the like for like formula collapses from within, a victim of the same vague and protean nature that gives it such appeal. When invoked to limit the reactive component of retribution, like for like becomes anybody's game. Which equivalence do we seek? Which is morally relevant: the victim's degree of suffering (as in the "literal" *lex talionis*), the social status of the person injured (as in the *Code of Hammurabi*), the social status of the person offended when he or she differs from the person injured (as in Aquinas's idea of sinning against God's eternal personality), the gravity of the right invaded (as in Kant's conception of categorical duty), and so on? Each of these conceptions of moral likeness has its time-honored defenders, yet each is inconsistent with its rivals.

Despite inadequacy from a rational point of view, like for like provides the warp for cultural reinforcement of *Homo sapiens*'s weak natural inhibition against intraspecies violence. One basis, of course, for the relative weakness of this inhibition is the strength of our desire for vindictive solace. We want positively and palpably to see those who have wronged us suffer in a manner commensurate with our sense of the gravity of the offense. Historically, the quest for this kind of solace underlies the practice (in both ancient Near Eastern and ancient Greek law) of assigning prosecution and punishment of offenders to relatives of the slain or injured. Though arguably a source of stable retributive order within the confines of tribal organization (e.g., in the blood feud cooled by infrequent contact among rival groups), giving primacy to vindictive solace within larger and more complex units of civilization creates intractable problems. Self-help and vigilantism provide only fleeting solace as opportunities for retaliation multiply.

Thus emerge strategies for and arguments over appropriate channeling of vindictive passion. The Erinyes are tamed to sit, albeit fiercely, beneath the Areopagus. The grievance of offending against the state takes primacy over inflicting harm on any of its individual citizens. Theatre is alternately praised as an imaginative catharsis for revenge and castigated for keeping revenge alive in the hearts and minds of theatregoers. The blood feud, infused with the high-mindedness of death before dishonor, is transmuted into the code of honor and its institutional accomplice, the duel. Dueling, in fact, so successfully sublimates vindictive passion that we hardly recognize it. Because the duelist seeks first and foremost to vindicate his honor, proof that his adversary is a coward serves equally with injuring him or fighting him to the death. What is from one perspective a mitigation (sparing life) may be from another perspective an ample satisfaction (the life spared is worthless, stained with dishonor). Furthermore, if the tactics of King James I and Sir Francis Bacon are any indication, banishing the duel by force of law and moral persuasion requires reinterpreting rather than abandoning the code of honor. Duelists are labeled cowards, given the lie, and challenged to repulse the allegation by foreswearing single combat.

This last point may be generalized into an important insight about retributive webs and their placement in specific social and cultural contexts. Under pressure from reformers, retributive institutions change over time. Like generals fighting the last battles of an old war, reformers find it convenient to embrace certain doctrines from an inherited retributive web. The past is replete with allegiances— some of them rational, some not. Reformers work with the language and the concepts they are given, leading them to depict the new order partially in the rhetoric of the old. Time and again the promise recurs to wipe vindictiveness from the web of civilized belief and practice, but time and again it is smuggled unseen and unappreciated into what men and women newly fashion as morally acceptable in administering criminal justice. Time alone informs us of our blasted hopes, revealing hitherto undisclosed vindictive elements in our innovations for dealing with those who do injury or cause offense. Following Plato, we may strive to "cure" rather than to "punish" offenders—all the while innocently supposing that pain is essential to achieving our aim.

One lesson, then, is that however much retributive passion may embarrass our rational reconstructions of morality, we must not overlook it in designing institutions of criminal justice.[5] Shunning the worst manifestations of vindictive solace (as in exact retaliation unmediated by judicial authority) does not commit us to shunning all its manifestations. On the contrary, to the extent the conclusions of Part I are correct, cultures work by sanctioning some forms of vindictive solace and disapproving of others. In some uses of moral theory in authorizing legal punishment, we side with Dostoevsky to stress the nonrational factors pervading a given society's conception of just deserts.

Mention of Dostoevsky suggests a transition from vindictive solace to the solace of self-control. Here, too, we have ample grounds for skepticism. A conscience regulated by internalized forces of guilt and shame may be indispensable to civilized life, but it is also fraught with difficulty. We may supplement our doubts about the metaphysical underpinnings of vindictive solace by questioning analogous metaphysical underpinnings of guilt and shame. The image, for instance, of the atheist as psychopath, a person inevitably devoid of conscience, may appeal to the shallow moralist and the unimaginative dramatist, but otherwise is not to be heeded. The idea in which this image is grounded—that morality cannot exist without ultimate providential sanction—lacks all foundation in human experience.[6] One dram of present and palpable penal suffering has always had more deterrent value than an infinity of portended but deferable penal suffering.

Valuable as it is, conscientious self-control stands ever in need of external corroboration. Morbid forms of the fully retributive conscience may lead one person to chastise herself for an offense inconceivable to others (as, for instance, when a member of a strict religious sect commits the "sin" of dancing). The standards of righteousness, honor, and self-esteem prescribed by the retributive conscience are derived in part from celebrated cultural ideals. Some people may aspire to imitate schematic lives of the saints—all precept and no passion.[7] Even when their actions are above reproach, such persons may judge themselves harshly for simply harboring illicit desires. The saints, they mistakenly believe, must have been as pure in thought as in deed.

An individual retributive conscience may swing from excess to deficiency, or lodge permanently near one pole or the other. It may also stabilize near the mean, producing rare and happy persons who feel no urge to dispense evil against those who do them injury. Though praiseworthy, such individuals have little effect on the unmerited suffering of others; they are at once an inspiration and an irrelevance. Their example most inspires those who are most like them, and therefore least in need of correction. Persons committed to the deliberate infliction of suffering—whether for gain, malice, sadistic pleasure, or the pursuit of justice—can no more be deflected by conscientious example than a hurled plastic explosive can be deflected by a magnetic field.

Like the other varieties of retributive solace, a peaceable conscience is good or bad depending on its constitution. One who is placid but unreflective, shying from self-judgment, can hardly be ranked with one who earns ease of conscience through intense engagement with and perceptive forgiveness of other people. Nor should we think that conscientious solace, actively achieved, is incontrovertibly a good. If the standards by which a person judges himself and others are too restrictive, the result is haughtiness rather than ethical example. Certain people maintain falsely high-toned impressions of themselves by castigating everyone else for falling short of some narrow-minded ideal, a gain for sanctimony but a loss for moral persuasion.

Though we could advance our study of retributive webs by elaborating further on metaphysical solace, vindictive solace, or the solace of self-control, we henceforth restrict our attention to the solace of duty. It bears most directly on the moral evaluation of legal punishment, for we like to think of ourselves and our government officials as wholly exculpated in the administration of retributive suffering. Positing a first-order moral duty of inflicting legal punishment aids in overcoming the natural inclination to sympathize and commiserate with those who suffer. The extended argument of the present and remaining chapters is that we should beware of exculpatory solace in administering criminal justice in the same measure as we should beware of other kinds of retributive solace. The inclination to sympathize with those who suffer, even if they happen to undergo a just punishment, should not be deflected by the solacing thought that we are only doing our duty. Belief in a first-order moral duty legally to punish may foster the arrogant assumption that the punisher can do no wrong. By contrast, the correct view that legal punishment is merely permitted—a necessary evil—encourages the healthy reflection that permissible hard treatment shades all too easily into impermissibility.

Legal Punishment and Moral Justification

Philosophers are fond of posing as a problem something called "the justification of legal punishment"; yet, when we probe the meaning of this phrase, we confront a bewildering array of interpretations. One source of perplexity lies in settling on a definition of "punishment," another in settling on a characterization of "justification." Sometimes "punishment" connotes any kind of hard treatment; at other times hard treatment imposed for the sake of a perceived moral fault in an offender; and at still other times hard treatment imposed because one has violated a legal rule. Even ostensibly neutral definitions of punishment may impinge on "justification" in subtle but important ways.[8] For instance, it is one thing to justify punishment as an evil imposed for alleged moral fault, another to justify punishment understood as an evil imposed for a violation of legal rules.

Recognizing that definition and (as I shall henceforth prefer) "authorization" of legal punishment go hand in hand, I shall here stipulate a definition whose merits will unfold as the argument against a duty-bound logic of justification develops. By "legal punishment," then, I mean any hard treatment exceeding mere censure or social stigma imposed on an offender for an offense against legal rules. Though such a person may be said to suffer from the censure or stigma associated with a guilty verdict, if this is *all* he or she suffers (as in a suspended sentence), then there is, by this definition, no legal punishment. Though censure and stigma are retributive in nature, the issue of morally authorizing these reactions is importantly different from the issue of authorizing legal punishment. Any sort of moral fault may be grounds for censure or stigma, but not all moral fault is grounds for imposition of additional hard treatment. Conversely, violation of legal rules may fail to involve moral fault (as in offenses of strict liability or offenses perpetrated in conscientious objection to an odious law), but even in the absence of such fault there may still be moral grounds for imposing legal punishment.

By focusing on "something extra" (e.g., a fine, flogging, imprisonment, or death) imposed in addition to censure and stigma, we capture the institutional nature of legal punishment. Punishment itself may be an activity,[9] but any *legal* punishment worthy of the name is constrained by rules, guidelines, and administrative procedures. One group of people is authorized to inflict hard treatment on another, but they may not do so at their unbounded discretion or without checks on their behavior. When it comes to authorizing legal punishment, the relationship between persons punished and those who administer punishment must be kept ever in the foreground. Our moral authorizations may differ depending on their addressee. If we wish to persuade the person punished of the rightness of our act, we may construct an argument which emphasizes that he ought rationally to consent to punishment even if he fails actually to consent. If, by contrast, the one who punishes is our addressee, we may emphasize a moral duty to protect the public—a duty that may apply in lieu of or in conjunction with the resolve to administer hard treatment according to what the offender is conceived retributively to deserve.

But why "authorization" rather than "justification"? What's in a word? The answer lies in a synopsis of the tie between justification and a conception of moral theory that is too rigorous and formalistic to pass scrutiny.

The concept of justification is at home in two main spheres. The first is that of epistemology and philosophy of science, where philosophers speak of rationally justifying beliefs, scientific laws, and the like. The second sphere is that of the speech act, where philosophers talk of justification as rebutting a charge against one's conduct. In both spheres the idea of *explanation* is central, as is the idea of a *defense* against some kind of challenge. One justifies a scientific law against skeptical charges of inadequacy, incompleteness, and the like, whereas one justifies conduct against charges of immorality. Nonetheless, providing a warrant for holding a belief is vitally different from providing a warrant for conduct. A person who holds the contrary of a justified belief after having the evidence explained is quite simply irrational. There is no alternative way of describing his persistence. If, on the other hand, a person continues to act immorally even in the face of justified challenges to his conduct, the question of irrationality is raised but not answered. Our subject may be irrational *or* he may be acting according to different moral precepts than the ones invoked to challenge him.

Some conceptions of moral theory attempt to assimilate moral to epistemological justification by providing unambiguous criteria of duty. Conduct falls into three classes: morally right, morally wrong, and morally indifferent. One is justified if her conduct is morally right; unjustified if it is morally wrong; and neither justified nor unjustified if the conduct is morally indifferent. If we ask for a test of what is morally right, we are told that it is prescribed by the concept of duty. One has a duty, as with Kant, to act always in accordance with the categorical imperative or, as with John Stuart Mill, to produce the greatest happiness summed indifferently across all individuals affected by one's act.

Such powerful conceptions of moral duty make the logic of justification gratifyingly easy to apply, at least in principle. A justification becomes a moral trump. If conduct is challenged, one simply shows that he acted in accordance with duty; what appeared wrong was, at bottom, right, and no more need be said. In the famous parlance of J. L. Austin, moral justifications are distinct from excuses in exactly this measure. Justifications deny directly and successfully that the conduct was wrong; excuses concede that the conduct was wrong but plead extenuation, giving reasons why the wrong thing was, in this instance, an understandable and perhaps forgivable thing to have done.[10]

If the preceding picture of moral justification is to command assent, the moral theory on which it rests must be, in principle, complete, consistent, and determinate. Conflicts of duty must be resolvable by classifying one duty as higher than its rivals. Accordingly, a person is only justified if her conduct accords with this highest duty. If she acts on a lower duty (say, running an errand for a friend during an hour she has promised to devote to charity), she may have an excuse—even a good excuse—but not a justification. She is justified only when her highest duty is fulfilled.

The two leading competitors in the philosophy of punishment, classical retributivism and classical utilitarianism, share this stern view of the nature of moral justification. The main versions of both theories subscribe to the tenet of optimal duty, along with the allied doctrine that moral theory is complete, consistent, and determinate. The retributivist maintains that the dutiful response to wrong is to liken legal punishment to offense; the utilitarian, by contrast, holds that the dutiful response to wrong is to choose that response which provides the most favorable balance of good consequences over bad. In some cases, the optimal utilitarian response will be legal punishment; in other cases not. For both retributivist and utilitarian, however, the severe logic of justification applies: Specific instances of legal punishment are either morally justified or not. There is no middle ground.

To the extent retributivism and utilitarianism each subscribe to the stern doctrine of moral justification, each gravitates toward value monism. That is to say, one value is held to surpass all others in adjudicating disputes over moral conduct. For the retributivist, the value of meeting evil with its morally measured likeness becomes the ultimate criterion of judgment. For the utilitarian, the value of pleasure trumps all others. In neither case is there an answer to the question, What justifies meeting evil with its like? or to the question, What justifies pursuing the greatest sum of pleasure? Since retributive redress, in the one case, and pleasure, in the other, are the ultimate values invoked in justifying moral conduct toward wrongdoers, their pursuit is axiomatic. Meeting evil with its like and maximizing pleasure are first principles that can be used to justify, but can—as a matter of logic—never *be* justified. Asking to justify them is like asking to prove premises in a logical deduction by means of the deduction itself.

Space does not permit further excursion into the relationship between value monism and the logic of justification. Suffice it to say that value monism—insistence that one ultimate value trumps all others—is one means of rendering moral theory complete, consistent, and determinate.[11] By adjudicating conflicts, the ultimate monistic value of a moral system renders its justification decisive: There is, in principle, a final justification of conduct exactly as there is, in principle, a decisive justification for rational belief.

In seeking solace for suffering, the preceding picture of moral justification has its attractions. Challenges to our conduct are unsettling, leading us to desire the strongest vindication possible. In cases of deliberately visiting evil on others, the problem is particularly acute. We must explain our conduct both to ourselves and to the person who will suffer from it. To believe that our action accords with an unequivocal moral duty is to exculpate ourselves in the strongest possible way. Both addressees of the justification (the one punished and the one who punishes) must accede to the argument, if valid, that legal punishment is a first-order moral duty. Moral theory becomes an idealized grid of truth. When compared to this grid, our conduct either accords or fails to accord with it. If found wanting, we must seek excuse or forgiveness while promising to reform; but if found to be right, we enjoy an unassailable repose. If someone protests against our conduct, so much the worse for him: We are, after all, *only doing our duty*.

The image of a grid of moral truth is a product of the philosopher's tendency to prize logic above all else. The grid is an artifact of reason, its spaces regular and predictable, like the mesh of a filter manufactured to exacting tolerances. As such, the image clashes with that of a retributive web, which is opportunistic, spun to accommodate the vagaries of its environment rather than constructed to suit a rational prototype. Not surprisingly, then, devotees of the study of retributive webs must find an alternative to the stern logic of justification—raising, in the process, disquieting doubts about the solace of duty in administering penalties under law.

Legal Punishment and the Logic of Permission

Moral theory is and should be a body of serious reflection about the standards of human conduct. It need not, however (in concert with the stern justificatory view) be a body of thought that is complete, consistent, and determinate, rendering an unambiguous answer to every case presented to it. Rather, the body of serious reflective judgments constituting moral theory may well contain points of indeterminacy. On controversial issues, then, not only may our emotional promptings and gut-level intuitions differ, but so also may our mature, considered verdicts of right and wrong. Acknowledging ineradicable differences in fundamental moral precepts requires us to abandon the tidy idea of a grid of truth for measuring and declaring conduct to be either moral, immoral, or morally indifferent. We must instead think of conduct (and the precepts for guiding it) as falling into four categories: morally right, morally wrong, morally indifferent, and morally problematic.

Moral conflict and disagreement are of course common at the level of conduct. Prior to mature and impartial reflection, human beings tend to favor their own selfish interests over the recommendations of morality. On reflection, however, most of us agree to the outlines of a morality that, if followed, will preclude most conflicts. If all fundamental moral values were commensurable, perhaps our considered moral judgments could be rendered consistent, as in Kant's doctrine of a rational realm of ends. To be faithful to experience, however, we must allow for irresolvable conflicts in considered moral judgments. Taken together, the historical studies of Part II constitute an argument for Isaiah Berlin's thesis of the radical incommensurability of any robust set of fundamental human values.[12] Consistency and completeness are logically possible only for a relatively spartan assortment of values. Once the pluralism characteristic of culturally induced human desires and aspirations is unloosed, we find that conflicts and dilemmas rise to the level of mature and impartial judgment.[13]

Take as a first example of indeterminacy in mature moral reflection the grievous split among U.S. citizens over the morality of elective abortion. The familiar arguments for each faction tend to presuppose a duty-bound logic of justification. One side insists that abortion is an inherent moral evil, always unjustified as a violation of the duty to preserve life; the other claims that abortion is morally justified (at least in certain instances) and not a violation of moral duty. Individuals differ at an emotive level, yet moving to the plane of unimpassioned moral judgment settles nothing. Even after applying all the tricks of the moral trade— exchanging viewpoints with one's opponent, walking a mile in his moccasins, and so on—the conflict persists. Abortion is a critical practical dilemma precisely because it is a critical theoretical dilemma, pitting the value of life against the value of autonomy.

So too with the dilemma of assisted suicide of the terminally ill. A powerful argument emphasizing the value of autonomy and the aim of alleviating suffering can be made for morally authorizing loved ones to help a principal who wishes to die but is physically incapable of suicide. At the same time, arguments to the contrary (emphasizing the sanctity of life and the dangers of legally tolerating one who acts with deliberate intent to cause another's death) are equally compelling. The happy view that we can resolve our dilemma at the level of reflective deliberation pans out only if we select principles based on one set of fundamental moral values rather than another. As rational criteria fail us when we confront a choice between respecting autonomy and preserving the sanctity of life, the most honest measure is to incorporate certain dilemmas into the body of reflective moral thought.

Once the ethically problematic rises to the level of reflective deliberation, the traditional logic of moral justification must be discarded. When bound to the concept of duty, justification applies to conduct in a mutually exclusive fashion: An act or practice either is justified or it is not. Furthermore, there is no degree in justified acts—so, strictly speaking, no role for the expression "more or less justified." Like perfection, justification is an optimal concept, not admitting of degree. One may be more or less unjustified (or imperfect), but once the top of the scale is achieved, discrete stages no longer exist.

Justification, then, presupposes a clear and uncontroversial highest duty. Lacking this, we cannot trump challenges against our conduct. We may still argue and remonstrate, still plead our case, but we can no longer claim duty as our guide. To substitute for the stern logic of justification, we need a more flexible logic—that of permissibility.

In the view of moral theory as complete, consistent, and determinate, permissions are restricted to morally indifferent choices. One is permitted to do that which is neither prescribed nor forbidden by moral duty. There is thus little of consequence that hinges on the logic of permissibility. By contrast, in a view of moral theory that includes the morally problematic at the level of reflective moral judgment, the concept of permissibility has much broader application. To declare conduct or institutional practice morally permissible is to give it tentative sanction, short of saying that it is prescribed by duty. To declare conduct or practice impermissible is similarly tentative, stopping short of declaring a violation of moral duty.

The logic of permission is especially at home in morally evaluating institutions and practices where the canons of duty remain controversial, and yet a choice must still be made, a policy set. We need a logic that gives voice to our uncertainty, keeping us from enjoying the self-congratulatory sense of "only doing our duty" in cases where we may, in fact, be mistaken. For such instances a logic of permission commends itself over a logic of justification. The change in language declares that our actions may or may not be a matter of duty—that it perhaps surpasses human wisdom to know what our duty is in difficult cases of this kind. Unlike justification, permission allows for degree. After due reflection and consideration of the interests involved, we may declare conduct to be permissible, but we can nonetheless envision factors that, if true, would make it more or less so. Enough of these factors, if they were to come to light, might lead us to revise our judgment and to declare formerly permissible conduct to be impermissible—which category, incidentally, also admits of degree.

In producing a logic of tentative sanction, the concept of moral permissibility is especially at home at the juncture between moral and political theory. Even individuals who believe themselves to possess a logic of justification may yield to a logic of permission for a morally detested policy when major institutions of their society have endorsed that policy. Opponents of abortion, for instance, believe it a grievous moral wrong, unjustified according to a moral view that gives decisive weight to the value of human life. Even so, all but the most intransigent opponents of abortion concede that abortions are permissible if the relevant major institutions of the society declare them to be so. To most opponents of abortion, doctors who perform them still do a grievous moral wrong, but not as bad a moral wrong as if civil authority prohibited rather than permitted abortion.

We must keep in mind that for cases of the morally problematic—of which abortion is a prime instance—a logic of permissibility commends itself because individuals differ, not merely at the level of intuitive moral response, but also at the level of moral principle. Both opposition to and support for abortion may be the result of mature moral reflection. Respect for the serious weight of arguments on both sides of the issue ought to lead us to hold our conclusions more tentatively than the stern logic of justification allows. We may decide that, on balance, abortion is morally permissible or not; but by thinking and speaking in these terms, we leave ourselves open to continuing debate and possible revision of our views. By contrast, thinking and speaking in terms of justification tends to do exactly the opposite, cutting off further debate and precluding new ideas.

It would be well to note that adopting the logic of permission in morally problematic cases does not entail its universal adoption. That is, we may still possess demonstrable and uncontroversial moral duties that remain subject to a logic of justification. We have a first-order moral duty not to inflict gratuitous pain on human beings and other sentient creatures, and to honor this duty is always to be vindicated morally. Failing to honor this duty may sometimes be excused, but it is never permissible in the way that I have argued applies in the realm of the morally problematic.

The moral issues surrounding legal punishment are as complex and controversial as those surrounding the abortion debate or the debate over assisted suicide. Here, too, we ought to adopt a logic of permission rather than of justification. The first stage in establishing this point requires showing that there can be no first-order moral duty of legal punishment. Chapter Thirteen begins by arguing for this claim.

THIRTEEN

Permitting Legal Punishment

Some visions of moral theory conceive of it as, in principle, a complete, consistent, and determinate guide to conduct. Our duties can be ranked in a definite order and any conflicts among them resolved by rational moral criteria. For every possible moral choice, then, we can be presumed to have a first-order moral duty to act in a certain way. Such a duty is one that trumps all others—a duty that can be shown to be superior by unequivocal moral criteria.

Adherents of a justificatory approach to legal punishment believe that its morality must be analyzed by appeal to moral rights and duties. In Kant's case, for instance, the duty to punish all legal offenders retributively is a categorical imperative. To fail to punish legal offenders is a moral wrong, a violation of a first-order moral duty. When we ask to whom this duty is addressed, the most plausible answer seems to be that it is addressed to those agents of the state who must administer the sentence. Yet, curiously enough, Kant and others following him write as if the addressee of the justification is the offender himself.[1] It is the offender who, through his act, has willed his own punishment. If we think of the offender's having a moral duty subsequent to his offense, it would be that of consenting to what a court decrees.

The view that a legal offender has a duty to consent to his punishment allows Kant to tie the justification of punishment to his favored core example of a first-order moral duty, that of keeping a promise. Given the absolute weight he accords the value of autonomy, the tactic of assimilating problematic duties to the unproblematic moral duty of promise keeping is understandable. One who gives an unforced promise to another commits himself in a way that leaves no question of the proper addressee in justifying the duty to fulfill the promise. This duty cannot (*logically* cannot) lie with anyone else.

Unfortunately, morally authorizing legal punishment is not so tidy as morally enforcing a promise. As a consequence, we must rest content with the negative assertion that the legally innocent possess a right *not* to be punished, dispensing for reasons cited in the next section with the assertion of a first-order moral duty to punish the legally guilty.

Moral Duty and Legal Punishment

There are three basic alternatives in arguing that legal punishment is an unequivocal moral duty. First, one may follow Kant to insist that the duty legally to punish follows from the implied consent of offenders insofar as they are participants in a rational realm of ends. Second, one may follow Hegel to argue that the duty to punish is correlative with a right to be punished. Third, one may argue that the duty legally to punish is an imperfect duty, contingent neither on consent nor correlative with a right. Each of these alternatives fails to achieve its objective.

If persons consent to their own legal punishment, our worries about authorizing punitive hard treatment seem at an end. Kant believes that universalizability is sufficient to persuade the rational personality of any legal offender to consent to what the state decrees. The incommensurability of ultimate moral values is one ground for challenging the Kantian thesis, but there are other grounds as well. Suppose the punishment in question is excessive or imposed for an act that the state is wrong in criminalizing. In these cases offenders are not obliged to accede to the state's justification of its action. The best we can say is that offenders have the duty to consent to legal punishment only if they have in fact, both legally and morally, committed an offense.

Even under these conditions, however, the case of legal punishment cannot be readily assimilated to Kant's favored case of promise keeping. The defective promisor is a proper subject of censure and criticism; in Kant's view, it is a wrong *not* to censure him. The offender against legal rules, by contrast, is both censured and made to suffer an added penalty. As someone else must administer the additional hard treatment, agents of the state become addressees of our putative logic of justification. After all, we ask them to do something (deliberately impose suffering on another) that is a prima facie wrong. In some cases (e.g., a servile person's plea to be beaten), consent is insufficient to override the obligation one has not to impose avoidable suffering on another. Agents meting out hard treatment must thus ponder constraints independent of consent, whether actual or ideally rational. These constraints sometimes deny them the moral standing to do to another what that person fervently desires. If consent is beside the point, then the alleged duty to inflict suffering beyond censure must rest elsewhere.

An alternative but unnecessarily paradoxical way of making justificatory sense of the duty possessed by civil agents to punish legal offenders is proposed by Hegel.[2] The duty to punish is, Hegel asserts, correlative with a moral right of the offender. When civil authorities fail to punish, they do a serious moral wrong because they invade a serious moral right—the right of the offender to his punishment. Unfortunately, the right to legal punishment is a right that few, if any, of us would claim; and, as Joel Feinberg demonstrates, there is no plausible role in moral discourse for rights divorced from claims.[3]

Proponents of the logic of justification may still be reluctant to abandon the thesis that civil authority has a first-order duty legally to punish. After all, not all duties on the part of one person are correlative with a right possessed by some determinate other person.[4] There are imperfect duties where one may possess a moral duty generally, but not in regard to a particular identifiable rights holder. The general moral duty to be charitable does not confer on any specific person a right to be the object of that charity. Similarly, trained civil authorities may have a moral duty to rescue people whose lives are in jeopardy without those same people, especially if they have been negligent, having a moral right to be rescued.

Partisans, then, of the view that legal authorities have a moral duty to punish legal offenders may sensibly hold such a position without committing themselves to the belief that offenders have a correlative right to be punished. Invocation of a right on the part of one person makes establishment of a correlative duty in others much easier, for the duty is derivable from the validity of the right. When, as in the case of legal punishment, we cannot invoke a correlative right, establishing a duty (now imperfect) must proceed in some other way.

How might we establish the existence of a general imperfect moral duty of civil authority legally to punish offenders? Utilitarian moral theory cannot ground such a duty, for it cannot even establish that all voluntary moral fault ought to meet with hard treatment. Only if hard treatment produces the greatest overall balance of good consequences is it justified in any given case, according to the utilitarian. Despite efforts at articulating varieties of rule utilitarianism that invoke values other than utility, the doctrine is and must remain act oriented.[5] The main strength of utilitarianism is that its justifications are particular. First-order moral duties are determined by the outcome of a calculus, and if an outcome in one set of circumstances differs from the generally prescribed rule, this is merely to show that one has the strongest reason possible for not following the rule—namely, a justification according to the principle of utility.

So the utilitarian answer to determining the moral duty of authorities to punish holds that the duty is contingent on the likely consequences. No general binding duty may be presumed. Rather, each case must in principle be taken separately, even if after experience we learn to group cases into convenient general categories. As with any other human act or institution, legal punishment is justified on utilitarian grounds only by accurate aim at the greatest balance of happiness. If this aim includes punishing an innocent person, or only apparently punishing a guilty person, so be it.

Thus, to find a means of grounding a general first-order moral duty of civil authority to punish legal offenders, we must look to retributive thought. The problem here is that the retributive license is too general. Classical retributivism is warranted in holding that moral wrong deserves to be met with hard treatment, but not all hard treatment is legal punishment. The doctrine has no independent criterion for separating offenses that deserve legal punishment from those that do not. As a result, its tendency is to make all moral offenses legally punishable, at least in principle.

Because the implications of utilitarianism are too selective to coincide with our ideas of moral desert, while the implications of retributivism are not selective enough to separate moral from legal fault, some philosophers conclude, paradoxically, that legal punishment is necessary but morally unjustified. Alan Goldman, for instance, argues that defensible theses from both utilitarianism and retributivism generate an irreducible paradox: To provide a sufficient level of deterrence (and hence safety for the public at large), we must punish each offender whom we convict in excess of what justice—on retributive grounds—requires.[6] The paradox surfaces most obviously in crimes against property, where the severity of the favored punishment of imprisonment generally exceeds the pecuniary interest invaded by most thieves apprehended and brought before a court. Though conceding a great deal to utilitarian and consequentialist considerations, Goldman generates his paradox by assuming a stern logic of justification that sees every human action or institution as either demonstrably in accordance with duty or not. Viewing moral theory as complete, consistent, and determinate, he concludes that everyday practices of legal punishment are unjustified. At the same time, justification (or lack of it) seems merely an object of thought; when it comes to action, we are morally required to do what is unjustified.[7]

There is something compelling in the wish for moral theory to be complete, consistent, and determinant. How can moral theory provide a means of criticizing practice if it contains potential areas of silence, inconsistency, or indeterminacy? We have enough of these qualities in life as we know and live it. Why import incompleteness and the rest into the primary instrument for ordering and judging moral conduct?

The only answer to this question is that the price of maintaining completeness, consistency, and determinacy in moral theory is unacceptably high. We purchase these qualities by embracing value monism, making one moral value the supreme arbiter, decisive at all points of conflict. Utilitarians do so with the production of pleasure and prevention of pain—*it* becomes final arbiter. Libertarians make do with liberty, egalitarians with equality. The moment plural values are admitted as desirable, each in its own right, moral theory loses its determinacy. In a genuine value pluralism, moral dilemmas are exactly what they seem—dilemmas. They cannot be resolved by deeper thinking, by redescribing circumstances, or by explaining away apparent conflicts. Such dilemmas, within the body of considered moral judgment, constitute those morally problematic cases where the logic of permission comes to the fore.

My contention is that many, if not most, cases of legal punishment fall into the category of the morally problematic. Moral theory alone cannot and should not be expected to demonstrate their justifiability. Sharing in the mistaken view that civil authority can be shown to have an unequivocal moral duty to punish, both classically utilitarian and classically retributive theories hold that particular instances of legal punishment are either justified or not. It is, however, far better to think of legal punishment as permissible: Civil authority *may* legally punish wrongdoers, but it has no first-order moral duty to do so. Instead, its first-order moral duties are to condemn wrongdoing and to protect innocent members of the public. Civil authorities may not claim the exculpatory solace of believing they have a timeless first-order duty to inflict hard treatment. They are morally permitted to punish, but this sanction is tentative and undogmatic; what is permissible today may prove impermissible in the considered moral judgment of a later age.

The coherence of legal punishment with the retributively authorized hard treatments of censure and criticism will be discussed in the following section. It remains here to say a few words in elaboration of the kind of moral permission that allows civil authority to impose legal punishment.

In nonmoral contexts, the concept of permission allows persons to do or to not do a thing according to their own best judgment. Persons with permission are not duty bound to do the thing that they have permission to do. The need for permission is the simple need to gain the consent of those in authority, but, once gained, the permission need not be used. The same latitude, I believe, characterizes the moral permission by which legitimate civil authority punishes its citizens. Pardon is (and should be) reserved to the executive so that, in principle, any offender is a candidate to have his legal punishment annulled. More important, alternative forms of and substitutes for legal punishment ought constantly to be explored. It is far from self-evident that current institutions optimize the multiple aims of deterring crime, protecting the public, and reintegrating offenders into society.

All these things said, it does not do to leave legal punishment to the unbounded discretion of civil authority. Abandoning the logic of moral justification obliges us to apply moral theory in a new way. Permission is the kind of tentative moral sanction agents have when engaged in actions conducive to one important moral value, but violative of at least one other important moral value. The case for punishment as ethically permitted differs from the case for actions that accord with a first-order moral duty. Legal punishment is authorized as a response to wrongdoing because, first, insofar as it is stigmatizing, it coheres with other morally authorized retributive practices, and, second, insofar as it inflicts suffering beyond that of stigma, legal punishment is a unique and irreplaceable means of reinforcing the seriousness with which we view the moral values protected by criminal law. Stage one of this argument follows in the next section; stage two (which amounts to showing that legal punishment is not *im*permissible) follows in the section concluding this chapter.

Coherence of Legal Punishment with Censure and Criticism

Moral analysis of retributive practice proceeds along two dimensions. First we must assess the *desert* of candidates for hard treatment; second, the moral *permissibility* of the treatment to be given. Classical retributivism combines these two dimensions by supposing that some feature of the agent's transgression is grounds for establishing both desert and permissibility of response.[8] The idea of the doer suffering what he does is the basis for this connection. A murderer is thought morally to deserve death, because death is what he caused—an imposition of the like for like formula supposed to render this particular punishment a first-order moral duty.

Breaking the spell of like for like in retributive thought forces us to separate desert from permissibility. Desert is a function of the agent and her act. The questions relevant to desert concern such aspects of conduct as motives, mental states, and degree of external coercion. Perhaps an act was done with malicious intent, perhaps with recklessness or insufficient care. In any case the agent's will is the proper object of scrutiny in determining retributive desert.

Unlike desert, the moral permissibility of any given response to wrongdoing depends on the way various kinds of hard treatment accord with cultural sensibilities. As these sensibilities are fashioned by nonrational factors, they are difficult, if not impossible, to assimilate into moral theory. One may hope that such moral values as respect for human dignity and protection of the innocent shape a culture's canons of permissibility, but ensuring that such values predominate is far from easy.

The case for separating canons of desert from canons of permissibility is best made by examining retributive practices other than legal punishment. Accordingly, I shall consider what is perhaps the most general among authorized retributive practices, namely, distribution of censure.

In moral life censure and criticism are the most common varieties of retributive hard treatment. People have every right to protest criticism for acts that they did not do, or for which they lacked the relevant state of mind to be held substantially responsible. These considerations indicate the extent to which desert is fundamental to so commonplace an enterprise as the distribution of blame.

Suppose a moral reformer were to propose divorcing censure from its perceived grounds of desert in the defective will of the person censured. We should, the reformer might propose, no longer react with hostility to negligence, malice, or recklessness. We should no longer resent such acts against ourselves, nor feel indignant when we hear of their commission against others.

Such a proposal collapses from the weight of its own contradictions. Either the reformer means that we should abolish censure, blame, and criticism entirely, or she means that we should cease distributing them according to desert. The first option is fruitless unless one envisions creatures physically and emotionally different from human beings. Perhaps if malicious, reckless, or negligent acts did not have injurious and sometimes lethal consequences, we might in fact be able to dispense with censoriousness. If some *deus ex machina* (as in Euripides' *Orestes*) were reliably to intervene the moment any of us tried to act out his defective will toward another, we could perhaps get along without the practice of censure. Care must be taken, however, lest we believe that a thought experiment of this sort "proves" that the case for censure is wholly forward looking and consequentialist. Reason tends to be forward looking because we lack means of changing the past, but this fact does not mean that reason figures solely or even predominantly in shaping our moral responses. As vulnerable creatures needing sometimes to react without delay, we are educated into an array of culturally sanctioned reactions to various threats. While reason may aid morality in disclosing grounds for condemning a certain kind of retributive practice (as in the campaign against dueling), condemnation alone is insufficient. The condemnation must be felt as well as articulated, working its way into a culture's nonrational modes of guiding conduct.

Abolishing censure altogether would, then, abolish a primary means of reforming impermissible institutions—far too high a price to pay. Our imagined reformer's second option is to maintain censorious practice but to divorce it from the concept of desert. Perhaps, it might be thought, people need to let off steam by blaming, criticizing, and railing against others. We will not try changing our retributive emotional fabric, but we will alter the targets for its expression. But now the question arises, What are the new targets to be? If we include among them acts of a good, kindly, and other-regarding will, we undermine practices of praise and reward. What is the point of praise if the same act that earned it once is likely to be condemned next time around? To avoid this implication, our reformer might propose morally neutral targets for censure. Perhaps we rail at people for falling ill, as in Samuel Butler's *Erewhon*, or create stone censure icons that we pull out four times a day to criticize for simply existing. However therapeutic such tactics might be, they lose all moral force. If censure is not of a fault or a defect, it loses its nature entirely. It is like the promise made with fingers crossed behind one's back—not a promise at all.

Censure, blame, and criticism are thus inherently retributive. There is more to this point than the mere logical observation that only a wrongdoer *can* be blamed. If words alleging fault are spoken to an innocent person, the logical observation tells us that he is not really being blamed. Instead, he is the victim of a mistake or an injustice. Even though blame logically connects with fault, harsh words alone are insufficient to tell us whether or not a person is being blamed. The point of retributivism is to insist that the person guilty of a fault *ought to* be blamed. Thus if we knowingly exempt from blame someone deserving it, we ourselves are guilty of a moral fault. We contribute, in however small a way, to undermining the integrity of reciprocal relations. As shown in the reductio ad absurdum of the reformer who would do away with censure, we debase praise by the same currency with which we debase its opposite.

We thus reach the first stage in our argument for authorizing retributive practices, among which we will soon find a place for legal punishment. In effect, we have provided high-level reflections in favor of the basic intuition that moral fault deserves hard treatment. Blame is the minimum retributive response, and is likely to feature in every other form of moralized retribution as we proceed upward along the scale of severity. Yet not every kind of blaming is morally permissible, for canons of permissibility are distinct from canons of desert. In criticizing those who deserve it, we must be sensitive to other moral values constraining our behavior. For example, the fault of another, however grievous, does not permit us to be rudely tendentious in our criticism. Certain kinds of blaming are morally offensive irrespective of the desert that occasions them.

In general, one who criticizes another ought to measure her response in light of a host of nonretributive moral considerations. Among these are a concern for the other person's dignity, an assessment of how best to use criticism as an incentive to improve conduct, and how frequently the fault in question has manifested itself in the past. Such factors influence the severity with which we may permissibly express ourselves. They also affect the all-important emotional coloring of our response. Effective criticism is tailored to the mental constitution of its recipient. Morbidly sensitive people ought, all things considered, to be treated more delicately than those with a normal degree of self-assurance. Out of this complex of factors emerges an important moral constraint on one who criticizes—namely, that she should use the least harsh means available for accomplishing her objective. If two sharp words will induce someone to reform, each additional sharp word is morally suspect.

A key point in assessing the morality of censure is to see that the moral standing of the person who expresses the censure is an important variable, independent of the desert of whomever is criticized. No matter how much a person deserves a scolding, the upbraiding she receives may be morally impermissible simply because the one who proffers it behaves wrongly. In legal punishment, too, maintenance of the requisite moral standing by those who administer punishment is important. It is here, properly speaking, that nonretributive aims of legal punishment (e.g., reform of the offender, protection of the public, and minimizing of suffering) have their force. Those agents of the state who superintend its population of criminal offenders maintain the moral authority to do so by striving to accomplish aims other than the meeting of evil with evil. In a well-designed system of legal punishment, the retributive aim needs no special reinforcement. It permeates punishment in the way that repudiation permeates censure.

Insofar as it is morally stigmatizing, then, legal punishment is morally authorized because of its coherence with other authorized retributive practice. Retributive canons of desert are absolute in addressing the question, Whom, morally, may we punish? The answer, without exception, is only those guilty of an offense. Identifying this class, however, does not mean that each and every legal offender ought to be legally punished. Some may qualify for hard treatment short of this mark. What is more, the "something extra" in legal punishment (e.g., the evils of enforced boredom and separation from loved ones attendant on incarceration) is prima facie impermissible. The state is not morally authorized to inflict such evils on anyone it chooses. To clinch our case, then, we need to establish that at least some evils of legal punishment are not impermissible.

Permitting Punishment: Fairness and Desert

Our objective is to establish the legitimacy of serving in, superintending, and supporting institutions that deliberately impose suffering beyond public censure and stigma on legal offenders. At the same time, however, we must be wary of duty-bound justificatory routes to this end. To view punishment as a first-order moral duty involves the untenable presumption that the evil of punishment is actually a good. To seek a justification of punishment is to seek, in the words of H. L. A. Hart, a "mysterious piece of moral alchemy in which the combination of the two evils of moral wickedness and suffering are transmuted into good." [9]

Yet when reduced to the scope of proving legal punishment to be permissible, our task is none too easy. Whatever else is true of contemporary forms of legal punishment—fines, incarceration, and death, for example—they have this much in common: If done in the ordinary course of life, they are morally impermissible. Normally, to fine someone is to extract money from him against his will, to incarcerate someone is to hold him against his will, to execute someone is to kill him against his will. If done by other than state authority, each of these things is either a crime or a fit subject for criminal investigation. Extracting money from someone is extortion or theft, removing someone's liberty is kidnapping or hostage taking, killing another person is murder or manslaughter. Even when permissible (as in slaying in self-defense), individuals bear a heavy burden of proof in undertaking such actions, for they must deflect the prima facie charge of impermissibility. One who slays another may legally exonerate herself only by, in the judgment of civil authority, having exhausted all means of escape or of otherwise disabling her antagonist. To be sure, prosecutors, juries, and judges may make allowance for rash decisions induced by fear and the impulse for self-preservation, but the fact remains that a plea of self-defense is an excuse rather than a justification. We rightly think that one has done a moral wrong in killing someone else—then judge that moral wrong, retrospectively and with regret, to have been permissible.

Behind the precept requiring the use of least force in self-protection lie two important moral principles. The first is that suffering should be economized—necessary evil kept to a minimum. The second, which I take from Hugo Adam Bedau, is that if a risk of excessive suffering is to be apportioned between two or more parties, the innocent party (if one exists) ought to bear the least risk.[10] These two principles regulate the burden of proof in cases where one human deliberately imposes suffering on another. By the first principle, any deliberately imposed suffering is a prima facie wrong; by the second, the risk of error in moral policies and practices ought not, as far as possible, to be borne by the morally innocent. Taken together, the two principles are neither wholly consistent nor wholly inconsistent; rather, they both support and oppose each other in the tension characteristic of retributive webs.

In noncriminal contexts, licensing procedures are a means of protecting members of the public against undue risk. If we are sufficiently uncritical, there appears to be a powerful parallel between revoking a license and sanctioning the infliction of a legal punishment. The parallel is attractive because to seek and hold a license is a sign of voluntary participation in a regulated system. Given this voluntary dimension, grossly to violate regulations simply is to declare oneself undeserving of a license.

Licenses are, of course, permissions par excellence. In any system of licensing, there are rules to be obeyed, standards to be attained and maintained, and sanctions imposed for neglect or disobedience. Sometimes, of course, the penalties are criminal, but for the sake of clarity I shall here consider only the sanction of license revocation.

There is no question that loss of a license—whether to fish, drive, or practice medicine—is a variety of hard treatment. People request and hold licenses because the activity in question is important to their livelihood or enjoyment. Loss of a license imposes a measure of suffering, and we must seek to impose its burdens fairly and impartially. We do so, in part, by conceptually tying the holding of a license to positive desert and the revocation of a license to negative desert.

Both conceptually and in practice, the machinery of licensing an individual is separate from that of withdrawing a license. The former power typically resides with an administrative arm of the executive, the latter power with a court or some quasi-judicial body subservient to court authority. Because of this separation of powers, we can reasonably ask what is the general aim or purpose of each body. For the licensing bureau itself, we would give a utilitarian answer: to promote individuals doing what they want while keeping danger to others to a minimum. When we ask the general aim of the body empowered to remove a person's license, we find that it is and should be retributive: to see that those and only those who deserve to lose their licenses do so. By the time we invoke the enforcement mechanism, utilitarian concerns of the greatest good or the greatest happiness are, as it were, out of court. We could perhaps, in a given instance, promote greater happiness by removing or failing to remove a license irrespective of desert, but the point is past for expressing, endorsing, or even considering this aim.

We may thus put the case as follows. Enforcement of licensing standards is authorized by appeal to the logic of retributive desert. Who should lose a license? Only those who deserve to do so, those who have violated a rule of sufficient gravity or who have failed to maintain a required proficiency. If an enforcement institution is to maintain its integrity and satisfy the moral expectations of the public, its eye must be on desert and desert alone. Why else do we try, with greater or lesser success, to insulate such institutions from transient political pressures? Why else are standards of evidence, due process, and appeal maintained at enormous expense? The answer can only be that fairness to the individual is in this context more important than the general good.

We sometimes lose sight of the importance of desert in such institutions because the upshot of deserved hard treatment more frequently than not *does* protect the public. An incompetent doctor or a reckless driver loses his license—good, we are all better off. But this only means that the aims are compatible, not that the one (a focus on desert) is subservient to the other. Suppose a driver seriously at fault in a crash is so badly injured that he will never physically be able to drive again. Do we let him keep his license? We do not. The revocation of driving privileges has a symbolic and expressive function above and beyond its production of pleasure and its prevention of pain. The meting out of a just desert, irrespective of particular consequences in a given case, lends credence and integrity to a procedure that must win its support by adhering to canons of fairness rather than of utility.

Perhaps, then, the licensing analog suggests that civil authority has a similar warrant to impose legal punishment on the legally guilty. Perhaps we may conclude that the enforcement arm of a licensing authority has a first-order moral duty to revoke the licenses of those who, to a serious degree, abuse their privileges.

On inspection, however, the analogy misleads at exactly this point. Any alleged moral duty of authorities to revoke licenses is either a second-order duty to administer fairly, or uncritically embraced as a first-order moral duty because of the compelling "fit" between offense and sanction. Licensing is a cooperative scheme created by civil authority for public benefit, and the possessor of a license has subscribed to the scheme on her own initiative. For abuses, then, the most appropriate mode of treatment is forfeiture of the license.

Occasions for imposing legal punishment are not so tidy. In the first place, we should resist the implication that an offender (or, indeed, any citizen) only possesses privileges granted him by civil authority. In the second place, when it comes to determining an appropriate response to criminal wrongdoing, the quandary of whether to impose legal punishment is analogous to the treatment of non–license holders who usurp the privileges of license holders. It cannot plausibly be said of such persons that they have consented to a cooperative scheme. What sort of hard treatment is it our moral duty to impose on non–license holders who usurp privileges to which they are not entitled? The "fitting" answer is denied us, for we cannot revoke licenses that people do not possess. As a consequence, we must ask whether mere censure and reproach will do the job or whether an added measure of legal punishment is required. Consent again fails to bridge the gap between desert and permissibility of legal punishment, for consent falls away in the case of the non–license holder. He has done nothing to endorse the scheme subscribed to by others.[11]

Even so, the non–license holder typically benefits from the cooperation of others. An unlicensed driver's life is safer to the degree that fellow drivers are unlike him—that is, willing to subject their skills to public scrutiny. A physician with false credentials prospers in a world where people are trusting—that is, a world in which most such credentials are genuine. These considerations suggest that a principle of fairness in the distribution of benefits and burdens is what connects retributive desert to the permissibility of legal punishment.

Herbert Morris is the main exponent of linking retributive justice to fairness in the distribution of benefits and burdens.[12] Viewing the criminal law as a public good, Morris assumes that the same free-rider problem applies to it as to other public goods—namely, that a selected few who shun the burden of compliance gain at the expense of the many who are law abiding. Legal punishment of criminals thus redresses a distributive injustice. The law abiding assume a burden of compliance with law, benefiting equally from everyone else's compliance. The criminal, by contrast, assumes no such burden, while exploiting the excess benefits of noncompliance. Consent falls away in Morris's conception of legal punishment, for the relevant measure of the deserved degree of punishment is the size of the criminal's illicit advantage, whether she actually subscribes to the cooperative scheme or not. Morris assumes that when it comes to the benefits and burdens of obedience to the criminal law, all persons ought to share equally.[13] Departures from this state of equality must be made up for by what George Sher calls a principle of "diachronic fairness."[14] According to this standard, a person's unequal share of a good related to compliance with criminal law during one period should be compensated for by an appropriately lesser or greater share in a subsequent period. We must not, however, let the principle operate retrospectively: Earlier burdens must not be allowed to compensate for a criminal's present benefits of noncompliance.

Once we appreciate the grounds for temporal asymmetry in our principle of fairness, we cinch the case for the permissibility of legal punishment. The criminal, Sher notes, has gained more than a simple material advantage over others. Whatever the economic value of his crime, it must be measured first and foremost on a scale of moral value. In fact, its economic value is a sole derivative of its negative moral value, for if everyone were equally dishonest or dissembling, the criminal's act would gain him nothing. Sher argues that we must thus apply a moral measure to the advantages of failing to comply with criminal law. Rather than view compliance as primarily a psychic burden and noncompliance as primarily an economic gain, we must look at both as derivatives of moral wrong. Such a view puts legal punishment into proper perspective, for the hard treatment it imposes is normally a moral wrong:

> By treating the wrong-doer in what is ordinarily a forbidden way, we strip away part of the protection that moral restraints on our behavior would ordinarily have afforded him. Thus, we remove precisely the worth of advantage he has gained. Because the resulting disadvantage can be assessed in terms of its usual moral wrongness, it can be weighed on the same scale as the wrongdoer's unfair advantage. Thus, it is commensurable with the wrongdoer's extra benefit as his previous hardships are not.[15]

Following this reasoning, we may conclude that legal punishment is permissible when a legal violation passes a certain degree of seriousness measured by the moral gravity of the offense. Offenders deserve legal punishment in redress of their unfair advantage when and only when other retributive responses are insufficiently commensurate with the moral gravity of the prohibition violated. The "something extra" of legal punishment—the discomfort in addition to the suffering of censure or stigma—is morally authorized by "something extra" in the offense.[16] The more forbidden an act, the more permissible a punitive response to it becomes.

These considerations are reinforced by the distributional principle that, where possible, the risk of mistake ought not to be borne by the legally innocent. The possibility for error in criminal sentencing is ever present; someone must bear it. When we fail legally to incarcerate an offender, the risk of mistake is borne by the legally innocent, one or more of whom may become the offender's next victim. If we do incarcerate, we likewise risk a mistake—perhaps this particular offender has learned her lesson from the stigma of being found guilty, and will endanger no one if simply placed on probation. Even so, the burden of risk lies with the offender. The more grave our moral assessment of her crime, the less persuasive the case for shifting that burden to nonoffenders.

Recall that a stern duty-bound logic of justification applies to conduct in mutually exclusive, on–off fashion. There is no middle ground—a person is either justified or not. Both permissibility and impermissibility, however, admit of degree. When we contemplate the range of possibilities covered by any legal definition of an offense, we discover that admitting of degree is an added reason to favor a logic of permission over one of justification. This positive feature of the logic of permissibility is enhanced as the criminal act in question approaches the category of the morally problematic in our reflective deliberations. To make this point, let us return to the example of assisted suicide.

Compare the following two instances of homicide. In the first a woman gives her husband an overdose of sleeping tablets to be rid of him and to collect a large sum of insurance. In the second a woman gives the overdose to her incapacitated and terminally ill husband, who has repeatedly begged her to put him out of his misery. Let us assume that the morally right thing to do is to preserve life. By the logic of justification, then, both women are unjustified, though perhaps in different degrees. But how do we determine these relative degrees? One answer is denied us: We cannot measure by the degree of variation from the opposite state—that of being morally justified. By stipulation, both women are only and equally justified (that is, duty bound) in *not* administering the sleeping pills. We are thus driven to conclude that each woman's relative lack of justification cannot be measured by its opposite—the justified decision to preserve life.

With the logic of permissibility, however, we have a ready measure of the difference between the two acts. Still presuming that both women do wrong, we now mean that each acts in a morally impermissible way, and we may sensibly assert that the first woman's act is morally *more* impermissible than that of the second woman. It is also important that when we describe each woman's counterfactual failure to administer sleeping tablets we likewise come up with a judgment that can be measured by degree. We are now able to say that though both act permissibly in failing to administer the sleeping tablets, the second woman acts *less* permissibly than the first. There is a moral case (though, by stipulation, not a decisive one) that the second woman ought to relieve her husband's suffering by doing as he requests. This reflective moral judgment lessens the impermissibility of killing her husband in the same measure as it lessens the permissibility of her failure to kill him. Correspondingly, the same judgment weakens the permissibility of responding to her offense with legal punishment. We thus correlate a difference in the degree of permissibility of our response to wrongdoing with a difference in the degree of permissibility of the wrong itself—exactly the correlation lacking when we apply a duty-bound logic of justification.

The preceding analysis goes deeper than merely to explain a difference in degree of legal punishment that we may elect to administer to the two women. A justificatory approach allows for such a difference by viewing the second woman's act as partially excused (length of punishment serving as the proper dimension for recognizing excuses). But the challenge of assisted suicide to the definition of homicide is far more radical than the justificatory view allows. Many reflective persons (my reflective self among them) would hold that the second woman ought not to be legally punished at all. The case against legally punishing her is, in concert with Sher's view of desert, a case that her act lacks sufficient moral gravity. We may, by a narrow margin, decide otherwise, but this decision does not give us the warrant of a duty-bound justification. Whatever length of sentence we impose, we ought to have more reservations about legally punishing the second woman than we do about legally punishing the first. We best capture this difference by applying the logic of permissibility. Given the clash of values inherent in deliberately imposing suffering, we lack assurance of moral rectitude in our response to virtually any case, but our moral standing is far stronger vis-à-vis the first woman. We judge that she deserves hard treatment commensurate with the moral wrongness of her act because that act is well above the threshold where the gravity of moral judgment requires reinforcement by legal means.

One reason for mistaking the permissive nature of legal punishment may be illuminated by analogy to the classifying of highly confirmed inductive truths. At the core of moral wrongdoing lie acts whose viciousness is uncontroversial—and that any modern criminal code will prohibit. So certain are we of our morality in condemning these acts that we feel equally certain of our legally punitive response. After all, we have grown up to accept a culture that responds punitively in the way it does exactly as we have grown up to accept a culturally induced feeling of revulsion at the mere thought of the prohibited act. Similarly, we feel as certain that the sun will rise tomorrow as that a half-full barrel is half empty. Nonetheless, the first truth differs in kind from the second. The first is a highly confirmed inductive generalization, the second a deductive truth. Unless we are careful, our feeling of certitude will mislead us when classifying the two statements. Similarly, our feeling that an act is morally unjustified (i.e., that it violates a first-order moral duty) may lead us to the mistaken judgment that we are justified in our legally punitive response to it. The mistake is especially resonant when the language used to characterize the core of morally vicious acts also describes acts outside that core. Thus "first-degree homicide" understood as "the deliberate and premeditated taking of human life in the course neither of war nor self-defense" includes assisted suicide as clearly as it includes murder for hire, riches, or revenge. To argue that assisted suicide is a morally permissible act is, in effect, to argue for a legal definition of homicide that would include it, along with killing in war and in self-defense, among morally relevant exceptions. Even if such a definition were accepted, however, the argument would go on, for there would still be a strong case for the moral impermissibility of assisted suicide.

At this point, though, a note of caution: Too great a focus on ethical dilemmas in the body of reflective moral judgment may lead us to overstate our case. Moral theory is permissive rather than justificatory in the philosophy of legal punishment because moral theory cannot, by its nature, be complete, consistent, and determinate. Yet we must not exaggerate the degree of uncertainty that our theoretical scruples mandate. Just as it would be irrational to fail to put credence in a highly confirmed generalization simply because it is inductive, it is likewise irrational to think that every permission to punish legal offenders of a certain category is on the verge of crumbling. Though no one can forecast what innovations psychology or sociology might produce in respect to penal practice, odds are that imposition of deliberate suffering beyond censure and reproach will always pervade our morally approved modes of legal punishment. It is as difficult to imagine otherwise as it is difficult to conceive of penal practices that fail to be morally impermissible in the ordinary course of life. Jailers hold convicts against their will, executioners deliberately kill those sentenced to death. As Sher argues, we are capable of underscoring our gravest prohibitions only by doing normally forbidden things to those who violate them.

Retributive desert understood according to a principle of diachronic fairness fixes one pole in the argument for permitting legal punishment of legal offenders. At the same time, however, retributive desert is only one moral value among many. For legal punishment, as for the other varieties of hard treatment, the canons of permissibility are affected by values other than the generalized return of evil for its like. We may learn a great deal from pondering the way in which moral values influence the authorization of hard treatment independently of whether such treatment is deserved. Indeed, for permissive retributivism to break the spell of like for like, yet remain distinct from utilitarianism, close attention must be paid to the intersection between canons of desert and canons of permissibility. Chapter Fourteen begins with an analysis of the moral permissibility of hard treatment, both deserved and nondeserved. This analysis, then, serves as a springboard for clarifying the place of retributivism within the setting of a larger value pluralism.

FOURTEEN

Legal Punishment
and Moral Standing

The concepts of moral right and moral duty serve well when commending us to act in ways beneficial to others. Positive obligations incurred through our own consent form a core of cases that moral theorists favor in illustrating the binding force of rights and duties. A promise to help someone is a tidy moral practice combining respect for autonomy with a concern for the welfare of others. It is small wonder, then, that promising forms the conceptual heart of contractarian thinking about the obligations owed among individuals in civil society.

Unfortunately the harmonious picture of moral rights and duties elicited from a contractarian view of promising does not apply in morally authorizing the state to punish one of its citizens. Legally to punish someone inflicts an evil to which the person in all likelihood does not consent. In addition, the evil prompting us to judge that a retributive response is warranted has already occurred. A positive ethics of rights and duties tells which evils are wrong, advising conscientious agents to avoid them. Yet once the evil is ineradicably a part of the past, in what way are we morally authorized to treat the agent responsible for it?[1] Whatever she has done, she has the same right as anyone else not to have evil deliberately inflicted upon her. To hold that she forfeits this right in committing her offense and that the authorities are therefore justified (i.e., duty bound) to punish her is to concede too much. The logic of this position strips offenders of their humanity, encouraging agents of the state to believe that their powers are unbounded. It is reminiscent of Aquinian theology in arguing that the damned in hell must never, in justice, be allowed surcease of pain.

A satisfactory moral view of legal punishment must not only explain the need for deliberate imposition of evil, but must also place satisfactory limits on agents of the state who investigate crime, try probable offenders, and administer the sentences of those found guilty. Since reflective moral judgment on the morality of punishment ranges from hard-line classical retributivism to the considered view that punishment is itself a crime,[2] we are unlikely to achieve consensus. Thus the moral evaluation of punishment, like the moral evaluation of abortion, proceeds best by invoking a logic of permission.

In seeking something less strong than a duty-bound justification of legal punishment, we abandon the solacing thought that in legally punishing criminals we are only doing our duty. In one sense this abandonment is a loss, for noncriminals lose a moral skyhook "justifying" them in supporting institutions that, by policy and deliberation, mete out suffering to fellow human beings. In another sense, however, abandoning the quest for an unequivocal solace of duty is a gain, for the standards of proof are less daunting; it is easier to establish that legal punishment is permissible than that it is justified by an unambiguous logic of moral duty.

So far we have argued that retributive desert qualifies legal offenders for legal punishment, whereas permissibility constrains both the degree and the kind of legal punishment that civil authority may employ. Focusing on canons of permissibility breaks the spell of like for like in morally authorizing legal punishment— a point substantiated by locating legal punishment in relation to other morally authorized hard treatment.

Desert, Permissibility, and Hard Treatment

Retributive desert can fail to apply to a person in each of two ways. Suppose someone receives hard treatment and we ask whether or not it is deserved. Perhaps the person is innocent, his will failing to be defective in the way alleged. Here the concept of desert is invoked but does not fit. The individual is said to be *un*deserving of his hard treatment. More generally, however, a person might be due hard treatment for reasons that have nothing to do with desert. Pain inflicted in the course of medical treatment is an example. Here the hard treatment is neither deserved nor undeserved; it is not a question of culpability or innocence. I shall speak of *nondesert* as encompassing both cases, though in the discussion to follow the distinction between *un*desert and the inapplicability of the concept remains relevant.

Establishing what an agent deserves is only part of the picture in morally authorizing hard treatment. The moral status of the person administering an agreed-on hard treatment must likewise be considered. Sometimes greater moral harm is done by allowing the wrong person to mete out a deserved hard treatment than in letting the offender off the hook. Such, for instance, is the case with vigilante "justice." Only agents of the state have the relevant moral standing to enforce legal punishment, however strongly it may be deserved.

Combining the dimensions of desert and permissibility, then, we may logically distinguish four possibilities. Hard treatment may be (1) deserved and permissible, (2) nondeserved but permissible, (3) deserved but impermissible, or (4) nondeserved and impermissible. The second and fourth possibilities require two subdivisions, for here the distinction between *un*deserved treatment and treatment where the concept of desert does not apply is morally relevant. This additional distinction yields a total of six categories. In order to end with the first category, which contains the family of hard treatments inclusive of legal punishment, I treat the categories in reverse order.

Not a Matter of Desert and Impermissible

This category is the first subdivision of hard treatment that is nondeserved and impermissible. Inappropriate medical procedures that involve pain and suffering are an example. Such hard treatment is imposed for reasons unconnected with moral guilt or innocence. In addition, the person who imposes it—a quack, say, or a licensed physician exceeding the bounds of her expertise—lacks the proper credentials. People may seek out and consent to such hard treatment because of wishfulness or desperation, but the controlling feature in judging its illegitimacy is the lack of moral standing of the one who imposes it.

Undeserved and Impermissible

This category (the second subdivision of hard treatment that is nondeserved and impermissible) includes evils resulting from malicious intent, recklessness, or failure to exercise proper care. Innocence of the victim is required for distinction from the preceding category. In the purely moral realm, thoughtless or biased censure of a person unrelated to his or her actual merits would be an example. In the legal sphere, most crimes would qualify (e.g., any use of force, theft, or fraud against an innocent person). Also qualifying would be certain harms amenable to redress via the tort system (e.g., libel or slander). Finally, we must include excesses perpetrated by civil authorities (e.g., undue duress or torture). Though technically criminal, assault in the course of legal interrogation presents a different set of difficulties from other crimes, for it is rarely prosecuted. People sometimes believe, wrongly, that authorities have a special moral prerogative to employ such tactics—a mistaken presumption that, as we shall see in the next section, leads to mistaken views about the permissibility of legal punishment.

Both of these categories have their greatest significance as an index of negative desert on the part of the perpetrator. Anyone subjecting another to nondeserved and impermissible hard treatment is prima facie a candidate for hard treatment in return. The lack of moral standing governing impermissibility of treatment overwhelms the difference between whether one who suffers is *un*deserving (an innocent crime victim) or simply not a candidate for desert (a volunteer for some quack medical remedy).

Deserved but Impermissible

This category is made up of hard treatments that are in some sense unsuited to the offense. In the purely moral sphere, a person may deserve to be criticized for one thing but actually receive criticism for another. Having genuinely been wronged, one person may criticize another, yet fail to target the real fault. Jones slights his employee Smith's accomplishments. Jones deserves to be censured for his myopia, but Smith vacillates, perhaps fearing for his job. Resentment builds and comes out in other ways. Smith picks at Jones behind his back, or perhaps elects to be defiant over an issue that is no cause for defiance. It is impermissible for Smith to employ these wrong channels to get back at Jones, but not because Jones is undeserving of hard treatment.

The legal analog is a case of extralegal "punishment" of a known offender. Here the one who punishes lacks the relevant moral status, even if she happens to restrain her measures to exactly those a legitimate civil authority would impose. Again, the issue of proper moral status is crucial, a common element in both the moral and legal instances of this category. One may say, in the case of Smith's failing to censure Jones in the proper way, that his failure undermines his moral status to censure Jones in any way at all. If he cannot do it properly, he may not do it at all. Though in the case of private "punishment" of an offender the lack of relevant moral status is a constitutional issue, the same constraint holds: If the victim (or a sympathizer) cannot achieve justice properly—that is, by following institutionalized procedure—he may not achieve it at all.

Not a Matter of Desert but Permissible

This is the first subdivision of hard treatment that is nondeserved but permissible. It is the most varied and interesting category, including many kinds of deliberate infliction of evil that philosophers have thought relevant to authorizing legal punishment. Without claiming to be comprehensive, I shall discuss five varieties, all of which are permissible in light of values other than retributive desert.

Medical Treatment.   Despite welcome advances in anesthesia and in minimizing the intrusiveness of procedures, many medical treatments still involve the deliberate infliction of pain. Some readers might prefer to deny that medicine provides an example of hard treatment by arguing that pain is an unintended consequence. I would counter that pain is sometimes very much intended, as in a physician's poking or probing to locate the site, source, or nature of an ailment. That such pain is subservient to the greater end of achieving a cure makes it no less real or no less deliberately inflicted. Yet, even if one finds these observations unpersuasive, the fact remains that institutional punishment is so often contrasted with the medical art (witness Plato's curative theory) that we would be remiss for failing to explore the issues involved.

Irrational feelings to the contrary, physical disease is something that befalls one irrespective of desert. The good and the bad, the beautiful and the ugly, the faithful and the faithless—all fall ill in roughly the same proportion and for roughly the same reasons. What makes a person a candidate for medical treatment is having a physical disease. Nonetheless, simply being a candidate is insufficient to permit another person to apply the requisite remedy. First of all, the individual designated to give medical treatment must, save in extreme circumstances, have the status to do so. She must be, that is, a qualified medical professional operating within the limits of her competence. But even if this status condition is met, most adult candidates for medical treatment must give their consent before such treatment is permissible. Why? Plainly and simply because we give moral weight to personal autonomy. In fact, we give autonomy such emphasis that it characteristically outweighs, at a personal level, any argument from utility in favor of a given medical treatment. No matter how much less pain a person will suffer in the long run by undergoing a medical procedure, this fact alone does not permit its infliction against the patient's will.

Sport.   Boxing, rugby, American football, and ice hockey are games that permit contestants deliberately to inflict pain on each other. However incidental to the objectives of the game, punching, tackling, blocking, body checking, and so forth are thus examples of deliberate hard treatment. Unlike the case of medical treatment, where patients might gladly surrender the experience of pain, it is not at all clear that players (or their fans) would consent to the removal of pain from their contests. Despite this difference, however, the pain is permitted on much the same grounds as that of medical treatment. One who administers it must have the status of being another player (a tackle from an onlooker is assault), and the one to whom it is administered must consent to participate in the contest.

Paternalistic Protection of Individuals.   Consent falls away in this variety of permissible hard treatment. Children and adults lacking substantial self-control must sometimes be treated harshly to prevent harm to themselves. Since individuals rarely consent to their own legal punishment, this sort of permissible hard treatment seems a more promising source of analogy than either of the preceding varieties.[3] Perhaps as a result we have a strong tendency to think of offenders as impaired, less than fully rational and autonomous—sometimes for no other reason than that they have committed an offense.

If we consider paternalistic analogs in detail, however, we find them a source of as many troubles as advantages in the theory of legal punishment. To override claims of autonomy, an individual's lack of substantial self-control must be established independently of the act prompting us to administer hard treatment. Very young children present no difficulty, for their inexperience grounds a general presumption that they do not know better. We thus do not hesitate to jerk them away from precipices or to slap hands that play at electrical sockets. Even so, a respect for the growing autonomy of the child dictates that we use the least force possible. Protective hard treatment should also be accompanied by explanations so that children internalize, not the penalty, but the positive reasons for avoiding danger. The larger aim according to which hard treatment is morally permissible may thus include preventing physical injury, but only as part of the even larger aim of building the rational self-control known to be missing.[4]

With adults who lack full rational self-control the picture is less tidy. The same condition for restraint applies as for children: An adult must be known to lack rational self-control on grounds independent of the act that prompts us to consider the need for restraint. Yet, unlike children, many such adults (e.g., those incapacitated by age or suffering severe mental derangement) cannot be presumed to be in the process of developing rational self-control. Accordingly, we permit the administration of hard treatment solely for the individual's own protection (though sometimes also in conjunction with the protection of others). Even here, however, there is a strong moral case for using the least intrusive means possible, as well as for respecting a person's autonomy across whatever narrow band of choices it can operate without impairment. Accordingly, for adults lacking rational self-control and the capacity to give informed consent, the burden of moral deliberation shifts to assessing the status of persons administering the necessary hard treatment.

With children in dangerous situations, anyone perceiving the danger is permitted to intervene, subject to the constraint of using least possible force. The child's consent is not sought because there is no reason to believe it would be an informed consent. Many adults, however, court danger out of personal choice. A general license for anyone to intervene at the simple perception of another's danger would defeat the end of autonomy. Granting such permission becomes a matter for the proper exercise of civil authority, allowing placement of adults in self-protective custody only after a legal determination that they lack substantial ability to care for themselves.

Custody of the Legally Innocent.   Neither an innocent person held and interrogated by police nor a person placed under medical quarantine suffers hard treatment for reasons associated with desert. Their consent is not required, and though a case may be made that their own good is ultimately served by such measures, the arguments for this position are thin and uncompelling. A person under quarantine either already has a disease or is an immune carrier of it, so it is difficult to see how his good is served by the measure. The best we can say is that he has a remote general interest in seeing that other communicable diseases, which he does not have, are also dealt with by quarantine. Similarly, an innocent person in police custody may have a remote general interest in seeing guilty persons apprehended, but no interest at all in seeing a person apprehended for the crime of which he is suspected. Perhaps he is a car-parts salesman suspected of malicious vandalism of cars, a crime that independently of his encouraging it bolsters his livelihood. It is difficult to see how such examples can be assimilated to paternalistic self-protection.

We do far less violence to these cases by describing them in classically utilitarian terms as the sacrifice of one person's well-being for the greater well-being of others. Police must have reasonable scope for their inquiries, even when such scope inflicts hardship on the innocent and the guilty alike. The public must in certain cases be protected from contagious disease even though, from a moral point of view, its carriers are persons whom fate has touched with a condition that is neither deserved nor undeserved.

Dire Straits.   The final variety of permissible hard treatment has great but fundamentally misunderstood relevance to the philosophy of legal punishment. It deserves careful examination because its implications are easily distorted.

Unrelated individuals sometimes find themselves in circumstances where survival requires harsh discipline. Maroonings constitute the most prominent examples. When groups of people are cut off from civilization, leaders are morally permitted to use harsh means up to and including beatings and temporary enslavement of individuals whose noncooperation threatens the survival of others. Whether a leader's permissible power extends to killing and even to cannibalizing is more problematic, though sometimes the law takes an interestingly retrospective view of such instances. In *Regina v. Dudley and Stevens* (a case involving high-seas cannibalism)[5], the verdict of guilty with a recommendation of pardon perhaps counts as making the best of an insoluble dilemma.

Owing to the power of state-of-nature theory in moral and political philosophy, survival cases find favor for supposedly shedding light on what a government is justified in doing to its citizens. If anything, however, these cases favor the logic of permissibility far more than the logic of duty and justification. To whom is the duty of ensuring survival owed? Surely if to anyone, then to everyone. If someone in dire straits loses heart and opts to do nothing, what could possibly make his subjugation a duty? Perhaps he is correct to do nothing. Rescue may be around the corner—his option proving best despite the general contempt felt for it. The point is that in dire straits participants do not have answers. Vindication, if it comes, is entirely retrospective, giving a language of excuse the nod over a language of justification.[6] The harsh actions of a leader marooned with his followers are at best permissible, excused under the circumstances—but not a matter of duty.

Undeserved but Permissible

This is the second subdivision of hard treatment under the heading nondeserved but permissible.[7] Social policy sometimes dictates the imposition of burdens on individuals innocent of wrongdoing. Taxation and rationing of scarce goods are both examples. Virtue is irrelevant to setting the level of one's tax burden, whereas ability and willingness to pay (normally grounds for legitimate possession) are irrelevant to determining one's fair share of a rationed good. Burdensome market exchanges likewise fall into this category; the penniless saint, equally with the unrepentant sinner, may permissibly be evicted by her landlord.

An important implication of this category is negative—namely, that it fails to intersect with the class of permissible legal punishment. The point is in part the logical one that if desert is relevant to a certain category of hard treatment, it is wrong to impose that treatment in the absence of desert. To institute legal punishment simply *is* to declare desert relevant, thus separating legal punishment from any and all of the examples in the previous categories. Lack of desert exempts a person from legal punishment for the same reason that lack of promising exempts a person from the obligation to keep a promise. Desert is a constitutive feature of the practice, part of its authorization, and any imposition of hard treatment that neglects desert fails to be legal punishment in the same way that extracting a reward based on a false claim that a promise was made is something other than enforcing a promise.

Yet the retributivist says more than merely that desert is a logical condition for retributive hard treatment, including legal punishment. That is, she is not simply answering the question, To whom logically *can* we mete out retributive hard treatment? The logical point is a point of naming, of picking among the categories of hard treatment and sorting them into precise linguistic slots. If this were all the retributivist held, it would be very little. She also has the moral point that we *ought* to mete out hard treatment to those satisfying the conditions for retributive desert. Even so, nothing commits the retributivist to the claim that every kind of permissible hard treatment is retributive. She can as easily accede to other grounds for hard treatment as can a nonretributivist.

Deserved and Permissible

The breadth of this final category of hard treatment is too little recognized. It includes, importantly, legal punishment, but an exclusive focus on this subspecies may weaken the moral case for retributivism in that it precludes us from perceiving the degree to which institutions of legal punishment are coherent with other morally permissible retributive practice.

The legal warrant for legal punishment begins with formal declaration of guilt by a court or other judicial agency. This by itself is a retributive hard treatment, though it is not itself a legal punishment. Still, there is a strong case to be made that if the declaration alone serves all the other, nonretributive aims of legal punishment the state may permissibly rest content. A first offender who poses little danger to the public may be pronounced guilty and given a suspended sentence. By contrast, a recidivist convicted of the same crime as the first-time offender may be declared guilty and legally punished as well.

A classical retributivism that measures punishment according to some morally relevant feature of the crime cannot make sense of this difference between the sentence for a first-time offender and a repeat offender. The first-time offender must "pay for" his crime by punishment, and once he has done so the balance is clear. If he commits the same crime again, he must "pay for" it only what he owes, no more and no less. By contrast, as Andrew von Hirsch notes,[8] a retributivism freed from the spell of like for like makes sense of the reflective moral judgment that recidivists are due harder treatment for the same crime as nonrecidivists. Qualitatively speaking, each individual *deserves* the same (a return of evil for their evil done), but the moral authority of the state is different in the two cases. Recidivists pose a greater danger to the public than nonrecidivists, and agents of the state thus have their moral hand strengthened by this consideration.

Our review of desert and permissibility in the moral evaluation of hard treatment is at an end. The subject is complex, its lessons impossible to absorb into a view of legal punishment as a first-order moral duty. Whether or not desert is a factor, civil authority may at best be said to have permission—a tentative sanction—to impose hard treatment beyond censure and stigma. In the absence of retributive desert, certain kinds of hard treatment (notably legal punishment) can be shown to be morally impermissible even if a preponderance of other values suggests otherwise.

Punishment and Moral Pluralism

A duty-bound logic of justification drives the philosophy of legal punishment toward value monism. Classical retributivists assert that the value of meeting evil with an equivalent moral likeness trumps all other values when it comes to redressing wrong. Classical utilitarians, by contrast, assert that legal punishment is justified only when it conduces to the greatest overall sum of happiness. Between these poles we find so-called mixed theories of justification. Permissive retributivism, though not seeking a "justification" in the duty-bound sense, has much in common with these mixed views.

First among prominent efforts to provide a mixed theory of legal punishment is H. L. A. Hart's claim that the "general justifying aim" of punishment is utilitarian, while particular distributions satisfying that aim may proceed only on the basis of legal demerit—a view Hart calls "retribution in distribution." [9] When it comes morally to "justifying" legal punishment as an institution or a practice, we get one answer, but, when it comes to distribution of hard treatment within that practice, we get another answer.

If we think of law in its capacity to instruct and to persuade—informing, guiding conduct, and giving people reasons to do or not to do certain actions—the assertion that "the general justifying aim" of law is utilitarian is unexceptionable. Criminal law as positive pronouncement either serves such aims or is flaunted and ignored. But the question of how to treat someone who violates the criminal law is a different matter. Here the enforcement arm of criminal law comes into play, and if we seek to find "the general justifying aim" of enforcement institutions (police, criminal courts, and prisons) only a retributive answer is acceptable. These institutions are "justified" to the extent that utmost care is taken to apprehend, try, and punish *only* persons guilty of criminal offense. As with the earlier analogy to license revocation, there is little substance in insisting that the retributive aim serves or is subsidiary to a more general utilitarian purpose. In some vague sense this claim has its appeal, but there will always be particular cases where utilitarian considerations speak in favor of deliberately punishing an innocent person or of deliberately failing to apprehend a guilty person. Doing either of these two things in the enforcement arm of criminal law is not to make a retributive aim subsidiary to a utilitarian aim; rather, it is to abandon a retributive aim altogether. Much better, then, to say that the two aims, whether thought of as "justifying" or not, are simply different, characterizing different institutions at different levels of generality. The value of retribution has one particular sphere of influence, the value of utility another. Which value trumps the other will depend on context, on the institution in question, rather than on a moral skyhook propounding one weighing of values for all times, places, and circumstances.

Following along the same curve as Hart, John Rawls distinguishes between "justifying" an institution or a practice as a whole and justifying distribution of benefits and burdens within that practice or institution.[10] He views the institution of legal punishment as "justified" by generally utilitarian considerations of deterrence and social protection, whereas distributions of punishment are "justified" by retributive considerations—that is, punishment is distributed only to those guilty of offending against legal rules.

Rawls thus avoids the noxious implication of utilitarianism that authorities might sometimes have a first-order moral duty to punish the innocent, but this does not mean that his theory is a mixture of retributivism and utilitarianism. On the contrary, insofar as Rawls's theory is morally acceptable, it must be classified as permissive retributivism. The key to this point lies in asking what Rawls means by "justifying" the practice of punishment on utilitarian grounds. He certainly does not mean that we apply moral theory to institutions in such a way as to proclaim legal punishment an unequivocal first-order moral duty. Would it be a grievous moral wrong to have a society that lacked institutions of legal punishment? Clearly not, so Rawls must mean something like the following: On balance, given the kinds of persons produced by Western cultures, there are more good reasons to have institutions of legal punishment than not to have them. This sense of "justification" is weaker than the duty-bound sense, and fully compatible with the concept of moral permission.

By rejecting value monism in the "justification" of legal punishment, both Hart and Rawls prohibit retributive hard treatment of the legally innocent. The integrity of retributive institutions does not permit such treatment—a point easily obscured if we confuse legal punishment with the other categories of permissible hard treatment explored in the preceding section. Such a confusion haunts the "revised compromise theory" of C. L. Ten—another mixed theory of legal punishment. Ten fails to recognize the difference between hard treatment that is permissible but nondeserved and hard treatment that is permissible but deserved. As a result, his concessions to utilitarianism do not speak either to the morality of punishment in general or to the morality of legal punishment in particular. In disclosing his mistake, we simultaneously provide a lesson in the pitfalls of applying the logic of justification where that of permissibility is most apt.

Elaborating on an example from Antony Quinton, Ten believes that authorities may sometimes be justified in torturing an innocent person. Suppose someone has planted "a bomb in a large hospital, which no one but he knows how to defuse and no one dare touch for fear of setting it off." [11] Ten follows Quinton in thinking that torture by the authorities might be justified as a means of inducing the man to defuse the bomb and save the many lives at stake. (Presumably the hospital contains at least some people who cannot be evacuated save at the cost of their lives.) If this is so, then in a case where torture is ineffective—perhaps the bomb planter is very tough or faints when the torture is applied—could we then torture his wife? Perhaps the bomb planter cannot tolerate seeing her undergo even mild pain, and willingly defuses the bomb.

Under such circumstances, Ten thinks we may be justified in torturing the wife, though the justification is subject to more severe constraints than that of torturing the man himself. He is guilty, his wife is not. Still, if her pain would be very much less than the pain inflicted on the innocent persons in the hospital, we would still be justified in torturing her.

Ten believes that such examples have a bearing on the moral theory of punishment. They lead him in his revised compromise theory to articulate and defend the following exception to the retributive condition in punishment:

> Punishing an innocent person would be justified if and only if punishing him inflicts much less suffering on him than the suffering that at least one other innocent person would have experienced as an additional victim of crime had there been no punishment.[12]

The picture of sparing innocent blood at the lamentable expense of innocent blood is a compelling one, but is the infliction of pain in such cases punishment, or merely a permissible kind of hard treatment? There are a host of problems with enshrining at the level of moral principle this sort of exceptional and putatively justified infliction of pain on the innocent.

The logic of permissibility helps us sort through such cases better than the logic of justification. It is wisest to say that if an authority's reflective moral judgment favors torturing a legally innocent person, whether suspected offender or not, that authority enters a realm where it is at best excused for this action, but not justified. The moral claim that legal innocence is always a barrier to police torture is sufficiently compelling that we must view such cases as morally problematic. An authority's decision to torture or otherwise mistreat a person in custody ought always to be subject to formal review after the fact. The logic of permissibility mandates such inquiry. If, by contrast, the authorities are perceived to be exonerated by a misplaced logic of duty and justification, the hard treatment in question will appear to be a matter of course, nothing to cause concern. To be excused for doing something—retrospectively permitted to have done it—assumes that one is on the defensive in a way a justification of one's actions does not. If authorities, indeed, if anyone, inflict hard treatment on legally innocent persons, the case is overwhelming that they ought to be on the defensive.

But the broader question is whether morally permissible hard treatment of innocent people speaks to the issue of legal punishment at all. I argue that it does not because legal punishment is a variety of permissible hard treatment morally applicable only to those who qualify on the basis of desert. What light, then, do even plausible cases of permissible torture or killing of innocent persons shed on legal punishment? We should note that such cases almost always require quick decision and instant reaction. Bombs are about to go off, terrorists about to act, a deranged killer's whereabouts desperately sought. But what is the relevance of this kind of crisis management to the austere, deliberative, and ponderously slow processes of trial, incarceration, appeal, parole, and the like by which we manage institutions of legal punishment? What considerations of sparing innocent blood could ever excuse anyone for using these practices knowingly to condemn and punish an innocent person? None that I can see, for all such considerations are excluded by a morally decisive preoccupation with desert in institutions of legal punishment.

A sensitive and morally pluralistic view of punishment can make retributivism count where it should—namely, against legally punishing the innocent. Even so, the tough question persists—Why impose legal punishment in preference to some other form of deserved and permissible hard treatment? The aim of retribution morally licenses censure, but there are many varieties of censure short of depriving a person of life or liberty. Why not adopt one or another of these other forms of permissible hard treatment rather than fully fledged legal punishment?

The answer to this question has already been given—namely, that grave moral offenses require sanctions that underscore their gravity. Doing normally forbidden things to people who violate grave sanctions is a unique communicative act that is not duplicable by any other form of censure. Whatever moral faults may be involved in acts where legal punishment is a permitted response, the paramount consideration is violation of a legal rule.

Enactment of such a rule marks the great divide between the informal sanctions of morality and the formal, institutional sanctions of law. Both kinds of penalties are at least partly retributive, threatening evil against those who violate either a precept of morality or a legal rule. But in the case of a purely moral sanction the threatened evil is inherently vague. It depends on particular relations between particular human beings. Say a young child steals from another member of the family. The act is novel, the situation fluid, the sanction unspecified. Only the moral norm—stealing is wrong—has been pronounced. So how to respond? A reprimand and a stern lecture? Working so many hours to repay the value of the theft? Grounding for a week? Any of these counts as punishment, but one may be superior to the others according to the particular family history. As Elizabeth Wolgast points out, familial punishment cannot afford severing emotional bonds.[13] Nurture and caring must shine through the chosen penalty so that the child is both the object of punishment and of love. Though the stealing may be a new offense, the range of permissible punishments is constrained by past history and by a concern for the future. Values other than that of retribution shape the kind and degree of punishment to be given.

In legal punishment, of course, a moral concern with equal application of the law comes to the fore in a way that raises problems for any analogy to informal, noninstitutional punishment. Offenders against a legal rule have a right to complain if they are treated more severely than others who have committed the same offense. On inspection, this concern for equality is the formal analog of the parents' desire to communicate love for an offending child. How better can an authority show that an offender is both deserving of an evil and at the same time "one of us," completely human with full potential for reintegration into the community, than to limit the evil in a way that applies equally to all who commit the same offense?

We have in part followed Herbert Morris to view the value of equality in legal punishment as stemming from an abstract concern for fairness in some presumed ideal distribution of benefits and burdens. All persons should have an equal share in the benefits and burdens of obeying the law; thus, the law justly imposes hard treatment on those who have taken unfair advantage by shirking some of the burdens. At the same time, however, we must see that the deeper value underlying the law's concern with equality is that of respect for persons. Proportionality in legal punishment is best seen as a vote for the future—a legal authority's most effective way of communicating to offenders that they are moral persons with the potential of reintegration into the community. Only by deliberately restraining their power, by imposing on an offender no less and no more than on any other offender of that class, can legal authorities lacking emotional bonds with lawbreakers attain anything like the moral status required to be something other than a blind, avenging Erinys. Offenders against the law, no matter how heinous their crimes, have a dignity as persons that must somehow be recognized.

The upshot for a defensible retributive theory of legal punishment is that after pronouncement of legal guilt the permissible hard treatment meted out by legal authorities is a function of values independent of the value of returning evil for evil. Unless the spell of like for like is broken, this fact is unlikely to be perceived, for it will continue to be thought that retributive values determine not only the kind of treatment deserved, but its nature and degree also.

Let us first look at the values constraining the morally permissible nature of a legal punishment. Flogging, eye gouging, and display of offenders in a public stock are all examples of impermissible legal punishments in codes of justice with a humanitarian bent. These punishments, we think, are excessively cruel, though many of our not-so-distant ancestors thought otherwise. Whose moral intuitions are to be heeded, theirs or ours? The answer must be ours, but not because of some moral skyhook that "proves" that our scheme produces the greatest balance of happiness or best restores an abstract original balance of benefits and burdens. In the course of human experience, certain kinds of deliberately imposed suffering are deemed morally intolerable for a variety of reasons. If legal authorities neglect the public mood, they undermine their moral authority. Public confidence suffers, and offenders begin to be shielded from the law by otherwise law-abiding citizens. The test, if you like, is pragmatic, but it is a pragmatism driven by consensus on how best to express a complex range of values.

The logic of permissibility reflects the flexibility over time of a community's search for legally retributive responses that are likewise morally acceptable. We might always change our legal punishments, this logic says; indeed, we might morally be compelled to change. Even now, the reformer's voice might win us over, persuading us that our favored mode of punishment is inferior to some alternative. Again, the logic of permissibility is a confession that we lack complete wisdom. Here, especially, is where consequences count. It is always good evidence against a particular mode of punishment that it produces offenders more inclined to do evil than they were before its imposition. Yet, at the same time, it is always good evidence in favor of a particular mode of punishment that it protects the public. No doubt one reason such harsher means of legal punishment as flogging have been abandoned is that they do neither of these two things. Such treatments often return to the public individuals who are more bitter for their hard treatment—individuals more likely than ever to abuse the law if they think they can get away with it.

Similar considerations pertain to determining the permissible degree of legal punishment. The case for longer sentences for recidivists has already been mentioned. In any particular imposition of punishment on an offender, a respect for her autonomy must weigh against a concern for the safety of the public. If the offender persists in misusing her autonomy, why should a respect for it count as much as previously? Again, the logic of permission applies more than that of duty and justification. A duty-bound justification is held once and for all; permissions may weaken or grow stronger. Repeat offenders wear on the patience and tolerance of civil authority in its exercise of responsible moral authority. Allowing recidivists to be punished more gravely than first-time offenders follows from a correspondent enhancement in the moral standing of civil authority. Its agents are permitted greater discretion according to the principle commanding that where risk of impermissible hard treatment must be borne by someone, the legally innocent ought to bear least risk. There is no reason for a retributivism released from the spell of like for like to ignore an offender's past history, even if she is formally "paid up." Similarly, there is no reason for such a retributivism to ignore other values in determining the nature and degree of retributive response.

As we have seen, Hart calls for "retribution in distribution," on the grounds that the "general justifying aim of punishment" is utilitarian, whereas candidates for distribution of punishment are determined by their desert. There is, however, a sense in which we may legitimately reverse this formula to say that the general aim (not a "justifying" aim) of legal punishment is retributive, whereas the conditions for its distribution are determined by other values, many of them utilitarian in character. Sometimes legal punishment is the most morally permissible among retributive responses. A legal offense has been committed by a person possessing a normal capacity for self-control, among other positive qualities. What do we do? If the individual is found guilty, we legally punish in a way consonant with respect for his person and autonomy, as well as for the safety and welfare of the public. These nonretributive values determine the nature and degree of the retributive response.

Because respect is best communicated by proportioning an offender's treatment to the treatment of similar offenders, we may conclude that a legal authority violates its duty if it fails to treat like cases alike. We must be careful, however, not to reintroduce the logic of justification into our understanding of this claim. The duty in question is not a first-order duty to impose hard treatment, but a second-order duty to administer impartially. Those who superintend institutions of legal punishment must treat each offender of a given class neither more nor less harshly than the norm. But this constraint is no different from any other public administrator's duty to administer fairly and without prejudice. If a normal kind of hard treatment is morally impermissible, administering fairly and impartially is no defense. An offender's legal desert sometimes qualifies him for legal punishment, but not for every nature and degree of punishment. When we say that authorities have a duty to punish in a certain way to a certain degree, we have in mind a *legal* duty that presupposes the prior permissibility of the hard treatment attendant on the punishment.

Solace, Sentimentality, and Restraint of State Authority

The view of legal punishment as morally permitted deprives us of the comforting thought that we have an unambiguous mandate to impose suffering deliberately on persons convicted of crime. From the standpoint of the average citizen, deprivation of this exculpatory solace may seem inconsequential. Penal institutions are remote from the daily experience of most people in most modern societies. Even judges and police are insulated from the harsh realities of incarceration and programmatic death. Where distress is slight, so also is the need for solace in the face of it. We can thus, in our popular views, easily countenance circumscribing the state's moral authority legally to punish along the lines I have been suggesting.

Arguably, however, the same may not be true for the group that (in addition to inmates themselves) enjoys neither physical nor psychic distance from the spectacle of pain judicially imposed. I refer, of course, to jailers, prison guards, wardens, and, in the extreme, executioners. For these individuals, exculpatory solace is not an indifferent matter. From the standpoint of moral psychology, these individuals present an acid test for the thesis that whatever retributive web we ultimately embrace, we must keep from weaving into it a first-order moral duty to inflict suffering.

In the view prescribed by classical retributivism, prison guards and their colleagues are morally justified. Sympathy for the suffering of those condemned by criminal justice is mere sentimentality so long as that suffering is neither excessive nor capricious. In only doing their duty, guards do exactly their duty. Vindication is complete, distress at the sight of deliberately imposed judicial pain misplaced.

Modern proponents of this view will protest any diminishing of the state's moral authority to punish in the same strong terms as Kant condemned the sentimentality of sparing the lives of murderers. How, the advocate of permissibility will be asked, dare we require human beings to superintend penal institutions without arming them to the hilt against pangs of tender conscience? To assert that representatives of the state lack moral justification in meting out measured suffering is more than simply to excise an unwanted portion from a retributive web; it is, a critic might allege, to allow the web to unravel in its entirety. When prison officials are encouraged to feel morally uncertain about what they do, the economy of suffering is worsened. We must add to its sum, which includes the undeserved suffering of the victim and the deserved suffering of the criminal, the pangs of prison employees who are now uncertain about the requirements of justice. At a single stroke, concludes our critic, skepticism about the duty legally to punish offenders deprives solid citizens of their peace of mind while sentimentalizing the plight of criminals.

Fortunately, we need not accept the preceding unidimensional analysis of moral duty. Legal punishment serves multiple aims—the first-order moral duty of protecting innocent persons primary among them. Acknowledging our uncertainty about the best means of achieving this aim does no more to undermine the morale of prison staff than uncertainty about the best means of producing educated citizens does to undermine the morale of educators. On the contrary, such uncertainty is a proper spur toward improvement, a hedge against mediocrity and smug contentment. Unattainable though it may be, the aspiration to counter evil with good is a reforming spirit we can ill afford to squelch. It may never release us from the tragic condition of perceiving in retrospect concealed retributive features in reforms earnestly designed to rid us of retributivism, but to concede everything to the spell of like for like is to impoverish ourselves and our futures. We gain nothing by concealing our doubts and dilemmas with a patina of certitude.

Our scant wisdom about criminality tells us that however bad the worst of us, the best of us is not so good as to guarantee that we will never sink so low. We have all been temporarily cut from the circle of family and friends for our faults. The fortunate among us are soon reintegrated. Preserving as many relationships as we can is more permissible than cutting off relationships on the presumption that we are too wise or too good to err. Since each of us lacks the moral standing to pronounce finally on the depravity of others, so, by extension, do the representatives—the jailers and wardens and executioners—deputized to act on our behalf.

These considerations of fragility in moral judgment are reinforced by the need, in general, to articulate clear grounds for self-restraint on the part of public authorities. Where state authority is either limited or not an issue (as in trade retaliation or censure among colleagues), retributive practices are morally sound only when the parties are equal and the evil deliberately inflicted is otherwise morally permissible. Requiring equality keeps one party from pounding another into permanent subservience. But equality is not enough—duels, for instance, are fought among equals. Duels are morally impermissible because they fall afoul of the second condition. Inflicting or running the risk of inflicting grievous bodily harm on another is not a morally permissible evil, save in legitimate self-defense. Duels create an artificial need for self-defense among people who could otherwise avoid it. Even the mutual consent of equals thus fails to turn dueling into a morally permissible retributive practice.

However, when state authority enters into our thinking about permissible retributive practice, the condition of equality no longer applies. Possessing a monopoly on the legitimate use of force, the state is superior to every other party. This disparity in power and resources is grounds for holding the state to even higher standards than those to which individuals are held in the deliberate infliction of retributive evil. Individuals can legitimately protect themselves against harm inflicted by other individuals. We lock our homes and keep valuables out of sight—no use relying wholly on the moral self-restraint of others. But with the state such precautions are futile. If wanted by state authority, we may not permissibly go into hiding, and others are barred from harboring us. Given its monopoly on the legitimate use of force, the state's exercise of moral self-restraint is vital, providing a further reason to cede it no more than the revocable sanction of a moral permission legally to punish.

Permissive retributivism stresses that, under ordinary circumstances, citizens possess a right *not* to be punished. Determination of legal guilt results in forfeiture of this right by the individual found guilty, but does not issue in a first-order moral duty of the state legally to punish—a duty that is the source of the forfeiture. A moral right is forfeited because of a culpable act by the agent possessing it, not because of a stronger countervailing duty possessed by someone else.

This point can be illustrated by showing that no such thesis is necessary where hard treatment is permissibly meted out to people who are nondeserving of it. Assume that the police detain an innocent person on the mistaken but reasonable belief that she has committed a legal offense. If we want to hold that the police have a first-order moral duty to detain this woman, then they are morally justified; they have done the right thing and owe her no apology. Given that the woman is innocent, however, the police have done the wrong thing, excusable though it may be. It is far better, then—more protective of the moral rights held by individuals—to think of the police power as a permission. This way, at least, we make sense of the apology owed to the innocent detainee. The woman's forfeiture of a right not to be detained (based on the presumptive evidence against her) is only the beginning of a long story of numerous vital moral constraints on the prerogatives of the police in dealing with her.

By analogy, forfeiture of the moral right not to be punished is likewise only the beginning of a long story. Guarding against abuse of the state's monopoly of the legitimate use of force sometimes means that the satisfying spectacles of retributivism must be foregone. The legally guilty are deliberately and knowingly set free when the state exceeds the bounds of its permissive powers. A focus on procedure (e.g., on *Miranda* warnings, on the provision of adequate defense counsel, and so forth) characterizes our insistence that state officials preserve the requisite moral standing to inflict the hard treatment of legal punishment. Rather than lament that these measures result in the coddling of criminals, we should celebrate them as an index of our liberation from the spell of like for like. To defend a retributive web that fails to pay as much attention to suspension of evil as to its requital is to presume an imperial role for moral theory that neither history nor analysis will sustain. The moral standing legally to punish is not fixed, like a statue in a square. Instead, it is a dynamic enterprise—a maintaining of balance—like the movements of a gymnast on a beam or of a log roller on a spinning log. Propositional knowledge about "just deserts" takes us only so far; at some point, our balance depends on an intuitional knowing-how as much as on a propositional knowing-that.[14] Repeated practice based on a willingness to learn from our falls proves indispensable to the dynamics of maintaining moral standing.

Notes and Index

Notes

INTRODUCTION

1. Cited by Aristotle in *Nichomachean Ethics*, trans. Richard McKeon, *The Basic Works of Aristotle* (New York: Random House, 1941), p. 1010.

2. Details of the murders may be found on page 1, *New York Times*, April 13, 1989. The wrinkle of forcing one of the accused cult members to exhume the bodies is reported on page 4, Part I, *Los Angeles Times*, April 14, 1989.

3. Thus, for example, the essays by Jeffrie G. Murphy and Jean Hampton, *Forgiveness and Mercy* (Cambridge: Cambridge University Press, 1988) are devoted as much to the topic of retribution as to forgiveness and mercy.

4. See John Cottingham, "Varieties of Retribution," *Philosophical Quarterly*, 29 (July 1979), pp. 238–56.

5. Witness A. C. Ewing, *The Morality of Punishment* (London: Kegan Paul, 1929), p. 13: "The primary justification of punishment is always to be found in the fact that an offense has been committed which deserves the punishment, not in any future advantage to be gained by its infliction"; see also John Rawls, "Two Concepts of Rules," *Philosophical Review*, 64 (1955), pp. 4–5: "What we may call the retributive view is that punishment is justified on the grounds that wrongdoing merits punishment. . . . The state of affairs where a wrongdoer suffers punishment is morally better than the state of affairs where he does not; and it is better irrespective of any of the consequences of punishing him. . . . What we may call the utilitarian view holds that . . . punishment is justifiable only by reference to the probable consequences."

6. Roger Wertheimer, "Deterrence and Retribution," *Ethics*, 86 (April 1976), pp. 181–99, argues for the compatibility of "enforcement retribution" with considerations of future deterrence. In "Understanding Retribution," *Criminal Justice Ethics*, 2 (Summer/Fall 1983), p. 31, he makes the stronger point that to assume the consequentialist/ nonconsequentialist divide in justifying punishment ends in begging the question. A con-

sequentialist moral theory can give only a consequentialist (i.e., a circular) justification of itself; the same holds for a nonconsequentialist moral theory.

7. W. V. Quine and J. S. Ullian, *The Web of Belief* (New York: Random House, 1970).

8. Skutch offers predation as evidence in an argument that the natural order must *not* be the product of a benevolent creator. See Alexander F. Skutch, *Life Ascending* (Austin: University of Texas Press, 1985), pp. 68–69.

9. John Milton, *Paradise Lost*, I, 24–26:

> That to the highth of this great Argument
> I may assert Eternal Providence,
> And justifie the wayes of God to men.

10. The broader concept of hard treatment I take from Feinberg's, "Expressive Function of Punishment" in Joel Feinberg, *Doing and Deserving* (Princeton, N.J.: Princeton University Press, 1970), p. 95.

11. For an elaboration of this point, see Cottingham, "Varieties of Retribution," pp. 245–46.

12. For a full defense of this view, see Richard A. Posner, "Retribution and Related Concepts of Punishment," *Journal of Legal Studies*, 9 (January 1980), pp. 71–92.

13. The full title of Thomas Beard's treatise gives its flavor: *The Theatre of God's Jvdgements, wherein is represented the admirable iustice of God against all notorious sinners, both great and small, but especially against the most eminent persons of the world, whose transcendent power breaketh through the barres of humane iustice; deduced by the order of the commandments* (London: 1612).

CHAPTER ONE

1. In addition to a Stoic like Marcus Aurelius, Spinoza comes to mind as one who propounds a nonretributive solution to the problem of human suffering.

2. An example of unnecessary difficulties arising from failure to distinguish between retribution and revenge is provided by Susan Jacoby, *Wild Justice: The Evolution of Revenge* (New York: Harper & Row, 1983). As Jacoby observes (p. 4): "Advocates of draconian punishment for crime invariably prefer 'retribution'—a word that affords the comfort of euphemism although it is virtually synonymous with 'revenge.'" Well and good, but for the remainder of the book she is forced to speak of "measured retribution" in distinguishing attempts to achieve justice from mere vengeance. The qualifier is redundant if the idea of a measured response is assumed as part of the meaning of "retribution," as I believe it commonly is. For an expansion of this point, see Marvin Henberg, "Taming the Beast: Moral Views of the Criminal Law," *Duke Law Journal*, 85 (1985), p. 846.

3. The prime example of such recision is the Old Testament repudiation of collective punishment for sons whose fathers are guilty of iniquity. For the original collectivist doctrine, see Exod. 20.5; for its repeal, see Deut. 24.16, Ezek. 18, and Jer. 31.19.

4. I am indebted to Walter Moberly, *The Ethics of Punishment* (Hamden, Conn.: Archon, 1968), p. 111, for pointing out this ambiguity.

5. The earliest depiction of the balance beam is in an Egyptian drawing from the Papyrus of ANI (c. 1500 B.C.E.) showing the jackal-headed Anubis weighing the heart (symbol of conscience?) of a dead man against a feather (symbol of law?). See the frontispiece to E. A. Wallis Budge, *The Book of the Dead* (New York: University Books, 1960).

6. H. Diels, *Die Fragmente der Vorsokratiker*, ed. W. Kranz, 6th rev. ed. (Berlin: 1951), 12, fr. 1; translation in Hugh Lloyd-Jones, *The Justice of Zeus* (Berkeley: University of California Press, 1971), pp. 79–80.

7. Hampton discusses at some length an example from the advice column of Ann Landers, in which a woman deliberately infects a casual sexual acquaintance with AIDS. See Jeffrie G. Murphy and Jean Hampton, *Forgiveness and Mercy* (Cambridge: Cambridge University Press, 1988), pp. 76–79. More mundane issues in advice columns tend to center on emotional tit for tat designed to bolster the self-respect of people who have been emotionally wronged by loved ones. For intimate contexts, Hampton (pp. 124–38) develops a view of retribution in which punishment is perceived as "defeat" of a wrongdoer by an action that symbolizes his or her correct relative value to the victim—a valuation that the wrongdoing has upset. Parallels abound between Hampton's interpretation and the dominance rituals of nonhuman social mammals discussed in Chapter Two.

8. For a sensitive exploration of this theme, see Susan Sontag, *Illness as Metaphor* (New York: Farrar, Straus and Giroux, 1977). Among various punitive modes of thinking about disease, Sontag concentrates especially on illness as moral recompense and as a nonmoral (but still fitting) expression of character.

9. See E. P. Evans, *The Criminal Prosecution and Capital Punishment of Animals* (London: Heinemann, 1906).

10. Ibid., pp. 80–81.

11. Mark 11.12–14; 20–22.

12. Keith Thomas, *Religion and the Decline of Magic* (New York: Scribner's, 1971), pp. 554–55.

13. See, for instance, the law of deodands. Our age tends to look at the banishment of "contagious" inanimate objects as a long-dead superstition, but, as I write this note, a newspaper reports that the ferry *Herald of Free Enterprise*, salvaged and perfectly serviceable, is being towed to South Korea for scrap. No one is willing to buy or to use the ship because of its involvement in the 1987 Zeebrugge disaster. Even with a rechristening, the risks of putting a suspect vessel into service are prohibitive. *Guardian*, February 11, 1988, p. 2.

14. See Robert O. Keohane, "Reciprocity in International Relations," *International Organization*, 40 (Winter 1986), pp. 1–27.

15. The match between nuclear retaliation and a nuclear first strike differs from the usual case of deliberate revenge. Equivalence between the provoking act and the retaliation itself is the result, not of deliberate limitation of the latter, but of the massive and uncontrolled potential for destruction that nuclear weapons represent. This gives rise to unique conceptual difficulties, but we are nonetheless warranted in classifying nuclear strategy as a variety of retributive thought, even though its main aim is deterrence. For fuller exami-

nation of the conceptual difficulties raised by strategies of nuclear deterrence, see Gregory Kavka, "Some Paradoxes of Deterrence," *Journal of Philosophy*, 75 (1978), pp. 285–302, and Richard Wasserstrom, "War, Nuclear War, and Nuclear Deterrence: Some Conceptual and Moral Issues," *Ethics*, 95 (1985), pp. 424–44.

16. See Lawrence Alexander, "The Doomsday Machine: Proportionality, Punishment, and Prevention," *The Monist*, 63 (April 1980), pp. 199–227.

17. Matt. 5.38–39 This and all other passages of scripture cited are from the Revised Standard Version.

18. Matt. 7.14–15: "For if you forgive men their trespasses, your heavenly Father also will forgive you; but if you do not forgive men their trespasses, neither will your Father forgive your trespasses."

19. The same gap between act and intention that fuzzes the will to retaliate also fuzzes the will to dispense forgiveness. We may want to abjure a retaliatory aim, but dare we believe our adversary when he offers forgiveness? The question opens into a hall of mirrors the moment we consider that his offer may be disingenuous—part of a larger retributive strategy to allay suspicion and to strike when we are unprepared.

20. "Revenge is a kinde of Wilde Justice; which the more Mans Nature runs to, the more ought law to weed it out." Francis Bacon, "Of Revenge," *The Essayes or Counsels, Civill and Morall* (Cambridge, Mass.: Harvard University Press, 1985), p. 16. Bacon concludes his essay with a reference (p. 17) to the presumed link between retributivism and the occult: "Vindictive persons live the life of Witches; who as they are Mischievous, so end they Infortunate."

21. Chapter Three explores the underlying affinities between this formula in returning evil for evil and in serving as epistemological bedrock in the association of ideas; thus the use of the adjective "epistemic."

CHAPTER TWO

1. For an extended account of this tendency, see Mary Midgley, *Beast and Man: The Roots of Human Nature* (Ithaca, N.Y.: Cornell University Press, 1978), especially chap. 2, "Animals and the Problem of Evil."

2. The still classic study of these evils is Richard Hofstadter, *Social Darwinism in American Thought*, rev. ed. (Boston: Beacon, 1955). For an update, see Howard L. Kaye, *The Social Meaning of Modern Biology* (New Haven, Conn.: Yale University Press, 1986).

3. Steven Goldberg, *The Inevitability of Patriarchy* (New York: Morrow, 1973), p. 82.

4. This discussion summarizes arguments put forward by Richard Dawkins, *The Selfish Gene* (Oxford: Oxford University Press, 1976), chap. 9, and by Dan Freedman, *Human Sociobiology* (New York: Free Press, 1979), chap. 2.

5. "It is not surprising that the model of society that turns out to be 'natural' bears a remarkable resemblance to the institutions of modern market society, since the theorists who produce these models are themselves privileged members of just such a society." Sociobiology Study Group, "Sociobiology: A New Biological Determinism," in *Biology as a Social Weapon*, ed. Ann Arbor Science for the People Editorial Collective (Minneapolis, Minn.: Burgess, 1977), p. 133.

6. T. H. Huxley, "Evolution and Ethics," in *Evolution and Ethics and Other Essays* (New York: D. Appleton, 1897), pp. 79–80.

7. Edward Westermarck, *The Origin and Development of the Moral Ideas* (London: Macmillan; vol. 1, 1906; vol. 2, 1908).

8. J. L. Mackie, "Morality and the Retributive Emotions," *Criminal Justice Ethics*, 1 (1982), pp. 3–10.

9. Westermarck, *The Origin and Development*, vol. 2, p. 739.

10. Westermarck, *The Origin and Development*, vol. 1, chap. 5.

11. David Hume, *An Inquiry Concerning the Principles of Morals*, III, 1.

12. For a review of this controversy, see E. O. Wilson, *Sociobiology: The New Synthesis* (Cambridge, Mass.: Harvard University Press, 1975), chap. 5. See also M. Wade, "A Critical Review of the Models of Group Selection," *Quarterly Review of Biology*, 53 (1978), pp. 101–14.

13. Arguments for selective advantage work best for traits that avoid high risks and that produce high payoffs to individuals of a species. As John Byers has pointed out to me, warning cries are a low-risk/low-payoff proposition; perhaps because of this, explanations for their emergence constitute a cottage industry. Ingenious accounts are given by J. Maynard Smith, "The Evolution of Alarm Calls," *American Naturalist*, 99 (1965), pp. 59–63, and by Robert L. Trivers, "The Evolution of Reciprocal Altruism," *Quarterly Review of Biology*, 45 (1971), pp. 35–57. Trivers, in fact, proffers five explanations, each for birds living under different conditions. Richard Dawkins adds two more explanations in *The Selfish Gene*, pp. 182–83.

14. Dawkins indulges in polemic when he relegates human bodies to the status of "survival machines—robot vehicles blindly programmed to preserve the selfish molecules known as genes." *The Selfish Gene*, ix.

15. The point that "selfish" in Dawkins's title carries only the sense of "self-replicating" is made with vehemence by Mary Midgley in "Gene-Juggling," *Philosophy*, 54 (1979), pp. 444–58—a retort to J. L. Mackie's defense of Dawkins in "The Law of the Jungle: Moral Alternatives and Principles of Evolution," *Philosophy*, 53 (1978), 455–64. Both Dawkins, "In Defence of Selfish Genes," *Philosophy*, 56 (1981), pp. 556–73, and Mackie, "Genes and Egoism," *Philosophy*, 56 (1981), pp. 553–55, respond with complaints at Midgley's bad temper. Midgley apologizes for her tone, but not her views, in "Selfish Genes and Social Darwinism," *Philosophy* 58 (1983), pp. 365–77.

16. For a synopsis, see Donald A. Dewsbury, *Comparative Animal Behavior* (New York: McGraw-Hill, 1978), p. 70.

17. Ibid., p. 180.

18. Trivers, "The Evolution of Reciprocal Altruism," p. 40.

19. Robert Axelrod and William D. Hamilton, "The Evolution of Cooperation," *Science*, 211 (1981), pp. 1390–96.

20. Other strategies would have won the first tournament, consisting of fourteen strategies played in round-robin against each other for a total of two hundred moves. When these potential winning strategies were submitted in the second tournament, however, TIT FOR TAT came out on top. This competition differed from the first in that sixty-two strategies were submitted and in that the two hundred fixed moves were replaced with a probabilistic formula for determining the end of the game. Both these changes increased the tourna-

ment's realism, the first giving a more variegated environment of strategies, the second removing a temptation to defect toward the end of a game. For a detailed discussion of tournament results, see Robert Axelrod, *The Evolution of Cooperation* (New York: Basic, 1984), chap. 2. See also Douglas R. Hofstadter, "The Prisoner's Dilemma: Computer Tournaments and the Evolution of Cooperation," *Scientific American*, 248 (May 1983), pp. 16–26.

21. Axelrod and Hamilton, "The Evolution of Cooperation," p. 1392.

22. Ibid., p. 1393.

23. Ibid.

24. Wolves also communicate submissiveness in other ways, including vocalization, facial expression, and tail posture. See L. David Mech, *The Wolf: The Ecology and Behavior of an Endangered Species* (New York: Natural History Press, 1970), pp. 75–93.

25. See Konrad Lorenz, *King Solomon's Ring* (New York: Crowell, 1952), pp. 191–93, for an account of the lack of inhibition in conflicts between male roe deer.

26. See Dewsbury, *Comparative Animal Behavior*, pp. 115–20.

27. Jane Goodall, *The Chimpanzees of Gombe* (Cambridge, Mass.: Harvard University Press, 1986), chap. 17.

28. Goodall writes of the Kasakela males: "If they had had firearms and had been taught to use them, I suspect they would have used them to kill." *The Chimpanzees of Gombe*, p. 530.

29. For a summary of aggressive behavior in social animals and an extrapolation to the human condition, see Irenaus Eibl-Eibesfeldt, *The Biology of Peace and War*, trans. Eric Mosbacher (New York: Viking, 1979).

30. Midgley, *Beast and Man*, p. 41.

CHAPTER THREE

1. See James George Frazer, *The Golden Bough*, vol. 1, 3d ed. (London: Macmillan, 1926), pp. 245–55, for a host of examples of rain making based on sympathetic magic. Frazer attributes (p. 211) the power of what he calls "homeopathic" magic to the association of ideas by similarity and by contiguity in space and time. It is the association of ideas by similarity that I argue is fundamental in explaining the persistence of the retributive like for like.

2. Herbert Spencer, *Education: Intellectual, Moral, and Physical* (New York: D. Appleton, 1900), pp. 175–76.

3. Ibid., p. 178.

4. Ibid., p. 190.

5. Ibid., p. 147.

6. A related but converse idea is that the child's development "recapitulates" the history of humankind's emergence from barbarism. See Stephen Jay Gould, *The Mismeasure of Man* (New York: Norton, 1981), chap. 4, for a chilling account of the injustices following from this mode of grasping at supposed similarities between children and "primitives."

7. Cesare Lombroso, *Crime: Its Causes and Remedies*, trans. Henry P. Horton (Boston: Little, Brown, 1911). The first chapter of this book is devoted to the "criminality"

of animals, particularly apes. The remainder details fanciful physical parallels between human criminals and their "apish" counterparts.

8. Emile Durkheim, *Moral Education*, trans. Everett K. Wilson and Herman Schnurer (New York: Free Press of Glencoe, 1961), p. 171: "The primitive does not dream of attributing untoward things that befall him to the regularity of natural law for the very good reason that he knows nothing of natural law."

9. Hans Kelsen, "Causality and Retribution," in *What Is Justice?* (Berkeley: University of California Press, 1957), p. 304.

10. H. Diels, *Die Fragmente der Vorsokratiker* ed. W. Kranz, 6th rev. ed. (Berlin: 1951), 12, fr. 94; translation by Hans Kelsen, "Causality and Retribution," p. 309.

11. Kelsen, "Causality and Retribution," p. 309.

12. Spencer, *Education*, pp. 193–95.

13. For a defense of the link between a defective will and resentment, see P. F. Strawson, "Freedom and Resentment," *Proceedings of the British Academy* (1962), pp. 187–211.

14. For an account of the unacknowledged retributivism inherent even in reforms inspired by humanitarian considerations, see Michel Foucault, *Discipline and Punish: The Birth of the Prison*, trans. Alan Sheridan (New York: Pantheon, 1977), especially pp. 104–31, "The Gentle Way in Punishment."

15. Jane Goodall, *The Chimpanzees of Gombe* (Cambridge, Mass.: Harvard University Press, 1986); see p. 469 for a table of "relative frequency of observed copulations between maternal siblings versus mean number with non-related reproductively mature males during selected periods."

16. A more complicated theory posits secondary "epigenetic rules," which do not lead directly to sexual aversion to near relatives (after all, how would we recognize them?), but wait to be filled in by imprinting against anyone, relative or not, with whom we are raised in intimate proximity—thus, for example, explaining "incest" aversion among non-related individuals raised in the same kibbutz. See Charles Lumsden and E. O. Wilson, *Genes, Mind, and Culture* (Cambridge, Mass.: Harvard University Press, 1981), p. 370; see also Michael Ruse, *Taking Darwin Seriously* (Oxford: Blackwell, 1986), pp. 143–47. No matter how we complicate the biological substratum of a particular kind of behavior, however, we must recognize that culture may, *independent of that substratum,* provide powerful reasons for or against the behavior in question. At least some of the time these independent cultural reasons may prove decisive in guiding conduct.

17. For an extended discussion and refutation (on analytical rather than historical grounds) of the link between free will and retributivism, see Robert Nozick, *Philosophical Explanations* (Cambridge, Mass.: Harvard University Press, 1981), pp. 291–397.

CHAPTER FOUR

1. See Hubert J. Treston, *Poine: A Study in Ancient Greek Blood-Vengeance* (London: Longmans, 1923), pp. 1–3.

2. Treston's real interest in proposing the scheme is to introduce a thesis about two contending and incommensurable systems of blood vengeance in Homer: the Archaean, an

honor-bound scheme based on the restricted vendetta, and the Pelasgian, a mixed system of wergeld and exact retaliation. It is thus dangerous to attribute to him any generalized historicist or moral-developmentalist inclinations. True, he writes as if the four systems follow sequentially, but this may be as much a matter of rhetorical convenience as of wishing to commit himself to a developmental framework.

3. In the study of ancient Near Eastern law, G. L. Driver and John C. Miles, *The Assyrian Laws* (Oxford: Clarendon Press, 1935), pp. 501–2, and *The Babylonian Laws*, vol. 1 (Oxford: Clarendon Press, 1952), pp. 350–51, are the most notable exponents of an evolutionary scheme nearly identical to that of Treston. Others concurring with this concept are David Werner Amram, "Retaliation and Compensation," *Jewish Quarterly Review* (new series, 2), pp. 191–211, and Ze'ev W. Falk, *Hebrew Law in Biblical Times* (Jerusalem: Wahrmann, 1964), p. 80.

4. See, for instance, Colin M. Turnbull, *The Forest People* (New York: Simon and Schuster, 1961) for an account of a society (Congolese Pygmies) in which social ostracism appears to be the sole "legal" sanction.

5. Driver and Miles, *The Assyrian Laws*, p. 33.

6. Compare Deut. 19.19–21, discussed in the following section.

7. These two passages from the Hammurabic Code (and all other passages from non-Hebraic Near Eastern codes) are from J. B. Pritchard, ed., *Ancient Near Eastern Texts Related to the Old Testament* (Princeton, N.J.: Princeton University Press, 1955). Translators are Theophile J. Meek, *Code of Hammurabi* and *The Middle Assyrian Laws*, and Albrecht Goetze, *The Laws of Eshnunna* and *The Hittite Laws*.

8. This interpretation is that of Driver and Miles in *The Babylonian Laws*, vol. 1, p. 415.

9. For the lack of talion in Ur-Nammu, see S. E. Loewenstamm, "Review of A. Goetze, *The Laws of Eshnunna*," *Israel Exploration Journal*, 7 (1957), p. 194, and A. S. Diamond, "An Eye for an Eye," in *Jewish Law and Decision-Making*, ed. Aaron M. Schreiber (Philadelphia: Temple University Press, 1979), pp. 174–75.

10. C. H. W. Johns, *The Relations between the Laws of Babylonia and the Laws of the Hebrew Peoples* (London: Oxford University Press, 1917), p. 32.

11. J. J. Finkelstein, "Ammisaduqa's Edict and the Babylonian 'Law Codes,' " *Journal of Cuneiform Studies* (1961), p. 95.

12. See Moshe Greenberg, "Some Postulates of Biblical Criminal Law," in Schreiber, ed., *Jewish Law and Decision-Making*, p. 147.

13. The ancient Hebrew belief in pollution is similar in outline to that of the ancient Greeks. (A detailed account of the doctrine can be found in Chapter Five.) As this chapter focuses on the law of homicide and bodily injury, we resist excursion into such other issues relating to blood guilt as collective responsibility, vicarious suffering, spiritual atonement, and salvation.

14. This passage of scripture (and those that follow) is from the Revised Standard Version.

15. For this interpretation, see Hinckley G. Mitchell, *The Ethics of the Old Testament* (Chicago: University of Chicago Press, 1912), pp. 115–16.

16. Thus Philo's interpretation, based on the Septuagint: "If the child which was conceived within her is still unfashioned and unformed, he shall be punished by a fine. . . .

But if the child which was conceived has assumed a distinct shape in all its parts, having received all its proper connective and distinctive qualities, he shall die" (*De special legibus*, II, #19; quoted in V. Aptowitzer, "Observations on the Criminal Laws of the Jews," *Jewish Quarterly Review* (new series, 15), p. 81.

17. See A. S. Diamond, *Primitive Law* (London: Watts, 1950), p. 117.

18. "The solution can probably be got by paying attention to an idea that seems to have been of much importance in early times—and not only in the Bible: the idea that if you deprive a man of a certain power or faculty, this power or faculty becomes yours." David Daube, *Studies in Biblical Law* (Cambridge: Cambridge University Press, 1947), p. 121.

19. The Talmud argues that it is not the fact of exile that expiates the blood guilt, but rather the death of the priest; for if the priest dies after sentencing but before exile, the killer need never enter the city of refuge. Only death can expiate another death, vicarious as the expiation may be in the case of a high priest and the indefinite number of accidental homicides released on his demise see Babylonian Talmud, ed. Isidore Epstein (New York: Soncino, 35 vols., 1935–52) Makkoth, 11b. The argument is discussed by Moshe Greenberg in "The Role of the Tribe and Family in Applying Criminal Sanctions," *Journal of Biblical Literature*, 78 (1959), p. 125, and by Myer Galinski in *Pursue Justice: The Administration of Justice in Ancient Israel* (London: Nechdim, 1983), p. 347.

20. Babylonian Talmud, Makkot II.7, Makkot 12.a. See also the discussion by Boaz Cohen, *Jewish and Roman Law*, vol. 2 (New York: Shulsinger, 1966), pp. 626–27.

21. Mayer Sulzberger, *The Ancient Hebrew Law of Homicide* (Philadelphia: Greenstone, 1915), p. 94.

22. Johns, *The Relations between the Laws*, p. 73.

23. Daube, *Studies in Biblical Law*, p. 123.

24. For criticism of Daube's view of "taking back" the blood (and hence the powers) of the deceased, see Geoffrey MacCormack, "Revenge and Compensation in Early Law," *American Journal of Comparative Law*, 21 (1973), p. 76.

25. Driver and Miles, *The Assyrian Laws*, p. 34.

26. Babylonian Talmud, Yad Edut 20.8–9.

27. Babylonian Talmud, Yad Edut, 20.2. See also the discussion in Menachem Elon, ed., *The Principles of Jewish Law* (Jerusalem: Keter, 1975), pp. 516–17.

28. See J. J. Finkelstein, " 'Babel-Bible': A Mesopotamian View," in Schreiber, ed., *Jewish Law and Decision-Making*, pp. 115–19.

29. Babylonian Talmud, Bava Kamma, 83b–84a.

30. For an application of this myth of the Childhood of Man to Near Eastern law, see Philip Berger Benny, *The Criminal Code of the Jews* (London: Smith, Elder, 1880), p. 23. See also the discussion in Chapter Three of this book.

31. For a view that gross societal wealth rather than moral belief powers the shift from retaliation to compensation in early law, see Richard Posner, "A Theory of Primitive Society, with Special Reference to Primitive Law," *Journal of Law and Economics*, 23 (April 1980), p. 43.

CHAPTER FIVE

1. For a concise account of Ixion's fate, see Lewis Richard Farnell, *The Cults of the Greek States*, vol. 3 (Oxford: Clarendon Press, 1907), p. 67.

2. Passages cited in English from Aeschylus and Euripides are from David Grene and Richmond Lattimore, eds., *The Complete Greek Tragedies*, vols. 1 and 4 (Chicago: University of Chicago Press, 1959). Translators are Richmond Lattimore, *Agamemnon*, *The Libation-Bearers*, and *The Eumenides*; William Arrowsmith, *Orestes*; and Emily Townsend Vermeule, *Electra*.

3. Hesiod, *Theogony*, 178–85.

4. Erwin Rohde, *Psyche: The Cult of Souls and Belief in Immortality among the Greeks*, trans. W. B. Hillis (New York: Harcourt, Brace, 1925), p. 21.

5. Lewis Richard Farnell, *The Cults of the Greek States*, vol. 5 (Oxford: Clarendon Press, 1909), p. 439.

6. Gagarin argues convincingly that even in the time of Drakon, the Greek lawgiver whose name is synonymous with harshness in penal legislation, the preferred punishment for homicide was exile. See Michael Gagarin, *Drakon and Early Athenian Homicide Law* (New Haven, Conn.: Yale University Press, 1981), especially pp. 119–21.

7. Lewis Richard Farnell, *The Cults of the Greek States*, vol. 2 (Oxford: Clarendon Press, 1896), p. 495.

8. See Werner Jaeger, *Paideia: The Ideals of Greek Culture*, vol. 1, trans. Gilbert Highet (New York: Oxford University Press, 1945), especially pp. 150–69. This view is developed by Gregory Vlastos in "Solonian Justice," *Classical Philology*, 41 (1946), pp. 65–83, and in "Equality and Justice in the Early Greek Cosmologies," *Classical Philology*, 42 (1947), pp. 156–78. A more recent endorsement may be found in Hugh Lloyd-Jones, *The Justice of Zeus* (Berkeley: University of California Press, 1971), pp. 80–81.

9. See Arthur W. H. Adkins, *Merit and Responsibility: A Study in Greek Values* (Oxford: Clarendon Press, 1960), pp. 30–57; Michael Gagarin, *Aeschylean Drama* (Berkeley: University of California Press, 1976), pp. 12–20; and Eric A. Havelock, *The Greek Concept of Justice* (Cambridge, Mass.: Harvard University Press, 1978), pp. 251–54.

10. "The essential aspect seems to be that the person defiled by blood should once again come into contact with blood. The ritual is a demonstrative and therefore harmless repetition of the shedding of blood in which the result, the visible defilement, can equally demonstratively be set aside. . . . Comparable is the primitive custom where the murderer sucks in the blood of his victim and then spits it out again: he must accept the fact through intimate contact, and at the same time effectively free himself of it." Walter Burkert, *Greek Religion*, trans. John Raffan (Oxford: Blackwell, 1985), p. 81.

11. Euripides, *Iphigenia at Tauris*, 1233; translation by Rohde, *Psyche*, p. 296.

12. H. Diels, *Die Fragmente der Vorsokratiker*, ed. W. Kranz, 6th rev. ed. (Berlin: 1951), 12, fr. 5.

13. E. R. Dodds, *The Greeks and the Irrational* (Berkeley: University of California Press, 1951), p. 40.

14. Ibid., p. 36.

15. Lloyd-Jones, *The Justice of Zeus*, p. 71.

16. Hubert J. Treston, *Poine: A Study in Ancient Greek Blood-Vengeance* (London: Longmans, 1923), p. 141.

17. Robert J. Bonner and Gertrude Smith, *The Administration of Justice from Homer to Aristotle*, vol. 2 (New York: Greenwood, 1968), pp. 221–30.

18. Burkert, *Greek Religion*, p. 194.

19. See "Meaning, Metaphor, and Metaphysics" in Chapter One, pp. 18–21.

20. *Anthologia Palatina*, 10.123.

21. Farnell, *Cults of the Greek States*, vol. 3, p. 75.

22. Dodds locates this idea in late archaic and early classical writers, especially Solon, Aeschylus, and Herodotus; Dodds, *The Greeks and the Irrational*, pp. 30–31.

23. Adkins, *Merit and Responsibility*, p. 88.

24. Believing that Rohde, Dodds, Adkins et al. have overstated the connection between pollution and the irrational, Parker rejects "the idea that a culture's beliefs about pollution derive from anxiety or a sense of guilt. They are rather by-products of an ideal of order." Robert Parker, *Miasma: Pollution and Purification in Early Greek Religion* (Oxford: Clarendon Press, 1983), pp. 325–26.

25. *Odyssey*, 3.304–16.

26. *Nichomachean Ethics*, 5.5.

27. *Tetralogies*, Bd 8–Bd 9; discussed by Adkins, *Merit and Responsibility*, p. 106.

28. *Against Aristocrates*, 53; discussed by Adkins, *Merit and Responsibility*, p. 106.

29. *Oxford Classical Dictionary*, 2d ed., ed. N. G. L. Hammond and H. H. Scullard (Oxford: Clarendon Press, 1970), p. 303.

30. "The instinct for retribution is part of the nature of man, and channeling that instinct in the administration of criminal justice serves an important purpose in promoting the stability of a society governed by law." Justice Potter Stewart, concurring in *Furman v. Georgia*, 408 U.S. 238 (1972), note 3 *supra*, at 308.

CHAPTER SIX

1. All passages cited in English from Plato's dialogues, save those from the *Laws*, are contained in Edith Hamilton and Huntington Cairns, eds., *The Collected Dialogues of Plato* (New York: Pantheon, 1961). Translators include W. D. Woodhead, *Gorgias*; W. K. C. Guthrie, *Protagoras*; and Paul Shorey, *Republic*. Passages from the *Laws* are from Trevor J. Saunders, *Plato: The "Laws"* (Harmondsworth, Middlesex: Penguin, 1970).

2. For a clear exposition of classical retributivism, see Edmund Pincoffs, *The Rationale of Legal Punishment* (New York: Humanities Press, 1966), pp. 1–16.

3. Such is the course adopted by Stalley, who argues (p. 162) that Plato "rejects any element of retributivism and looks on punishment as a device for doing social good, chiefly by curing the criminal." Accordingly, for Stalley, the retributivism of Plato's eschatology is purely admonitory—a warning against falling into vice. See R. F. Stalley, *An Introduction to Plato's "Laws"* (Indianapolis, Ind.: Hackett, 1983). A similar view is endorsed by Philip Shuchman, "Comments on the Criminal Code of Plato's *Laws*," *Journal of the History of Ideas*, 24 (1963), pp. 25–40.

4. This apparent discrepancy between theory and practice leads MacKenzie, in the most thorough study available, to hold that divorcing Plato's eschatology from his theoretical penology is to accuse him of bad faith in the former. We must, MacKenzie argues, take Plato's eschatology at face value—though we still do not have to import any element of retributivism into Plato's theoretical views on punishment. For complex reasons that readers may wish to ponder on their own, MacKenzie argues that Plato is confused but sincere in his allegiance to both retributivism and the curative theory. See Mary Margaret MacKenzie, *Plato on Punishment* (Berkeley: University of California Press, 1981), especially pp. 225–44.

5. "Outright invention plays almost no part at all in his work . . . his creations are developments of beliefs and practices already in existence." Glenn R. Morrow, *Plato's Cretan City: A Historical Interpretation of the "Laws"* (Princeton, N.J.: Princeton University Press, 1960), p. 591. The view is shared by Huntington Cairns, *Legal Philosophy from Plato to Hegel* (Baltimore, Md.: Johns Hopkins University Press, 1949), p. 75.

6. D. M. MacDowell, *The Athenian Homicide Law in the Age of the Orators* (Manchester: Manchester University Press, 1963), p. 89.

7. Stalley points out the parallels between Wootton's views and those of Plato. Though instructive, these convergences must be regarded in the light of a signal difference between them: Nothing in Wootton's view requires pain in the course of her favored therapeutic model; but, as this chapter demonstrates, Plato's curative view does require pain. See Stalley, *An Introduction to Plato's "Laws,"* pp. 143, 164–65, and Barbara Wootton, *Crime and Criminal Law* (London: Stevens, 1963).

8. Saunders argues that Plato's eschatology develops toward automatic, impersonal, and cosmic retribution for the very purpose of grounding ethics in physics. Trevor J. Saunders, "Penology and Eschatology in Plato's *Timaeus* and *Laws*," *Classical Quarterly*, 23 (1973), pp. 232–44.

9. For a modern defense of this connection, advocating a return to corporal punishment, see Graeme Newman, *Just and Painful* (New York: Macmillan, 1983).

10. Morrow, *Plato's Cretan City*, pp. 243, 291.

11. Such is the essence of punishment, according to Fingarette. Understanding "suffering" in its etymological sense of "to be passively done to, to undergo," Fingarette argues that punishment is a humbling of the offender's will. See Herbert Fingarette, "Punishment and Suffering," *Proceedings and Addresses of the American Philosophical Association*, 50 (1977), pp. 499–525.

12. Stalley, *An Introduction to Plato's "Laws,"* p. 147.

13. For a survey of this controversy, along with an argument for a unitary soul that appears composite in conjunction with the body, see W. K. C. Guthrie, "Plato's Views on the Nature of the Soul," in *Plato: A Collection of Critical Essays*, vol. 2, ed. Gregory Vlastos (Notre Dame, Ind.: University of Notre Dame Press, 1978), pp. 230–43.

14. See Antony M. Quinton, "On Punishment," in *The Philosophy of Punishment*, ed. H. B. Acton (London: Macmillan, 1969), pp. 55–64.

CHAPTER SEVEN

1. For both the etymology and the Qur'anic substantiation of nature as *muslim,* see Fazlur Rahman, *Major Themes of the Qur'an* (Minneapolis, Minn.: Bibliotheca Islamica, 1980), p. 13.

2. Only one of the three chief original Arabic biographies of Muhammad has been translated into English: Alfred Guillaume, *The Life of Muhammad: A Translation of Is'hāq's "sīrat rasūl allāh"* (London: Oxford University Press, 1955). This work, full of both authentic detail and miraculous embroidery on the facts, is a primary source for the more critical Western biographies on which I have relied: W. Montgomery Watt, *Muhammad at Mecca* (Oxford: Clarendon Press, 1953) and *Muhammad at Medina* (Oxford: Clarendon Press, 1956); Maxime Rodinson, *Mohammed,* trans. Anne Carter (New York: Pantheon, 1971); and John Bagot Glubb, *The Life and Times of Muhammad* (London: Hodder and Stoughton, 1970). All passages cited from the Qur'an are from Maulana Muhammad Ali, trans., *The Holy Qur'an: Arabic Text, English Translation and Commentary,* 5th ed. (Lahore: Ahmadiyyah Anjuman Isha'at Islam, 1963).

3. "As the pre-Islamic proverb has it, *la dina illa bi'l muruwwati,* 'there is no religion but manliness.' " Cited in M. S. Seale, *Qur'an and Bible* (London: Croom Helm, 1978), p. 12. For the definitive discussion of pre-Islamic Arab ideas of virtue, see Ignaz Goldziher, *Muslim Studies,* vol. 1 (Chicago: Aldane, 1967.)

4. Goldziher, *Muslim Studies,* p. 24.

5. Ibid., p. 25.

6. Watt, *Muhammad at Mecca,* p. 137.

7. See Richard Bell, *The Origin of Islam in Its Christian Environment* (London: Macmillan, 1926), and Henry Preserved Smith, *The Bible and Islam* (New York: Scribner's, 1897).

8. Kenneth Cragg, *The Call of the Minaret* (Oxford: Oxford University Press, 1956), p. 89.

9. David Daube, *Studies in Biblical Law* (Cambridge: Cambridge University Press, 1947) chap. 4, "Communal Responsibility."

10. For Solomon see surah 2.102; for David see surah 38.24, along with Muhammad Ali's note 2136, p. 870.

11. "The Qur'an never enjoins love of God . . . because God Himself loves only the strictly pious. To love God one must presuppose that God is reciprocating the sentiment. And to presuppose that is to presuppose that one is perfectly pious. Such presumption the Qur'an never allows." Daud Rahbar, *God of Justice: A Study in the Ethical Doctrines of the Qur'an* (Leiden: Brill, 1960), p. 180.

12. See the discussion of *taqwa* in Rahman, *Major Themes of the Qur'an,* p. 28.

13. See 'Umar Austin, "Suffering in Muslim Religious Thought," *Islamic Quarterly,* 26 (1982), pp. 27–39.

14. A. J. Wensinck, *The Muslim Creed: Its Genesis and Historical Development* (Cambridge: Cambridge University Press, 1932), p. 170.

15. See *The Encyclopaedia of Islam,* new ed., vol. 1 (Leiden: Brill, 1960), p. 187; A. S. Tritton, *Islam: Belief and Practice* (London: Hutchinson's University Library, 1951),

pp. 179–80; and Jane I. Smith, "Reflections on Aspects of Immortality in Islam," *Harvard Theological Review*, 70 (1977), pp. 85–98.

16. See Maulana Muhammad Ali, "Jihad," in *The Religion of Islam* (Lahore: Ripon, 1950), pp. 545–99; see also S. Abdullah Schleifer, "Understanding Jihad: Definition and Methodology," *Islamic Quarterly*, 27 (1983), pp. 118–31.

17. Safia M. Safwat, "Offences and Penalties in Islamic Law," *Islamic Quarterly*, 26 (1982), p. 154.

18. Adultery, slander, inebriation, theft, highway robbery, apostasy, and rebellion. See ʿAbdur Rahman I. Doi, *Shariah: The Islamic Law* (London: Ta Ha, 1984), p. 223.

19. See Chapter Four above.

20. *The Encyclopaedia of Islam*, vol. 1, p. 1297.

21. See Joseph Schacht, *An Introduction to Islamic Law* (Oxford: Clarendon Press, 1964), p. 34.

22. Matthew Lippman, Sean McConville, and Mordechai Yerushalmi, *Islamic Criminal Law and Procedure* (Westport, Conn.: Greenwood, 1988), p. 60.

23. Syed Muʿassam Husain, "Effects of *Tauba* (Repentance) on Penalty in Islam," *Islamic Studies*, 8 (1969), p. 196.

24. See Muhammad Ali's note 693 to surah 5.38 in his translation of the Qurʾan, p. 252–53.

25. See Sheikh Mohammad ibn-Ibrahim al-Hewesh, "Sharia Penalties and Ways of Their Implementation in the Kingdom of Saudi Arabia, I," and Sheikh Omar ibn-Abdul Aziz al-Mutrak, "Sharia Penalties and Ways of Their Implementation in the Kingdom of Saudi Arabia, II," in *The Effect of Islamic Legislation on Crime Prevention in Saudi Arabia* (Riyadh, Saudi Arabia: Ministry of Interior, 1980), pp. 349–89 and pp. 407–64.

26. See al-Mutrak, "Sharia Penalties, II," p. 423.

27. See Franklin L. Ford, *Political Murder: From Tyrannicide to Terrorism* (Cambridge, Mass.: Harvard University Press, 1985), pp. 96–104.

28. Watt labels the religious orientation of pre-Islamic Arabs "tribal humanism." Because of its emphasis on collective values, tribal humanism was ill-suited to the growing individualism of commercial Mecca; thus, Watt argues, the region was ripe for the vision of Muhammad, whose doctrine of salvation was founded on the merits of the individual. See Watt, *Muhammad at Mecca*, pp. 24–25, 151–53.

29. See Guillaume, *The Life of Muhammad*, p. 300.

30. Maulana Muhammad Ali, *A Manual of Hadith* (London: Curzon, 1944), p. 382.

31. Doi, *Shariah*, p. 224.

32. The alleged poisoning occurred three years before Muhammad's death; see Glubb, *Life and Times of Muhammad*, p. 283.

33. No fewer than eight references to this dogma are found in *hadith* literature. See A. J. Wensinck, *A Handbook of Early Muhammadan Traditions* (Leiden: Brill, 1927), p. 54.

34. See Wensinck, *The Muslim Creed*, pp. 83–101.

35. The earliest Muslim thinker to deny the eternity of hell was Djahm, who is condemned by orthodoxy (Wensinck, *The Muslim Creed*, p. 119). Nonetheless, Muslims are today still divided on the issue; see Smith, "Reflections on Aspects of Immortality," p. 96.

CHAPTER EIGHT

1. Miguel Asin, *Islam and the "Divine Comedy"* (London: Murray, 1926), p. 174.

2. For a skeptical assessment of Asin's claims, along with citations from other detractors, see Leonardo Olschki, "Mohammedan Eschatology and Dante's Other World," *Comparative Literature*, 3 (1951), pp. 1–17.

3. Dante, *The Divine Comedy: 1, Hell*, trans. Dorothy L. Sayers (Harmondsworth, Middlesex: Penguin, 1949), 20.28–30.

4. Passages cited from Aquinas are from *Summa Contra Gentiles* [*S.C.G.*] or from *Summa Theologica* [*S.T.*]. Citations in parentheses following quotations or summaries refer to the following English translations: *The Summa Contra Gentiles of Saint Thomas Aquinas*, Literally Translated by the English Dominican Fathers from the Latest Leonine Edition, 5 vols., (London: Burns and Oates, 1923–29), and *Summa Theologica*, Literally Translated by Fathers of the English Dominican Province, 3 vols., (London: Burns and Oates, 1947, 1948). The Supplement (vol. 3) to *Summa Theologica*, on which this chapter draws heavily, was not composed in the same manner as the rest of the work. Aquinas died without completing *Summa Theologica*, leaving the Supplement to be constructed by one of his followers (probably Reginald of Piperno) from Aquinas's *Commentary on the Sentences of Peter Lombard*. As the views on hell and purgatory expressed in the Supplement agree in almost every particular with those expressed in *Summa Contra Gentiles*, I attribute them directly to Aquinas without recourse to qualification other than that presented in this note.

5. Aquinas defines punishment as "being contrary to the will, painful, and inflicted for some fault" (*S.T.* I-II, Q. 46, Art. 7). He also maintains that vengeance, when imposed by the magistrate, is a special virtue (*S.T.* II-II, Q. 108, Art. 2). As for the retributivism of purgatory, though Aquinas concedes that the fires of purgatory are cleansing, he insists that its punishments are imposed strictly because of the "debt of punishment" incurred by past (venial) sins (*S.T.* Appendix 1, Q. 2, Art. 5).

6. See Jonathan Edwards, *Freedom of the Will*, ed. Arnold S. Kaufman and William K. Frankena (Indianapolis, Ind.: Bobbs-Merrill, 1969), especially Part II, section 13, "God's certain foreknowledge of the future volitions of moral agents, inconsistent with such a contingence of these volitions, as is without all necessity."

7. Dante, *The Divine Comedy: 1, Hell*, 3.9.

8. Dante, *The Divine Comedy: 2, Purgatory*, trans. Dorothy L. Sayers (Harmondsworth, Middlesex: Penguin, 1955), 21.61–66.

CHAPTER NINE

1. For an account of Kyd's influence, see Fredson Thayer Bowers, *Elizabethan Revenge Tragedy, 1587–1642* (Princeton, N.J.: Princeton University Press, 1940), esp. chaps. 3 and 4. Bowers rightly points out that the more generic phrase "tragedy of blood" better characterizes the enormous body of Elizabethan and Jacobean drama devoted to violent themes. The revenge tragedy, properly speaking, is only a subset of this literature. None-

theless, "revenge tragedy" may also be understood generically (witness Bowers's own title); hence, I stick with this phrase throughout the chapter.

2. Thomas Heywood, *An Apology for Actors*, 1612. A century later Joseph Addison challenges this convenient notion, reviling the "ridiculous doctrine in modern criticism that they [authors] are obliged to an equal distribution of rewards and punishments, and an impartial execution of poetical justice. Who were the first that established this rule I know not; but I am sure that it has no foundation in nature, in reason, or in the practise of the ancients." *Spectator*, 40, 16 April 1711.

3. J. Green, *A refvtation of the "Apology for Actors,"* 1615, p. 44.

4. Thomas Beard, *The Theatre of God's Jvdgements*, 1612.

5. Other exempla were less high-minded. Many sensational accounts of individual murders, glossed by the patina of warning against crime, were sold to receptive audiences outside the prisons and at the gallows on hanging days. The title page of one is sufficient to give their flavor: "I.T., *A Horrible Creuel and Bloudy Murther*, committed at Putney in Surrey on the 21 of Aprill last, being Thursday, vpon the body of Edward Hall a miller of the same parish, Done by the hands of John Stelling, Peeter Pet, and Edward Streater, his seruants to the said Hall, each of them giving him a deadly blow (as he lay sleeping) with a pickax. Published by Authority. Imprinted at London for *John Wright* and are to be Sold without Newgate at the Signe of the Bible. 1614."

6. "Thus we see divine vengeance prosecuting these sons of blood and assassination, by whose treachery, dissimulation and breach of Oathes, the Kingdom was almost ruined. But the pit they digged for others they are fallen into themselves, and their mischievous device is fallen on their own pate." John Reynolds, *Blood for Blood or Murthers Revenged*, 1661, p. 321.

7. Revised Standard Version.

8. Reynolds, *Blood for Blood*, p. 316.

9. For an account of these various tactics in the revenge genre, see L. B. Campbell, "Theories of Revenge in Renaissance England," *Modern Philology*, 28 (1931), pp. 281–96.

10. Beard, *The Theatre of God's Jvdgements*, p. 295.

11. Ibid.

12. Ibid., p. 303.

13. Ibid., p. 305.

14. Ibid., p. 304.

15. Ibid.

16. Ibid., pp. 304–5.

17. Ibid., p. 305.

18. Heywood, *An Apology for Actors*, 1612.

19. Green, *A refvtation of the "Apology,"* p. 42.

20. "For my contempt of God, I am contemned of men: for my swearing and for-swearing, no man will beeleue me: for my gluttony, I suffer hunger: for my drunkennesse, thirst: for my adulterie, vlcerous sores." Quoted in Charles W. Crupi, *Robert Greene* (Boston: Twayne, 1986), p. 32. The letter may well be a forgery.

21. Beard, *The Theatre of God's Jvdgements*, p. 150.

22. Cited in Arthur Freeman, *Thomas Kyd* (Oxford: Clarendon Press, 1967), p. 26.

23. Beard, *The Theatre of God's Jvdgements*, p. 149.

24. All quotations are from Cyril Tourneur, *The Atheist's Tragedy, or, The Honest Man's Revenge*, ed. Irving Ribner (Cambridge, Mass.: Harvard University Press, 1964).

25. See F. L. Lucas, *Seneca and Elizabethan Tragedy* (Cambridge: Cambridge University Press, 1922), p. 12.

26. Nonorthodoxy was often branded as atheism. See G. T. Buckley, *Atheism in the English Renaissance* (Chicago: University of Chicago Press, 1932), and Strathmann, "Elizabethan Meanings of Atheism," in E. A. Strathmann, *Sir Walter Raleigh: A Study in Elizabethan Skepticism* (New York: Columbia University Press, 1951).

27. John Stephens, *Satyrical essayes, characters, and others, or Accurate and quick Descriptions, fitted to the life of their subjects*, 1615, p. 212.

28. This section owes a significant debt to Fredson Thayer Bowers, "Middleton's *Fair Quarrel* and the Duelling Code," *Journal of English and Germanic Philology*, 36 (1937), pp. 40–65. It was through this article that I became aware of the sizable Renaissance literature for and against dueling. I follow Bowers in recounting details of the code of honor, but the parallel between this code and the belief in pollution is mine alone.

29. *The Charge of Sir Francis Bacon Knight, His Majesties attourney generall, touching Duells*, 1614, pp. 11–12.

30. *Third Institute*, 1602, cap. 72; cited in Bowers, "Middleton's *Fair Quarrel*," p. 52.

31. "Among persons of reputation, Honor is preferred before life." William Segar, *The Booke of Honor and Armes*, 1590, p. 22. "Sith honor is not lesse, nay more than life to bee respected." John Selden, *The Dvello, or Single Combat*, 1610, p. 16.

32. "And therefore euery man that longeth for honour . . . must foster religion & the religious which procureth honour. . . . The truest gloerie is gotten by measuring all things by conscience, not doing any thing for ostentation and vanitie." John Norden, *The Mirror of Honor*, 1597, p. 21; "I obserue, besides the inward Contents of a peaceable Conscience, two things wherein a Christian excels all other men. In true Valor . . . that is, in a just quarrell: for if his cause bee naught, there is none more timerous than hee." Owin Felltham, *Resolues Diuine, Morall, Political*, 1623, no. 13, pp. 38–39; both cited in Bowers, "Middleton's *Fair Quarrel*," p. 53.

33. George Gyfford, *A Treatise of True Fortitude*, 1594, sigs. D4–D4v; cited in Bowers, "Middleton's *Fair Quarrel*," p. 60.

34. For the play's date, see George R. Price, "Introduction" to Thomas Middleton and William Rowley, *A Fair Quarrel*, ed. George R. Price (Lincoln: University of Nebraska Press, 1976), p. xvii. All passages cited are from this edition of the play.

35. Curiously, Ager does not follow the code of honor and give the lie to the Colonel's aspersion. This complicated artifice, used for locating the burden of dishonor in a formal challenge, seems an obvious device for underscoring Ager's scrupulous conscience. The lie (as summarized in Segar, *Booke of Honor and Armes*, p. 19) works as follows. *A* hears *B* make an aspersion touching the very core of *A*'s honor. *A* can either retire in shame or say something to the effect of "Sir, Thou liest." From this point on, *A* is cleared of all dishonor, the burden of which has shifted to *B*. Having been given the lie, *B* now faces the choice of retiring in shame or issuing a challenge. If he issues a challenge that

is accepted, he must yield to his antagonist (now the defender) the choice of weapons. Applied to the circumstances of the Colonel and Captain Ager, this protocol seems ideal. If formally given the lie, the Colonel would be forced to yield the choice of weapons to Captain Ager—the "fair" procedure, given the Colonel's belligerent nature.

Instead, the pair retires at the end of Act I with a vague agreement to meet the next day in single combat. Perhaps Middleton and Rowley thought the details of a proper challenge tedious and compressed them for dramatic purposes. Perhaps, too, sensitive to the king's edict, they deliberately avoided portraying a quarrel in cold blood. In the eyes of the code, a cold-blooded slaying was merely an unfortunate side effect of the defense of honor. By contrast, killing in the heat of an impassioned moment was unworthy of a gentleman. The law, however, reversed these judgments, viewing impassioned killing as the lesser offense. Under the king's edict, a cold-blooded duel provided proof of premeditation, clearing the way for prosecution as deliberate homicide.

36. Bowers, "Middleton's *Fair Quarrel*," p. 64; Price, "Introduction," p. xxvi.

37. Thomas Adams, *The Diuells Banket*, 1614, p. 58.

38. James I, *A Publication of His Majesty's Edict and Severe Censure against Priuate Combats and Combatants*, 1613, p. 118.

39. Ibid., p. 113.

CHAPTER TEN

1. All passages cited from Kant are from the following translations: Immanuel Kant, *The Metaphysical Elements of Justice* (Part I of *The Metaphysics of Morals*), trans. John Ladd (Indianapolis, Ind.: Bobbs-Merrill, 1965); and Immanuel Kant, *The Doctrine of Virtue* (Part II of *The Metaphysics of Morals*), trans. Mary J. Gregor (New York: Harper & Row, 1964). In case readers wish to consult the original German or the work of other translators, I follow the page number in the above-mentioned translations with the page number, in brackets, of the Königliche Preussische Akademie der Wissenschaften edition (Berlin, 1900–56) of Kant's collected works.

2. The distinction between a practical and a pathological interest is introduced in a footnote to Kant's discussion of obligation in the Second Section of *Foundations of the Metaphysics of Morals*. It resurfaces in the Third Section under the heading "Of the Interest Attaching to the Ideas of Morality." Application of the distinction to love is extensively discussed in Part II, Chapter 1, of *The Doctrine of Virtue*.

3. See Immanuel Kant, *Foundations of the Metaphysics of Morals*, trans. Lewis White Beck (Indianapolis, Ind.: Bobbs-Merrill, 1959), p. 47 [429].

4. See Kant's Third Antinomy in *The Critique of Pure Reason*, trans. Norman Kemp Smith (London: Macmillan, 1933), pp. 409–15 [A444–A452], and the Third Section of *Foundations*, pp. 64–67 [466–99].

5. This distinction is the key to dividing Kant's *Metaphysics of Morals* into Part I, *The Metaphysical Elements of Justice* (treating those laws that command externally), and Part II, *The Doctrine of Virtue* (treating those laws that command internally). See Kant, *The Doctrine of Virtue*, p. 36 [378].

6. See "Justice Is United with the Authorization to Use Coercion," Section D of the Introduction, Kant, *The Metaphysical Elements of Justice*, pp. 35–36 [232].

7. Perfect and imperfect duties are distinguished in Kant, *The Metaphysical Elements of Justice*, p. 46 [240].

8. Kant, *Foundations*, p. 40 [423].

9. Ibid., p. 41 [424].

10. Kant, *The Metaphysical Elements of Justice*, pp. 76–77 [312].

11. Kant, *The Doctrine of Virtue*, pp. 84–86 [420–22].

12. Kant, *The Metaphysical Elements of Justice*, p. 103 [333].

13. Kant, *Foundations*, p. 57 [439].

CHAPTER ELEVEN

1. Fyodor Dostoevsky, *Crime and Punishment*, trans. David Magarshack (Harmondsworth, Middlesex: Penguin, 1951), IV, 1. All of the ensuing passages are from this translation.

2. When Raskolnikov's mother first visits him, she exclaims, "What an awful room you have, Roddy! Just like a coffin!" Ibid., III, 3.

3. For elaboration of the proto-Nietzschean elements in Raskolnikov's character, see Ilham Dilman, "Socrates and Dostoyevsky on Punishment," *Philosophy and Literature*, 1 (Fall 1976), pp. 66–78.

4. Fyodor Dostoevsky, *The Notebooks for "Crime and Punishment,"* trans. Edward Wasiolek (Chicago: University of Chicago Press, 1967), p. 58.

5. See Joseph Frank, *Dostoevsky: The Years of Ordeal, 1850–1859* (Princeton, N.J.: Princeton University Press, 1983), especially chap. 10, "A New Vision."

6. See Fyodor Dostoevsky, *The House of the Dead*, trans. H. Sutherland Edwards (London: Dent, 1962), chaps. 4 and 5.

7. Hannah Arendt, *Eichmann in Jerusalem: A Report on the Banality of Evil* (New York: Viking, 1963).

8. The means contemplated is a bullet through the head. See Dostoevsky, *Notebooks for "Crime and Punishment,"* pp. 55, 64, 66, 243.

9. Quoted in Konstantin Mochulsky, *Dostoevsky: His Life and Work*, trans. Michael A. Minihan (Princeton, N.J.: Princeton University Press, 1967), p. 273.

10. For instance, Ernest J. Simmons, *Dostoevsky: The Making of a Novelist* (Oxford: Oxford University Press, 1940), proclaims the epilogue unconvincing, an artistic failure; whereas Maurice Beebe, "The Three Motives of Raskolnikov: A Reinterpretation of *Crime and Punishment*," *College English*, 17 (December 1955), pp. 151–58, declares that without the epilogue Raskolnikov's will to suffering would be unclear and contradictory.

11. Mochulsky, *Dostoevsky*, p. 312.

CHAPTER TWELVE

1. See, again, Edward Westermarck, *The Origin and Development of the Moral Ideas* (London: Macmillan; vol. 1, 1906; vol. 2, 1908), along with P. F. Strawson, "Freedom and Resentment," *Proceedings of the British Academy* (1962), pp. 187–211.

2. For an account of the social context of punishment, see Georg Rusche and Otto Kirchheimer, *Punishment and Social Structure* (New York: Columbia University Press, 1939).

3. George Ryley Scott, *The History of Capital Punishment* (London: Torchstream, 1950), p. 221.

4. The phrase "permissive retributivism" is J. L. Mackie's. See J. L. Mackie, "Retributivism: A Test Case for Ethical Objectivity," in *Philosophy of Law*, 3d ed., ed. Joel Feinberg and Hyman Gross (Belmont, Calif.: Wadsworth, 1986), pp. 622–29. A careful analysis of permissibility as it applies to one particular penalty—that of capital punishment—may be found in Tom Sorell, *Moral Theory and Capital Punishment* (Oxford: Blackwell, 1987), especially chap. 1.

5. "The sentence of the law is to the moral sentiment of the public in relation to any offence what a seal is to hot wax. It converts into a permanent final judgment what might otherwise be a transient sentiment." James Fitzjames Stephen, *A History of the Criminal Law of England*, vol. 2 (London: 1883), p. 81. Stephen later (p. 82) compares the sanctioning of vindictive passion by the criminal-justice system to the sanctioning of sexual passion in marriage. The idea that an unhealthy "revenge taboo" (a prohibition on being candid about the desire for revenge) is characteristic of modern sensibilities in the same way as the unhealthy Victorian "sexual taboo" is a major thesis for Susan Jacoby, *Wild Justice: The Evolution of Revenge* (New York: Harper & Row, 1983).

6. This case is made best by David Hume, "Of a Particular Providence and of a Future State," in *An Inquiry Concerning Human Understanding*.

7. The implications of the ideal of sainthood in moral theory are explored by Susan Wolf, "Moral Saints," *Journal of Philosophy*, 79 (August 1982), pp. 419–39.

8. As Hugo Adam Bedau points out in an instructive analogy, one's *justification* of punishment may turn on one's persuasive *definition* of punishment: "It is quite clear now, even if it was not some years ago, that the definition of 'civil disobedience' is not altogether independent of the justification of civil disobedience. So with 'punishment' and the justification of punishment." Hugo Adam Bedau, "Retribution and the Theory of Punishment," *Journal of Philosophy*, 85 (November 1978), p. 606.

9. For a view that "justification" ought to focus primarily on punishment as an activity, see John Kleinig, *Punishment and Desert* (The Hague: Nijhoff, 1973), pp. 18–21. The book also discusses in illuminating fashion many other problems of "justification." See also Antony Flew, "The Justification of Punishment," in *The Philosophy of Punishment*, ed. H. B. Acton (London: Macmillan, 1969), pp. 83–104.

10. J. L. Austin, "A Plea for Excuses," *Proceedings of the Aristotelian Society*, 17 (1956–57), pp. 1–30.

11. An alternative means might be an unambiguous priority rule, such as Rawls's "lexicographical" rule that liberty always takes precedence over economic welfare. See

John Rawls, *A Theory of Justice* (Cambridge, Mass.: Harvard University Press, 1971), pp. 42–45.

12. Berlin illustrates the thesis as follows: "Machiavelli's candid achievement is . . . his uncovering of an insoluble dilemma, the placing of a permanent question mark in the path of posterity. It stems from his *de facto* recognition that ends equally ultimate, equally sacred, may contradict each other, that entire systems of value may come into collision without possibility of rational arbitration, and that not merely in exceptional circumstances, as a result of abnormality or accident or error . . . but . . . as part of the normal human situation." See Berlin, "The Originality of Machiavelli," in Isaiah Berlin, *Against the Current: Essays in the History of Ideas* (New York: Viking, 1980), pp. 74–75.

13. My views on the significance of moral dilemmas for the body of deliberative moral theory are close to those expressed by Williams, "Ethical Consistency" and "Consistency and Realism," both collected in Bernard Williams, *Problems of the Self* (Cambridge: Cambridge University Press, 1973). Williams's views have not gone unchallenged. See Ruth Barman Marcus, "Moral Dilemmas and Consistency," *Journal of Philosophy*, 78 (March 1980), pp. 121–36; and Philippa Foot, "Moral Realism and Moral Dilemma," *Journal of Philosophy*, 80 (July 1983), pp. 379–98.

CHAPTER THIRTEEN

1. In identifying the offender as addressee of a Kantian justification, I follow Edmund Pincoffs, *The Rationale of Legal Punishment*, (New York: Humanities Press, 1966), p. 6.

2. See G. W. F. Hegel, *The Philosophy of Right*, trans. T. M. Knox (Oxford: Oxford University Press, 1942), pp. 70–71. The Hegelian theory is elaborated by Bernard Bosanquet, *The Philosophical Theory of the State* (London: Macmillan, 1920), pp. 201–11, and criticized by John Deigh, "On the Right to Be Punished: Some Doubts," *Ethics*, 94 (January 1984), pp. 191–211.

3. Joel Feinberg, "The Nature and Value of Rights," *Journal of Value Inquiry*, 4 (1970), pp. 243–57.

4. See David Lyons, "The Correlativity of Rights and Duties," *Nous*, 4 (1970), pp. 45–55.

5. See David Lyons, *Forms and Limits of Utilitarianism* (Oxford: Clarendon Press, 1965), for a demonstration that so-called rule utilitarianism is "extensionally equivalent" to so-called act utilitarianism once all "threshold-related effects" of acts are accounted for.

6. Alan H. Goldman, "The Paradox of Punishment," *Philosophy and Public Affairs*, 9 (Fall 1979), pp. 42–58.

7. "The paradox of punishment is that a penal institution somewhat similar to that in use in our society seems from a moral point of view to be both required and unjustified." Ibid., p. 42. Murphy argues for another kind of paradox by insisting that the only satisfactory moral theory of punishment is a retributivism based on the moral autonomy of the individual, but that such a theory applies only where social conditions for realizing full autonomy for everyone are met. Since distributive inequalities of wealth and status everywhere undermine the flowering of full autonomy, in Murphy's view, everyday insti-

tutions of legal punishment are also morally suspect. See Jeffrie G. Murphy, "Marxism and Retribution," *Philosophy and Public Affairs*, 2 (Spring 1973), pp. 217–43.

8. Thus, for instance, Mundle argues that the retributive claims that committing a moral offense is a sufficient reason for suffering and that suffering ought to be proportionate to the moral gravity of the offense together "provide an explication of the concept of *moral desert*." C. W. K. Mundle, "Punishment and Desert," in *The Philosophy of Punishment*, ed. H. B. Acton (London: Macmillan, 1969), p. 72.

9. Hart, "Postscript: Responsibility and Retribution," in H. L. A. Hart, *Punishment and Responsibility: Essays in the Philosophy of Law* (Oxford: Oxford University Press, 1968), pp. 234–35.

10. Hugo Adam Bedau, *Death Is Different: Studies in the Morality, Law, and Politics of Capital Punishment* (Boston: Northeastern University Press, 1987), p. 31.

11. The usurping non–license holder, then, is a bit like the community member who, in Nozick's challenge to H. L. A. Hart's principle of fairness, refuses "his" day to entertain, even though he has benefited from the compliance of each of his neighbors in a scheme in which they voluntarily take turns to entertain for a day. Considerations of distributional fairness for benefits received, Nozick correctly insists, cannot override the right of the individual to do as he chooses. The important difference between the two cases is that the usurping non–license holder may recklessly endanger others, whereas Nozick's libertarian refuser simply withholds a benefit. See Robert Nozick, *Anarchy, State, and Utopia* (New York: Basic, 1984), pp. 90–96.

12. Herbert Morris, "Persons and Punishment," *The Monist*, 52 (October 1968), pp. 475–501.

13. If the benefits and burdens of the fair-distributional scheme are interpreted psychologically (e.g., measured by the strength of one's inclination *not* to comply), Morris's scheme produces counterintuitive results. See Richard W. Burgh, "Do the Guilty Deserve Punishment?" *Journal of Philosophy*, 79 (April 1982), pp. 193–213. As Sher points out, however, the relevant measure of degree of benefit or burden is *moral* rather than *psychological*. George Sher, *Desert* (Princeton, N.J.: Princeton University Press, 1987), p. 81.

14. Sher, *Desert*, pp. 94–96.

15. Ibid., p. 84.

16. Having broken the spell of *like for like,* we must resist the temptation to proportion the suffering of legal punishment to some presumed morally relevant feature of the offense. The morally acceptable degree of retributive response can only be judged by nonretributive moral values.

CHAPTER FOURTEEN

1. See Wolgast, "Intolerable Wrong and Necessary Punishment," in Elizabeth Wolgast, *The Grammar of Justice* (Ithaca, N.Y.: Cornell University Press, 1987), pp. 147–68. I am much indebted to Wolgast's general view of the problem of punishment, agreeing in particular with her critique of the ideal of justice. What is palpable are injustices, which, once done, put us into a quandary about how to respond.

2. Supporters of a wholly therapeutic model for treating criminality take this view. See Karl Menninger, *The Crime of Punishment* (New York: Viking, 1963).

3. See, for instance, Herbert Morris, "A Paternalistic Theory of Punishment," *American Philosophical Quarterly*, 18 (October 1981), pp. 263–71.

4. See Jean Hampton, "The Moral Education Theory of Punishment," *Philosophy and Public Affairs*, 13 (Summer 1984), pp. 208–38.

5. *Queens Bench Division*, 1884, 14 Q.B.D. 273.

6. I model this account of the role of excuses in dire straits on that given by Paul Woodruff, "Justification or Excuse: Saving Soldiers at the Expense of Civilians," *Canadian Journal of Philosophy*, suppl. vol. 8 (1982), pp. 159–76.

7. The examples in this paragraph were provided by a reviewer for Temple University Press.

8. Von Hirsch divides seriousness of offense into the two dimensions of harm and culpability, insisting that recidivism has an impact on the latter but not on the former. Andrew von Hirsch, *Doing Justice* (New York: Hill and Wang, 1976), pp. 84–88. In a later article he revises his view to hold that recidivism authorizes authorities to punish in full measure, whereas first-time offenders are proper subjects for leniency. See Andrew von Hirsch, "Desert and Previous Conviction in Sentencing," *Minnesota Law Review*, 65 (1981), pp. 591–634. For a skeptical view of recidivism as grounds for differential sentencing, see George P. Fletcher, "The Recidivist Premium," *Criminal Justice Ethics*, 1 (Summer/Fall 1982), pp. 54–59. Michael Davis mounts a defense of the recidivist premium that is too clever by half, arguing along the lines of Herbert Morris's "unfair advantages" principle that the recidivist benefits from "the unfair advantage of taking more than one's share of unfair advantage." Michael Davis, "Just Deserts for Recidivists," *Criminal Justice Ethics*, 4 (Summer/Fall 1985), p. 41. Here, as elsewhere, Davis shows himself remaining under the spell of like for like, arguing that an idealized market which gives the highest bidder a license to commit crime can provide a price (and thus a relative ranking) to each category of offense. See also Michael Davis, "How to Make the Punishment Fit the Crime," *Ethics*, 93 (July 1983), pp. 726–52.

9. Hart, "Prolegomenon to the Principles of Punishment," in H. L. A. Hart, *Punishment and Responsibility: Essays in the Philosophy of Law* (Oxford: Oxford University Press, 1968), pp. 8–10.

10. John Rawls, "Two Concepts of Rules," *Philosophical Review*, 64 (1955), pp. 3–32.

11. C. L. Ten, *Crime, Guilt, and Punishment* (Oxford: Clarendon Press, 1987) p. 33; Antony M. Quinton, "Views," *The Listener* (2 December 1971), p. 758.

12. Ten, *Crime, Guilt, and Punishment*, p. 79.

13. Wolgast, "Punishing Our Own," in *The Grammar of Justice*, pp. 169–93.

14. For the distinction between "knowing-how" and "knowing-that," see Gilbert Ryle, *The Concept of Mind* (New York: Barnes & Noble, 1949), pp. 25–61.

Index